A
CENTURY
OF
AMBIVALENCE

SCHOCKEN BOOKS
New York
Published in cooperation with
YIVO Institute
for Jewish Research

A Century of Ambivalence

The Jews of Russia and the Soviet Union, 1881 to the Present

Zvi Gitelman

Map on p. xiii from *A Special Legacy: An Oral History of Soviet Jewish Emigrés in the U.S.* by Sylvia Rothschild. New York, Simon & Schuster, 1985.

Map on p. 3 from *The Jews of Russia: Their History in Maps and Photographs* by Martin Gilbert. London, National Council for Soviet Jewry of Great Britain and Ireland, 1976. © 1976, Martin Gilbert

Map on p. 182 from *The Final Solution: The Attempt to Exterminate the Jews of Europe, 1939–1945,* by Gerald Reitlinger. New York, Beechurst Press, 1953.

Copyright © 1988 by the YIVO Institute
for Jewish Research
Library of Congress Cataloging-in-Publication Data

Gitelman, Zvi Y.

   A century of ambivalence.

   Photographs from the collection of the YIVO Institute for Jewish Research, exhibited at the Jewish Museum in New York in Feb. 1988
   Companion vol. to: Image before my eyes / Lucjan Dobroszycki and Barbara Kirshenblatt-Gimblett, 1977.

   Bibliography: p.

   Includes index.
   1. Jews—Soviet Union — History. 2. Jews — Soviet Union — Pictorial works. 3. Soviet Union — Ethnic relations. 4. Soviet Union — Description and travel — Views.
   I. YIVO Institute for Jewish Research. II. Jewish Museum (New York, N.Y.) III. Title.

DS135.R9G444 1988 947'.004924 87-9822
ISBN 0-8052-4034-9

Manufactured in the United States of America
First Edition

All photos not explicitly credited are from the archives of the YIVO Institute for Jewish Research, New York.

Due to the complexity and diversity of languages used in this book, it proved impossible to follow consistent transliteration systems. Where possible, a modified version of the Library of Congress system was used for Russian and a modified version of the YIVO system for Yiddish.

Design by Blackpool Design, New York, N.Y.
Type by J. M. Post Graphics, Corp., Keansburg, N.J.
Printed and bound by Arcata Graphics, Halliday, West Hanover, Mass.

CONTENTS

ACKNOWLEDGMENTS

Like many other students of East European Jewry, for years I have used the treasure house that is the YIVO Institute for Jewish Research and have appreciated not only its vast and valuable holdings, but also its dedicated staff and that special East European atmosphere which they managed to transfer to New York from Vilna, where YIVO was founded in 1925. Therefore when YIVO's director, Samuel Norich, invited me to write a photographic history of modern Russian and Soviet Jewry, I welcomed the opportunity to implement an idea which I had often thought about. It has been a privilege and a joy to go through nearly 10,000 photographs now in YIVO's Russia/Soviet collection while writing this book. This collection has been supplemented by the efforts of Michael Gofman, a recent Soviet immigrant to America, who collected photographs from other immigrants. Konstantin Miroshnik, with whom it has been a pleasure to work over the years, tracked down hundreds of photographs in Israel with his usual ingenuity and conscientiousness. I was able to collect other photographs in the Detroit area and in Chicago. In Chicago Rabbi Yechiel Poupko, Liz Birg, and Henrietta Williams of the Jewish Community Centers were of great assistance in facilitating my collection efforts. YIVO's chief archivist, Marek Web, has been extremely helpful in ferreting out and arranging the materials. His knowledge of the collections and of the history of East European Jewry, and his cheerful cooperation and assistance in this enterprise, have made my task much easier and immensely enjoyable. Other YIVO archivists, especially Fruma Mohrer and Roberta Newman, were also helpful in gathering the materials from widely dispersed collections and arranging them for use in this volume.

The text was read most conscientiously by Profs. Mordechai Altshuler, Jonathan Frankel, and Samuel Kassow. Their expertise and willingness to share it were invaluable, and I am profoundly grateful for their collegial assistance. Bonny Fetterman, my editor at Schocken, struggled valiantly to transform academic jargon into understandable English. Her gentle criticism and wise suggestions are much appreciated. My wife, Marlene, Samuel Norich, Marek Web, and Myra Waiman also read the manuscript and made constructive comments. Needless to say, I alone am responsible for the interpretations and any errors of fact in the book. Lorraine Harvey of the Department of Political Science at The University of Michigan typed several versions of the book with good cheer and a discerning eye. Major funding for the project, which includes an exhibition at the Jewish Museum in New York drawn from the YIVO photographic collections, came from the J. M. Kaplan Foundation, to which I would like to express my gratitude. Additional funding was provided by the Judaic Studies Program at The University of Michigan, and the Edward Gerber Memorial Fund at YIVO, whose assistance I appreciate.

Z.G.

July, 1987

INTRODUCTION

A hundred years ago the Russian Empire contained the largest Jewish community in the world, numbering about five million people. Today the Soviet Union's two million Jews constitute the third-largest Jewish community in the world. In the intervening century the Jews of that area have been at the center of some of the most dramatic events of modern history—two world wars, revolutions, pogroms, political liberation, and repression. They have gone through dizzyingly rapid upward and downward economic and social mobility. In only one century Russian and Soviet Jews have expanded the literatures of Hebrew and Yiddish and made major contributions to Russian, Ukrainian, and Belorussian literatures, as well as to some of the other cultures of the area. When given the chance, they have contributed greatly to science and technology, scholarship and arts, industry, and popular culture. For these achievements they have been applauded and cursed, praised and envied. The Jews themselves have disagreed profoundly about where and how to make their contributions. Some dedicated their lives to the country of their birth, while others ultimately rejected it and sought to build up other lands.

This has been a century of great enthusiasms and profound disappointments. Jews have eagerly embraced programs to reform Russia or to leave it; to lose themselves within the larger population or to develop a distinctive culture of their own; to preserve traditional Jewish culture or to root it out completely. Probably most Jews throughout the period lived their lives without embracing any of the ideologies that competed for their allegiance. They settled for living their family and professional lives as best they could, just like most people in any society. But many wrestled with larger, more abstract questions. Throughout most of the period Jews felt that their situation was abnormal, in need of improvement. While some believed that this condition could not be changed, others were determined to find ways of improving their situation, whether by finding a general solution to the problems of Russia or by devising a particular one for the problems of the Jews. Throughout the century some Jews have sought to merge themselves into Russian society completely, either because they saw little value in Jewish culture or because they concluded that Jewishness was mostly a burden and the only way to escape from it was to cease to be Jewish. Others took the opposite tack, affirming their Jewishness and rejecting the larger society which, in their view, had rejected them. Zionists insisted on the value of Jewish culture and identity, rejecting assimilation as both undesirable and ultimately unfeasible. Even if the larger society could accept the Jews as equals, the only definitive answer to the "Jewish question" would be the restoration of a Jewish state where the Jewish way of life could flourish. Socialists before 1917, and political reformers and dissidents afterward, turned away from both assimilationist and Zionist programs. To assimilate into the surrounding society would be to accept its values and institutions, and these were seen as needing radical reform. To seek a specifically Jewish solution would be parochial, a betrayal of other peoples and probably a perpetuation elsewhere of the same inequities that drove Jews out of Russia in the first place. Therefore, the only true solution to the problem of the Jews and of all mankind was a worldwide socialist revolution. Most Jews subscribed to none of these ideologies and either made their way as best they could within Russian and Soviet society or "voted with their feet" against their situation, emigrating to North America, Western Europe, and Israel.

Russian Jewry's intensive search for individual and collective solutions played a decisive role in the development of the major trends in modern Jewish life. The immigration of millions of Russian Jews to the United States in the 1882–1914 period profoundly changed the character of American Jewry, not only by increasing its numbers manyfold, but also by infusing Russian Jewry's religious, social, and political traditions, as well as skills and occupations, into American life and into the American Jewish community. Russian Jewish immigrants, at first taking a back seat to the more established Jews of Sephardic, and especially German, origin, came to dominate the American Jewish scene as they acquired education, skills, wealth, and self-confidence. Russian Jews also were prominent in the first waves of Zionist settlers in Palestine. They transplanted their socialist ideas and their modes of political organization and behavior, as well as their music, dress, and food, from Russia to Palestine.

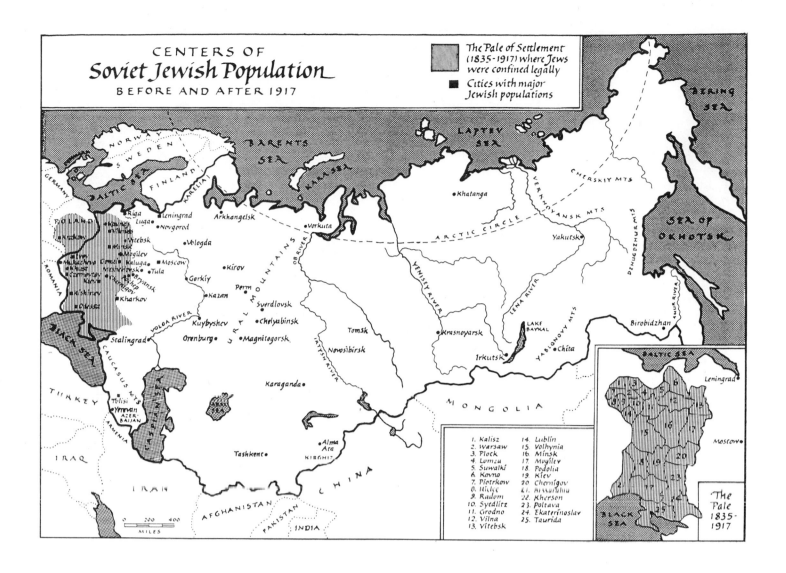

CENTERS OF
Soviet Jewish Population
BEFORE AND AFTER 1917

The Pale of Settlement
(1835-1917) where Jews
were confined legally

■ Cities with major
Jewish populations

1. Kalisz	14. Lublin
2. Warsaw	15. Volhynia
3. Plock	16. Minsk
4. Lomza	17. Mogilev
5. Suwalki	18. Podolia
6. Kovno	19. Kiev
7. Piotrkow	20. Chernigov
8. Hilce	21. Bessarabia
9. Radom	22. Kherson
10. Syedlitz	23. Poltava
11. Grodno	24. Ekaterinoslav
12. Vilna	25. Taurida
13. Vitebsk	

The Pale 1835-1917

For a long time the Israeli political parties and movements could trace their ancestry directly back to Russia. Smaller Russian immigrations placed their stamp on Western Europe and Latin America as well.

This turbulent century is only the second in which large numbers of Jews have been under Russian rule. There has long been a Jewish presence in territories of the present-day Soviet Union, but masses of Jews became Russian subjects only when the empire annexed eastern Poland between 1772 and 1795. Greek inscriptions in areas around the Black Sea attest to the presence of Hellenized Jews in the early centuries of the Common Era, and hundreds of years ago Jews migrated to Central Asia and the Caucasus as well. In the eighth century the rulers and upper classes of the Kingdom of the Khazars in the lower Volga and Crimea adopted Judaism. There were Jews in Kievan Rus in the tenth century and in the Crimea in the thirteenth. But the Russian tsars kept Jews out of their territories as much as they could. In 1727 all Jews were formally expelled from the country,

A scene in Ushitza, Ukraine. The woman in the window is said to have been the mother of the famous cantor Mordechai Hirshman, who served in Vilna (Vilnius) and the United States. PHOTO: Menakhem Kipnis.

and in 1739 all Jews were ordered to leave territories annexed by Russia from the Ukraine and Belorussia. Much of the animus against Jews stemmed from Christian beliefs that the Jews had killed Christ. The Tsarina Elizabeth, who ruled from 1741 to 1762, responded to merchants in the Ukraine and Riga pleading with her to allow Jews to trade there by writing, "From the enemies of Christ I wish neither gain nor profit."

But after the partitions of Poland nearly half a million Jews found themselves under Russian rule. In order to minimize the "damage" they might inflict on Russia, they were confined by law to the "Pale of Settlement," essentially those areas that they were already inhabiting but that had now come under Russian sovereignty. For the first half century after the partition of 1772 the Jews were able to carry on their traditional way of life pretty much without effective interference. But during this period, as the historian John

Klier has observed, "Russian Judeophobia was largely transformed from a simple, primitive hatred based on a view of the Jews as deicides into a set of more sophisticated, modern myths, encompassing a view of the Jews as participants in a conspiracy directed against the very basis of Christian civilization. This view predominated in the second half of the nineteenth century, but its foundations were laid in the period from 1772 to 1825."[1] Beginning in 1825 the tsars began to deal vigorously with what they saw as their "Jewish problem," setting off the cycle of repression and relaxation that was to create and re-create enormous Jewish ambivalence toward their homeland. It is in the last hundred years especially that Jews and the peoples among whom they have lived have been locked into a tempestuous, intense relationship from which none of the parties has been able to free itself completely, nor, in many cases, resolve their differences. On the other hand, that relationship has produced great achievements and advances for both Jews and others. Thus the modern history of the Jews in Russia and the Soviet Union is streaked with light and shadow. It is a story still unfolding, one likely to continue to tell of multiple ambiguities and complex ambivalences on the part of everyone involved.

CHAPTER ONE

CREATIVITY VERSUS REPRESSION:
THE JEWS IN RUSSIA, 1881–1917

Early Sunday afternoon, March 1, 1881, Tsar Alexander II left his palace in St. Petersburg to review the maneuvers of a guards battalion. He was known as the "Tsar Liberator" because he had emancipated millions of serfs, reformed the legal and administrative systems, eased the burdens of military service, and allowed more intellectual freedom. Nevertheless the revolutionaries of the Narodnaia Volia (People's Will) organization described him as the "embodiment of despotism, hypocritical, cowardly, bloodthirsty and all-corrupting. . . . The main usurper of the people's sovereignty, the middle pillar of reaction, the chief perpetrator of judicial murders." As long as he did not turn his power over to a freely elected constituent assembly, they pledged to conduct "war, implacable war to the last drop of our blood" against the sovereign and the system he headed.

Well aware of the danger to his life, the tsar usually varied his travel routes. On this cloudy day, as his carriage turned onto a quay along the Neva River, a young man in a fur cap suddenly loomed up in front of the royal entourage and threw what looked like a snowball between the horse's legs. The bomb exploded, but wounded the tsar only slightly. His Imperial Highness got out to express his solicitude for a Cossack and a butcher's delivery boy who had been severely wounded. Turning back to his carriage, he saw a man with a parcel in his hand make a sudden movement toward him. The ensuing explosion wounded both the tsar and his assailant. Rushed to the Winter Palace, the tsar died within an hour. His assailant died that evening without revealing either his name or those of his Narodnaia Volia co-conspirators. But the man who threw the first bomb, a recent recruit to the revolutionary ranks, informed on his comrades to the police interrogators. The sole Jew among those comrades was Gesia Gelfman, a young woman who had run away

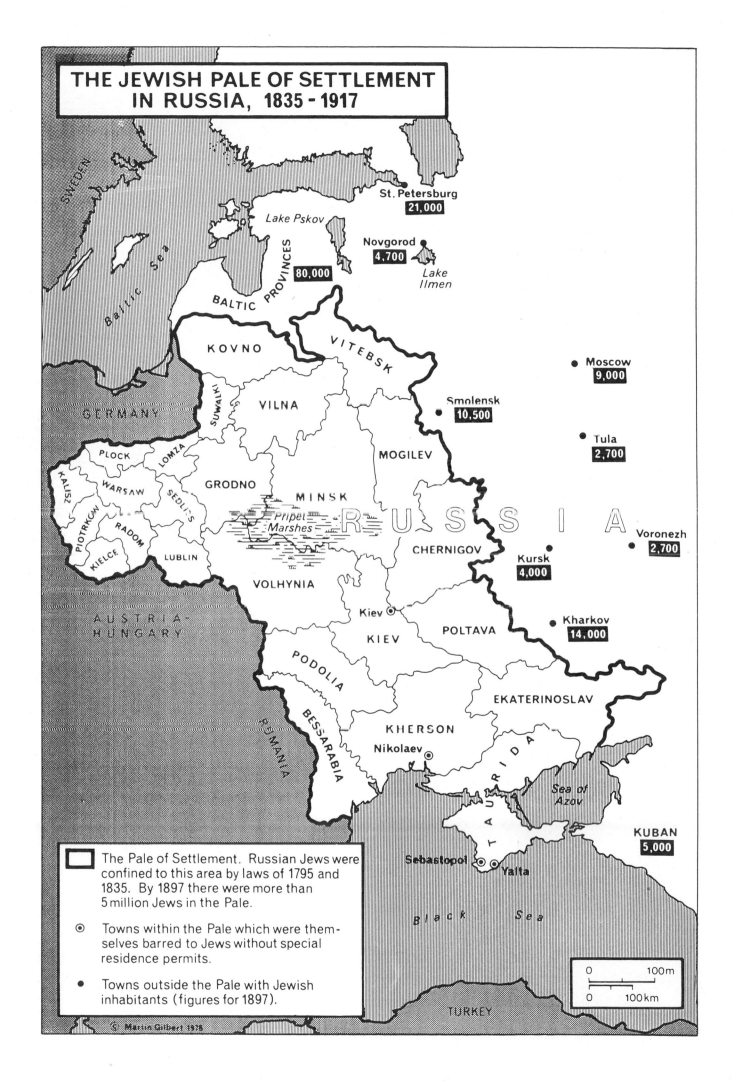

THE JEWISH PALE OF SETTLEMENT IN RUSSIA, 1835 - 1917

SWEDEN

Baltic Sea

GERMANY

Lake Pskov

St. Petersburg **21,000**

Novgorod **4,700**

Lake Ilmen

BALTIC PROVINCES **80,000**

KOVNO

VITEBSK

SUWALKI

VILNA

Moscow **9,000**

Smolensk **10,500**

MOGILEV

Tula **2,700**

PLOCK

LOMZA

KALISZ

WARSAW

GRODNO

SEDLES

MINSK

Pripet Marshes

R U S S I A

PIOTRKOW

RADOM

KIELCE

LUBLIN

VOLHYNIA

CHERNIGOV

Voronezh **2,700**

Kursk **4,000**

AUSTRIA-HUNGARY

PODOLIA

Kiev

KIEV

POLTAVA

Kharkov **14,000**

ROMANIA

BESSARABIA

KHERSON

Nikolaev

EKATERINOSLAV

T A U R I D A

Sea of Azov

KUBAN **5,000**

Sebastopol

Yalta

Black Sea

TURKEY

The Pale of Settlement. Russian Jews were confined to this area by laws of 1795 and 1835. By 1897 there were more than 5 million Jews in the Pale.

⊙ Towns within the Pale which were themselves barred to Jews without special residence permits.

● Towns outside the Pale with Jewish inhabitants (figures for 1897).

| 0 | 100m |
| 0 | 100km |

© Martin Gilbert 1976

Maria Grigorevna Viktorovich and her daughter, Esfir Aronovna, Tomsk, Siberia, 1914. CREDIT: Berta Rostinina.

The husband of Maria Viktorovich, Aron Abramovich, merchant of the first guild, a position which allowed him to live outside the Pale of Settlement, St. Petersburg, 1900. CREDIT: Berta Rostinina.

from her traditional home to avoid a marriage her parents had arranged for her when she was sixteen. She was found guilty of conspiracy to murder the tsar, as were another woman and four men. All were sentenced to hang. Because Gelfman was pregnant, her sentence was commuted to life at hard labor. She died a few months after giving birth, possibly because of deliberate malpractice, and her infant died at about the same time.

Soon after the assassination of Alexander II and the ascension to the throne of Alexander III, a wave of pogroms swept over Russia and the Ukraine, as the word spread that the Jews had murdered the "Little Father" in St. Petersburg. A quarter century of relative tranquility and modest progress for the Jews had ended. Jews had entered the Russian Empire in large numbers only a century before, when the imperial appetite of the tsars led them, reluctantly, to swallow unwanted Jews along with the coveted territories of Poland divided among the Russian, Hapsburg, and German empires. The huge Jewish population of the Polish territories was taken in, though barred from moving elsewhere in the empire and confined to the "Pale of Settlement." For about a hundred years thereafter they had experienced cycles of repression and relaxation. Sometimes the hand of the tsars would come down heavily on the Jews, while at other times it beckoned seductively and urged them to change their "foreign ways" and assimilate into the larger society. For nearly a century Russian society and its leadership had tried to change the Jews. Indeed, some of the Jews themselves preached a reform of Jewish ways so that they would be more acceptable to Russian society. But a few decades before the assassination of Alexander II a handful of Jews began trying to change not only themselves but Russian society and its political system as well. During the century following 1881 the dialogue between Jews and their neighbors was to be laden with ambivalence and distrust, but also with great hope and idealistic aspirations.

THE "IRON TSAR" AND THE JEWS

Nicholas I's ascension to the imperial throne in 1825 marked the start of the most difficult period for Russia's Jews. As the historian Michael Stanislawski has observed, "To Nicholas, the Jews were an anarchic, cowardly, parasitic people, damned perpetually because of their deicide and heresy; they were best dealt with by repression, persecution, and, if possible, conversion."[1] Through various decrees and restrictions, during the thirty years of Nicholas's rule large numbers of Jews were displaced from their traditional occupations and places of residence. But the harshest decree was issued in 1827 when the tsar ordered that each Jewish community deliver up a quota of military recruits. Jews were to serve for twenty-five years in the military, beginning at age eighteen, but the draftable age was as low as twelve. Those under eighteen would serve in special units called Cantonist battalions until they reached eighteen, whereupon they would begin their regular quarter century of service. As if a term of army service of thirty years or more were not enough, strenuous efforts were made to convert the recruits to Russian Orthodoxy, contrary to the provisions of religious freedom in the conscription law. A double catastrophe fell on the heads of Russian Jewry: their sons would be taken away not only from their homes and families, but in all likelihood also from their religion. Little wonder that all sorts of subterfuges were used in attempts to avoid military service. One can even understand the willingness of the wealthy, and of the communal officials whom they supported, to shield their own children from service by substituting others, as was allowed by law. The hapless substitutes were almost always the children of the poor and socially marginal. The decree fell upon them with especial cruelty, as they watched *khappers* ("snatchers") employed by the community tear their children, no less beloved though they were poor, from their arms. The oath of allegiance was taken by the recruits who were dressed in *talis* and *tfilin* (prayer shawl and phylacteries) as they stood before the Holy Ark in the synagogue, and was concluded by a full range of shofar blasts. This only further embittered the recruits and their families, not only toward the tsarist regime but also toward the "establishment" of the Jewish community. A Yiddish folk song of the time expressed the sentiment poignantly:

> Trern gissen zikh in di gassn
> In kinderishe blut ken men zikh vashn. . . .
> Kleyne oifelekh reist men fun kheyder
> M' tut zey on yevonishe kleyder.
> Unzere parneyssim, unzere rabbonim
> Helfen nokh tsu optzugebn zey far yevonim.
> Bei Zushe Rakover zeynen do ziebn bonim,
> Un fun zey nit eyner in yevonim.
> Nor Leye di almones eyntsike kind
> Iz a kapore far keholishe zind.

> Tears flow in the streets
> One can wash oneself in children's blood. . . .

Gertsl Yankl (Zvi Herts) Tsam (1835–1915). A former Cantonist who served in Siberia, Tsam appears to have been the only Jewish officer in the tsarist army in the nineteenth century. Though he turned one of the worst companies of his regiment into one of the best, Tsam was denied promotion until 1893 when, after forty-one years of service, he was made a full captain shortly before he retired. Tsam was unusual in that he never converted to Christianity and took an active part in Jewish affairs. CREDIT: Saul Ginsburg.

Little doves are torn from school
And dressed up in non-Jewish clothes.
Our leaders and our rabbis
Even help give them away for Gentiles.
Rich Zushe Rakover has sevens sons
But not one puts on the uniform.
But Leah the widow's only child
Becomes a scapegoat for communal sin.

Alexander Herzen, one of the first ideologists of the Russian revolutionary movement, encountered a group of Jewish recruits in 1835 and described the scene as "one of the most awful sights I have ever seen." "Pale, exhausted, with frightened faces, they stood in thick, clumsy, soldiers' overcoats . . . fixing helpless, pitiful eyes on the garrison, soldiers who were roughly getting them into ranks. The white lips, the blue rings under their eyes bore witness to fever or chill. And these sick children, without care or kindness, exposed to the raw wind that blows unobstructed from the Arctic Ocean, were going to their graves."[2]

Since most Jewish men at the time were married in their mid-teens, boys of twelve and under were often offered up to the authorities in order not to tear fathers and husbands away from their families. Between 1827 and 1854 about

70,000 Jews were conscripted, perhaps 50,000 of them minors. Perhaps as many as half the Cantonist recruits were converted to Christianity, passing out of their faith but remaining in the collective memory and folklore of the Jewish people as the *Nikolaevskii soldatn.*

In his attempt to convert the Jews, Nicholas I used the carrot as well as the stick. In 1841 he asked the "enlightened" (*maskil*) German scholar Max Lilienthal to try to persuade the Jews to accept the tsar's offer of modern Jewish schools which would teach both secular and religious subjects. Believing in the good intentions of the government and the need to bring the benefits of European civilization to the benighted Russian Jews, Lilienthal traveled the Pale, seeking to persuade skeptical communal leaders to subscribe to the program. Most Jewish leaders correctly suspected that this was but another scheme to convert the Jews. Clearly the schools were to promote loyalty to the autocratic system. One of the texts in the required religion class (*zakon bozhii*) went as follows: "In our souls we know that it is as great a sin to disobey the word of the King as it is to transgress the commands of God, and Heaven forbid that we should be ingrates or desecrators of His Holy Name and do so in public or in private."[3]

There was no rush to the new schools. Lilienthal left for America, where he served as a Reform rabbi. But by 1864 there were nearly 6,000 Jews in Crown schools (and over 1,500 attending Russian schools). These produced the first Russianized intelligentsia among the Jewish population. It is a great historical irony that many graduates of these state-sponsored schools, candidates for conversion to Russian Orthodoxy and loyalty to the autocracy, were caught up in the spirit of radicalism and rebellion infecting part of the Russian intelligentsia. They became the first Jews to seek ways of changing the tsarist system. Some were not consciously motivated by the plight of their own people, or at least they did not admit it, but others' dissatisfaction with the system was sparked initially by the miserable situation of their co-religionists. The first Jewish graduate of a Russian university (1884), Lev Mandelshtam, exemplified the ambivalence felt by some Jews who had benefited from exposure to Russian culture and had escaped the Pale, but could not escape their attachment to Jewishness and Jews.

> I love my country and the language of my land but, at the same time, I am unfortunate because of the misfortune of all my fellow Jews. Their rigidity has enraged me, because I

can see it is destroying their gifts; But I am bound to their affliction by the closest of ties of kinship and feeling. My purpose in life is to defend them before the world and to help them to be worthy of that defense.[4]

European culture was urged upon the Jews not only by the government, which wished to convert them, but also by Jewish reformers, who wished to "improve" them. The Haskalah, or enlightenment, had begun in Germany and had made its way eastward, passing through Galicia on its way to Russia. The *maskilim*, the enlighteners, sought to bring the benefits of European culture to the Jews and to infuse a new spirit into Jewish culture by reviving the Hebrew language—previously used only in religious texts and rabbinic responsa—for use in novels and scientific textbooks. Some of the *maskilim* advocated reforms in religion, while others were satisfied to maintain the traditional forms. Until the late 1870s the Russian *maskilim* maintained their faith in the goodwill of the tsarist authorities who, they believed, were working for the betterment of the Jews. Most religious Jews, and especially the Hassidim among them, opposed the *maskilim*, suspecting them of undermining traditional authority in the Jewish community and pulling the Jews down the path of acculturation into Russian culture. This, they presumed, could only lead to assimilation and religious conversion. Rejection of the Haskalah united the Hassidim and their traditional opponents, the *misnagdim*, but could not prevent young people, including *yeshiva* students, from delving into the "forbidden literature" and being seduced by the attractions of general European culture. *Maskilim* wrote novels in Hebrew, sometimes giving them biblical settings, and thereby stimulated the revival of Hebrew as a language of modern expression while simultaneously strengthening attachment to the ancestral homeland. The Zionist movement's modern political and cultural programs drew directly on the Haskalah. Others, however, were led by their contact with European culture to the larger, less "parochial" world of contemporary European culture.

Pauline Wengeroff, born in Bobruisk, Belorussia, in 1833, saw the transformation of part of Russian Jewish society in the eighty-three years of her life. In her memoirs she comments on the uncritical enthusiasm with which some Jewish youth embraced the opportunities offered them beginning in the 1840s. They "could not acquire the new, the alien, without renouncing the old and repudiating their unique individuality, and their most precious possessions. How cha-

A young Jewish woman, Genia Kogos Dolgin, in Orsha, ca. 1900.

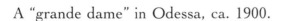

A "grande dame" in Odessa, ca. 1900.

otically these modern ideas whirled through minds of young Russian Jews! Traditional family ideals disappeared, but new ones did not arise in their stead." Women who wished to impart religious teachings and the ways of the tradition were brushed aside by their husbands. Wengeroff notes that the change in attitudes of the men went only so far. "They demanded not only assent from their wives, but also submission. They preached freedom, equality, fraternity in public, but at home they were despots."[5]

Vladimir Medem, a leader of the Jewish Labor Bund, was born in Minsk in 1879 to parents who had been baptized and who baptized their son at birth. He recalled that almost his entire family had been converted. "In the sixties, the springtide of Alexander II's regime, the attitude toward Jews was liberal, and the Jewish community responded ardently in its desire to fuse with the Russian people."[6] Medem's father, born in 1836, was able to study in a Russian *gym-*

nasium and even in a military academy. As an army doctor, he had little to do with Jewish life, and later on, finding his career blocked by anti-Semitism, he joined the Lutheran church at the age of fifty-six.

Leon Trotsky (Lev Davidovich Bronshtain), born in the same year as Medem, came from a family that had not converted, but as farmers who had benefited from one of the tsars' periodic grants of land to Jews, they were removed from the intensive Jewish life of the Pale. In his autobiography Trotsky asserted that "In my mental equipment, nationality never occupied an independent place, as it was felt but little in everyday life." He claimed that "national bias and national prejudices had only bewildered my sense of reason," and that his Marxist convictions deepened his belief that "internationalism" was the only reasonable posture one could assume.[7]

A family in Letichev, Ukraine, turn of the century. CREDIT: Rose Gold.

Peysekh and Leye Zilberman of Bar, Ukraine, where they moved after being forced out of their village by the May Laws of 1882. All six of their children emigrated to the United States, never to see their parents again. CREDIT: Beatrice Silverman Weinreich.

Thus in the last decades of the nineteenth century Jews began to display a variety of attitudes toward their national identities. The vast majority remained firmly rooted in their traditional, primordial Jewish identity, something which was as much a part of them as their own skin, assumed, unquestioned, and perhaps unexamined. Others had examined their Jewishness and found it wanting. They turned to enlightenment in an attempt to synthesize Jewishness and modernity, or they abandoned Jewishness altogether for Christianity and Russian culture, or for socialism and "internationalist" culture. For all of them the traumatic events of 1881–1882 marked an important way station in their journeys of search and self-discovery.

Tsarist Repression and Jewish Reaction

The sanguine expectations and aspirations of Jews who sought escape from the Pale in an enlightened Judaism within an enlightened Russian society were dashed cruelly by the government-inspired pogroms that rolled over the Ukraine and neighboring areas following the assassination of Tsar Alexander II. In the large Ukrainian cities and in Warsaw, in the small towns of the Ukraine and Belorussia, mobs roamed through the streets, attacking Jews, looting their homes and stores, smashing furniture, and generally terrorizing the people, often with policemen looking on. Only after a few days of this would troops be called out to restore order, and the Jews would begin the task of putting their bodies, homes, and lives together. A few hundred lives were lost and there was great material damage, but the psychological impact was greater than the physical one. As Pauline Wengeroff observed, in 1881 "the sun which had risen on Jewish life in the fifties suddenly set. . . . Anti-Semitism erupted; the Jews were forced back into the ghetto. Without ceremony, the gateways to education were closed."[8] In May 1882 laws were passed which prohibited Jews from settling outside the towns and *shtetlekh* (hamlets). Even those who were already residing permanently in rural areas were forced out under various pretexts, so that the countryside would be "cleansed" of Jews. A Jew who left his home for a few days ran the risk of being barred permanently from his residence. Jews were also forbidden to conduct business on Sundays or Christian holidays. Since they did not work on Saturdays or Jewish holidays, they were severely disadvantaged in the competition with non-Jewish businesses, and the subsistence standard of living of large masses was even further reduced. A *numerus clausus*, or quota system, was introduced in Russian schools. An upper limit of 10 percent was established for the proportion of Jewish students in secondary schools in the Pale and 5 percent outside it, 3 percent in Moscow and St. Petersburg. Later these quotas were reduced even further. The logical extension of these restrictions was to limit Jews in the professions, and this was duly enacted. In 1890 the police chief of Moscow ordered that signs on Jewish stores and workshops must carry the full Hebrew names and patronymics (father's name) of their owners. These were to be displayed in bold type only. Lest there be any doubt about the chief's intent, he added that proper names, such as Moisei, not be used; instead, the insulting diminutives (like "Moshka") were to be displayed.

With the same sense of cruel irony the government ordered the expulsion of Jews from Moscow on the first day of Passover, 1891. Coming on the holiday of national liberation, which celebrates the exodus from Egypt, this new exodus left only a few privileged, longtime Jewish residents in the historic city. It was just in 1891 that the grand synagogue had been constructed in Moscow, and now the authorities issued successive edicts constantly changing its permissible functions. It could not be used for worship, and had to be transformed constantly to serve different charitable purposes, each change necessitating reconstruction and driving what was intended to be a showpiece into near bankruptcy. The only institution not harassed was the cemetery. "The police did not impose their invariable limitations on this branch of Jewish life. They evidently recognized the Jewish cemetery as a useful institution."[9]

These persecutions crushed many hopes, closed off the options that had begun to develop only a few decades earlier, but led Jews to explore new ways out of their dilemmas. The Russian statesman Pobedonostsev, tutor to the tsars, was believed to have predicted that Russia's "Jewish problem" would be solved by having one-third of them killed, one-third of them converted to Christianity, and one-third made to leave the country forever. Indeed, in the 1880s there may have been some acceleration of the tendency to abandon Judaism as a hopeless burden and to pay the price for admission to respectability and civil society. In Wengeroff's view, "In the eighties, with anti-Semitism raging all over Russia, a Jew had two choices. He could, in the name of Judaism, renounce everything that had become indispensable to him, or he could choose freedom with its offers of education and a career—through baptism. Hundreds of enlightened Jews chose the latter. These apostates were not converts out of conviction, nor were they like the Marranos of an earlier age. These apostates disbelieved in all religions. . . . " She adds, poignantly, "The baptism of my children was the hardest blow of my life."[10]

Even baptism was not a guaranteed passage out of the stigma of Jewishness. Medem recalls that, unlike in earlier times, after 1881 "No matter how hard one . . . tried to forget one's former Jewishness, the outside world refused to allow it." In his Christianized home, "A sort of code was developed which only the family could understand. Instead of using the word 'Jew,' they said 'Italian,' or 'our kind.' . . . My Jewish origin was a burden. It was a shame, a degradation, a sort of secret disease about which no one should know."[11] This baptized, second-generation Christian was attracted to Jewish friends involved in socialism. He visited synagogues in Minsk on Yom Kippur, and his wanderings around the poor Jewish quarters of the city on Friday nights made a deep impression on him. Gradually he was drawn back to his ancestral people and sought their liberation through socialism, which would liberate all the oppressed, irrespective of nationality or religion. "When did I clearly and definitively feel myself to be a Jew? I cannot say, but at the beginning of 1901, when I was arrested for clandestine political activity, the police gave me a form to fill in. In the column 'Nationality,' I wrote 'Jew.'"[12]

The Moscow Choral Synagogue on Arkhipova Street. PHOTO: Gary Eisenberg.

The Dobrakin family, including the mother, wife, and three daughters of a man who had emigrated to America, 1915. They were separated by World War I. There were many cases of families separated by the war or by the desertion of husbands who emigrated and never sent for their families. CREDIT: Sonia Bronthman.

Emigration was much more popular than conversion as a way of escaping from the disabilities imposed by Russia. Though this solution entailed enormous physical, financial, and emotional hardships, increasing numbers of Jews were driven to give up on the lands of their birth, abandon loved ones, and seek their fortunes across the seas. Between 1820 and 1870 only some 7,500 Russian and Polish Jews had settled in the United States. Between 1871 and 1890 the number of those who went to America rose to 40,000, but in the decade following the 1881 pogroms it jumped to 135,000. The stream became a torrent between 1891 and 1910, when nearly one million Jews fled the Russian Empire for the United States. Tens of thousands of others emigrated to Canada, Western Europe, Australia, South America, and South Africa. The very high birth rates of Russian Jews, combined with mortality rates that had dropped dramatically in the nineteenth century, kept the population large despite the emigration. The first comprehensive census ever taken in the Russian Empire counted over five million Jews in 1897.

The anti-Semitic wave of the 1880s and thereafter, coming both from the peasantry "below" as well as from the tsar and the aristocracy "above," engulfed Jews of all political and cultural persuasions. The great majority of Jews remained loyal to their traditions and expected little from the surrounding world—for was it not taught that "Esau is always an enemy of Jacob"? Ironically, anti-Semitism was perhaps more painful to those who had hoped that education and enlightenment, both that of the Jews as well as of their neighbors, would gradually wipe it out. Some had placed as much faith in the new ideologies as their forefathers had placed in the old. But the old faith seemed more resilient than the new when shocked by the new persecutions.

The idealism and faith of some of the "new men" is exemplified by Solomon Wittenberg, son of a poor artisan, who was arrested and sentenced to death in 1878 for planning to lay a mine in Odessa harbor in anticipation of a visit by the tsar. He refused to accept Christianity as a way of having his sentence commuted, despite the pleadings of his Jewish mother. In his last testament, he explained his convictions:

> Of course, I do not want to die . . . but this should not cast a shadow on my faith and the strength of my convictions. . . . If it cannot be otherwise, if, in order for Socialism to triumph, it is necessary that my blood be shed, if the transition from the present order to a better one is impossible without stepping over our corpses, then let our blood be shed, in redemption, for the good of humanity.[13]

Jewish socialists were almost all *narodniki* (populists) until the 1890s, and based their hopes on an enlightened, self-liberating peasantry. Thus they were greatly shocked by peasant pogroms. They were jolted into confronting the "Jewish question," which many had believed to be only ancillary to the larger question of political and economic liberation. One of the early Jewish socialists, Aaron Zundelevich, said of the *narodniki* of the 1870s: "For us . . . Jewry as a national organism did not represent a phenomenon worthy of support. Jewish nationalism, it seemed to us, had no *raison d'être*. As for religion, that cement which combines the Jews into one unit, it represented to us complete retrogression. . . . For a Jewish *narodnik* the motto—'Go to the people'—meant go to the Russian people."[14]

What stunned some of the Jewish *narodniki* even more than the peasants' behavior was the attitude of their fellow revolutionaries. The bulletin of Narodnaia Volia, the organization that had arranged the tsar's assassination, commented on the "anti-Jewish movement" that it was "not originated or shaped by us" but was "nevertheless, an echo of our activity" for it showed that the peasant could be roused to rebellion. A leaflet in Ukrainian, published in August 1881, said: "You have already begun to rise against the Jews. That is fine. For soon a revolt will start all over Russia against the tsar, the landowners and the Jews." One revolutionary commented on the pogroms that "we rejoice in the educational effects of such occurrences. . . . Let us remind our readers that the French Revolution, too, began with massacres of Jews. It is a sad fate, which is apparently unavoidable."[15] In pogromizing the Jews, the theory went, the peasantry was learning to assert itself, to strike out against its oppressors. It would eventually learn that the real enemy was not the Jews but the exploitative system presided over by the autocracy, and it would come to realize that its proper target ought to be that system. But if in the learning process some Jews had to be sacrificed, so be it.

Many Jewish radicals could not accept this reasoning with equanimity. The Jewish wife of Georgii Plekhanov, a Russian *narodnik* who was to lead many of his disillusioned comrades from populism to Marxism, described the feelings of many Jews when she wrote: "Deep down in the soul of each one of us, revolutionaries of Jewish birth, there was a sense of hurt pride and infinite pity for our own, and many of us were strongly tempted to devote ourselves to serving our injured, humiliated, and persecuted people."[16] Some who yielded to this "temptation" moved toward Zionism, an ideology which argued that the liberation of the Jews could not come about simply as part of general social emancipation

Jewish socialists, 1875 or 1876. Seated third from the right is Aron Liberman, a *maskil* and socialist, who published the first Hebrew socialist journal, *HaEmet* (The Truth) in 1877. Active in socialist activities in England and Europe, Liberman shot himself in Syracuse, N.Y., in November 1880.

but needed to be fought for on its own. Others went over to Marxism, which persisted in seeing the solution to the Jewish question in the general emancipation of the oppressed but which placed its revolutionary faith in the emerging proletariat rather than in the peasantry. Still others drifted away from political activism altogether or, like hundreds of thousands of others, gave up on Russia and emigrated. A minority persisted in their belief in peasant revolution and the ultimate vindication of the *narodnik* cause.

THE EMERGENCE OF THE BUND

Though Jews were barred from much of the heavy industry developing in Russia toward the end of the century, their cottage industries had expanded to small workshops and modest factories. Probably a third of the Jewish labor force was employed in industry and handicrafts by the end of the century; another third were traders, storekeepers, peddlers, and the like; more than 10 percent were day laborers, domestics, and private employees; and the rest were scattered among the professions, agriculture, the military, and transport. Nearly 10 percent were judged to have no specific vocation at all. They were the *luftmentshn*, "people of the air," who lived by their wits, latching on to any opportunity that might present itself, but with no stable means of earning a living. Their ranks were periodically swelled by those who were dislocated from among the artisans, craftsmen, and petty traders.

By the end of the century there were some 300,000 Jewish industrial workers, only about 50,000 of whom were employed in the medium and large-scale factories, and the rest in workshops. In cities such as Warsaw and Lodz in the Polish territories, in Vilna and Bialystok in the northwest, and in Odessa in the south, the Jewish proletariat was an important social and political force. In Bialystok in 1887, for example, all the tobacco and pigskin factory workers, and nearly all the workers in lumber mills, machine shops, and tanneries, were Jews. The Jewish proletariat, like the Russian, eked out a meager existence in miserable conditions. In Gomel in the late 1890s the working day was between sixteen and seventeen hours long; in Minsk's sugar-refining factories at the turn of the century Jewish girls worked twenty hours a day. Sanitary conditions were primitive, pay was often not received on time, and job security was nonexistent.

In the 1880s the Jewish intelligentsia who had tasted Russian culture and who had drifted to Marxism from populism, or who had come directly to Marxist social-democracy, began to reach out to the Jewish proletariat. They organized small groups of workers in study circles in which economics, history, and other nontraditional subjects were studied. Building on the credit and loan associations that the Jewish workers had established, the socialist intelligentsia began to construct the infrastructure of a mass movement. The earliest leaders, having come from the Russified intelligentsia, were not concerned with forming a specifically Jewish movement. Timofei Kopelzon, one of these leaders, recalls that "We were for assimilation; we did not even dream of a special Jewish mass movement. . . . Our task was developing cadres for the Russian revolutionary movement."[17] Confined to the Pale, these Jewish socialists had no choice but to work with Jewish laborers. But they were influenced "from below," and their followers forced them to acknowledge the reality of specifically Jewish concerns and disabilities. Thus when a national organization of these social-democratic (Marxist) labor organizations was formed in 1897, it declared itself the "General League [Bund] of Jewish Workingmen in Russia and Poland" (Lithuania was added to the name in 1901). A year later the Bund was instrumental in bringing together several Marxist groups, including one that had been led by Vladimir Ilyich Lenin, to found a national Russian Social-Democratic Labor Party. The Bund entered that party as "an autonomous organization, independent only in matters which specifically concern the Jewish proletariat." It claimed to need such autonomy so that it could propagate socialist ideas more effectively among the Yiddish-speaking workers. The Bund was admitted to the RSDLP as the "sole representative of the Jewish proletariat."

As more Jewish workers joined the Bund, the intelligentsia leadership was forced to revise its assimilationist position in favor of a more explicitly national program. From Marxists in the Hapsburg Empire the Bund borrowed the idea of "national-cultural autonomy," incorporating it into its official program. This would give each nationality the right to conduct its own cultural affairs in a future democratized state. Meanwhile the socialists of different nationalities would remain part of the general socialist movement and would share with all nationalities the commitment to overthrow tsarism by means of a socialist revolution. Both Vladimir Ilyich Lenin, who became leader of the Bolshevik faction in the RSDLP, and Iulii Martov, who emerged as

H. Leivick (pseudonym of Leivick Halpern, 1888–1962) as a political prisoner. Leivick was arrested in 1906 in his hometown, Ihumen (Minsk province), for participating in a Bundist demonstration. He refused to defend himself at his trial because, as he told the court, "Everything I did, I did in full awareness. I am a member of the Jewish revolutionary party, the 'Bund,' and I'm doing all I can to bring down the tsarist autocracy, the bloody hangmen, you included." He was sentenced to four years at hard labor and permanent exile in Siberia. With money smuggled to him by friends in America, he escaped, wandered about Siberia, and finally arrived in America in 1913 at the age of twenty-four. Earning his living as a wallpaper hanger and a garment worker, Leivick soon gained recognition for his Yiddish poetry and dramas. One of his best-known works was "The Golem." Leivick flirted with Communism, but broke with the party in 1929 and, definitively, in 1939. CREDIT: H. Leivick.

the leader of the Menshevik faction—he was a grandson of Aleksandr Tsederboim, editor of the first Hebrew and Yiddish periodicals in Russia, published in the early 1860s—agreed that the Bund's demand for future national-cultural autonomy and its insistence on organizational autonomy now would harm the revolutionary cause. Therefore, at the Second Congress of the RSDLP in 1903, the Bund was expelled and severely criticized for its slide into "nationalist positions."

The expulsion of the Bund only strengthened the trend toward a more assertively Jewish posture. Jewish workers were attracted to the Bund not only by the promise of liberation from economic misery but also because it organized self-defense units against the pogroms. The Bund also offered them an opportunity to gain a general education, however informally. One of the Bund's more colorful leaders, the volatile Esther Frumkin, recalled how she led a "circle" of young women workers who would meet secretly after the workday:

> With what rapt attention they listened to the talks on cultural history, on surplus value, commodity, wages, life in other lands. How many questions they would ask! What joy would light their eyes after the circle leaders produced a new number of *Yidisher arbeter* [Jewish Worker, an early Yiddish socialist newspaper] . . . or even a brochure! How proud a girl was when she would be given a black book to take home![18]

A Bundist self-defense group in Odessa with three of their slain comrades, 1905. CREDIT: H. Kulkin.

The Bund also fulfilled a psychological need by giving the Jewish workers—whose low status and increasing radicalism isolated them from the "respectable" Jewish community—a sense of dignity and a reassuring feeling of belonging to a cohesive, supportive group. More and more the Bund became a kind of "counterculture," offering cultural and social opportunities and evolving an alternative Jewish identity and social life. Especially after the failed revolution of 1905, when political activity was vigorously suppressed, the Bund turned to cultural activity, largely in Yiddish. It organized musical, literary, and dramatic societies, expanded its press, planned for secular Yiddish schools, encouraged Yiddish writers, and tried to create for its adherents a vibrant cultural life which drew only indirectly from the religious tradition. The Bund generally saw religious belief as a private matter, but condemned institutionalized Judaism in Russia as a creation of the wealthier classes and a toady to the authorities. Drawing on the resentments that had emerged around the Cantonist episode, the Bund tried to wean its constituency away from the "respectable" elements, without shame or apology, and to provide them with a dignified and dynamic alternative.

The Eighth National Conference of the Bund, Petrograd, 1917. In the front row, from left to right, are: Alexander Tshemerinsky, later prominent in the Jewish Sections of the Communist Party; Isaak Tumin; Henryk Erlich, later shot by the Soviet NKVD; Raphael Rein-Abramovitch, active in the socialist opposition to the Bolsheviks; Rakhmiel Veinshtain, who committed suicide in a Soviet prison; Mark Liber, a socialist opponent of the Bolsheviks; Moishe Rafes, author of important scholarly studies of socialism, who joined the Communist Party; A. Litvak, later a Bund leader in Poland; and Esther Frumkin, a leader of the Jewish Sections of the Communist Party who died in a Soviet labor camp in 1943. CREDIT: Lazar Epstein.

ZIONISM:
ESCAPISM OR SALVATION?

The Haskalah movement simultaneously lauded the benefits of contemporary European civilization and the glories of the biblical past. Much of the prose and poetry of the Haskalah had biblical themes and the Hebrew of the *maskilim* was permeated with the biblical idiom. Dreams of a dignified and glorious past contrasted ever more sharply with the deterioration of the Jewish condition in the Russian Empire. Not surprisingly, some began to muse on the possibility of escaping the present by drawing on the past to create a better future. While some had emigrated and others hoped that universal solutions would cure Jewish ills, Zionists were skeptical of the ability of socialism or any other general remedy to cure the Jewish condition. Distressed by an emigration which they regarded as trading one exile for another, they dared to propose a specifically Jewish solution, one which would entail purposeful emigration with the goal of founding a Jewish state, thereby achieving international respectability for Jewry. Such a state would put an end to the myth of "the wandering Jew" and establish the Jews as a people possessing the attributes of a modern nation with its own territory, language, economy, and state.

Leon Pinsker of Odessa, a physician, was the first East European to prescribe Zionism as the remedy for the ills of the Jews. The pogroms of 1881 had shocked him into reconsidering his earlier attraction to assimilationism. In the following year, writing as "A Russian Jew," he published a pamphlet, *Autoemancipation*, in which he argued that anti-Semitism was a disease endemic to Europe, that its fundamental irrationality made it immune to education and rational arguments, and that, therefore, the Jew had no option but to leave Europe. The Jew, "everywhere in evidence but nowhere at home," frightened the non-Jews who could not explain this persistent yet inferior being, except through the most fanciful theories of conspiracy. Since there was no hope of integrating Jews into European society, Jews should not wait for their problems to be solved by others but should begin acquiring a territory which would attract Jewish migrants from all over the world. This would be the physical base for the reestablishment of a Jewish commonwealth.

Pinsker's contemporary, Moses Leib Lilienblum, had gone from a traditional religious education to Haskalah and then to a fascination with Russian radicals such as Chernyshevsky and Pisarev. After the pogroms of 1881, he, too, turned to a nationalist solution, rejecting assimilation. Writing to the famous *maskil* poet, Judah Leib Gordon, Lilienblum asked, "Why should we Jews relinquish our nationality and assimilate with the people we live among? . . . The name of Israel will be erased, but the division of nations will remain and humanity will gain nothing from this." The pogroms had shown that "we are aliens, not only here, but in all of Europe, for it is not our fatherland. . . . We were aliens in Europe when religion flourished because of our religion; now when nationalism reigns, we are aliens because of our origin. We are Semites among Aryans, the sons of Shem among the sons of Japheth, a Palestinian tribe from Asia in the European lands." America was also no solution: "Why . . . flee to America and be alien there, too, instead of to the land of our fathers?" Lilienblum repudiated his old ideal of education as the cure-all. "Our misfortune is not the lack of general education but that we are aliens. We will still remain aliens when we will be stuffed with education as a pomegranate is with seeds."[19]

In a curious way, those who came to Zionism out of frustration with what had turned out to be the chimeras of enlightenment or assimilation remained consistent in their attempts to conform the Jews to be like other peoples. Echoing the ancient Israelites who had demanded that Samuel the Prophet anoint them a king so they could be *kechol hagoyim* (just like the other nations), the intellectuals who had "converted" to Zionism believed that it would solve the Jewish problem by giving the Jews the same characteristics

A Zionist group in Bobruisk, Belorussia, 1902.

LEFT: Rabbi Isaac Jacob Reines (1839–1915), who founded the religious Zionist movement, Mizrachi.

RIGHT: Rabbi Samuel Mohilever (1824–1898), a founder of religious Zionism.

as the other nations. Therefore it can be said that one strand in Zionism was "assimilationist," since it sought to make the Jewish people like all others. This was the dominant Zionist tradition in Western Europe; but in the Russian Empire, where the great majority of Jews adhered to the religious tradition, a far more powerful impetus to Zionism was the age-old messianic dream of a return to Zion. The "assimilationist" argument may have attracted the acculturated intelligentsia, but it was the daily repetition of prayers, and the annual marking of festivals, both of which expressed the longing for a return to Zion, that pushed the masses in the direction of the Promised Land. Many rabbinic authorities looked askance at Zionism because it seemed to propose that the Jewish future could be determined by man, not God, and it tried to advance the messianic age earlier than had been intended by God. Other rabbis, particularly in Lithuania and Belorussia, welcomed Zionism as a movement which would secure badly needed refuge for Jews and would create a social and cultural environment more conducive to observance than the diaspora. Among the early leaders of Zionism were Rabbis Samuel Mohilever and Isaac Jacob Reines, whose writings influenced the development of a religious variant of Zionism for many decades.

In the early part of the twentieth century attempts were made to combine socialism and Zionism, synthesizing two of the most powerful movements of the day. No longer would

Jews have to choose between socialism and Zionism. Nachman Syrkin advocated a non-Marxist socialism emphasizing social welfare and justice. Class struggle in the orthodox Marxist sense would be too costly to the Jews who, oppressed as they were, could ill afford internecine warfare. On the other hand it was the poor Jewish masses who stood to gain most from Zionism, for they had little to gain from remaining in the diaspora. They would establish a society based on the principles of socialism. This would be a far more equitable society than the feudal societies of the European empires or the capitalist ones of Western Europe.

The highly talented Ber Borochov, a pioneer in Yiddish linguistics as well as in Marxist thought, believed that even the Marxist version of socialism could be combined with Zionism. Scrutinizing the Jewish condition in the diaspora—primarily in Russia—he was distressed by the abnormality of the Jewish social structure. Whereas "normal" capitalist society had a large peasantry and/or proletariat at its base, a bourgeoisie in the middle, and an aristocracy at the top, the Jewish world appeared to be an "inverted pyramid." There was hardly any peasantry to speak of, there was no aristocracy, but there was a very large class of petit bourgeois, the small shopkeepers and *luftmentshn* of uncer-

Ber Borochov (1881–1917), (seated, right), with his cousin, Misha Zusmanovitch (seated, left), and his brother-in-law, Meltser, Poltava, Ukraine, 1901.

tain vocation and even less certain future. The proletariat was small, weak, and concentrated in only a few industries. With such a distorted social structure the Jews could not possibly go through the usual social development described by Marx: a growing proletariat, increasingly exploited, rises up against its bourgeois oppressors and makes a socialist revolution. Through no fault of their own the Jews had been denied the basic ingredient of a normal social situation—land. Without land no peasantry could arise, capitalism could not develop as in "normal" societies, and therefore socialism would not evolve. The obvious solution was to find land for the Jews so that the pyramid could be set aright and the usual social evolution ensue. Once the Jews were settled on their own land, the rest would follow naturally. The next logical step, therefore, was to find the land for the Jews. Borochov asserted that "stychic" (spontaneous) processes would drive the Jews out of Europe and toward their own land. Happily, he continued, the ancestral homeland of Palestine was largely underpopulated, and since "nature abhors a vacuum," the Jews—especially the poor—would be attracted to Palestine, where they could proceed to normalize themselves, eventually passing through the capitalist phase by way of class struggle to the promised land of socialism. While some orthodox Marxists scoffed at Borochov's "Talmudic reasoning," his theory attracted many who were intellectually committed to Marxism and emotionally attracted to Zionism. The Poalai Zion Party was formed in 1906 to implement this synthesis of the two ideologies.

Some Russian Jews, largely from the wealthier groups, persisted in believing that they could find their place in a liberalized, not revolutionized, Russian political order. They urged that civil rights be extended so that Jews could have a normal existence in Russia. In 1905, 6,000 Jews signed a "Declaration of Jewish Citizens" which stated, "We expect to secure our civic equality not because it would make the Jews more useful as citizens and benefit others . . . [not] because of our centuries-old residence in the Russian Empire,"[20] but because Jews were human beings who had the right to be accorded fundamental human rights. A noted lawyer, Henrik Sliozberg, reflected in his memoirs that from early childhood he considered himself first of all a Jew, but at the same time "a son of Russia." "To be a good Jew did not mean that one could not be a good Russian citizen and vice versa." Though a non-Zionist, he still considered Jews a "nationality." "We did not think of ourselves as Russians of Mosaic faith, but as Russian Jews. . . . We were not a foreign element. . . . One culture complemented the other.

Yaakov Zrubavel (left), Yitzhak Ben-Zvi (center), and Shlomo Kaplansky, socialist Zionists, in their student days in Poltava, Ukraine, 1906. Zrubavel became a leader of the movement; Ben-Zvi was the second president of the State of Israel; Kaplansky became head of the Technion-Israel Institute of Technology, Haifa.

Dr. Chaim Weizmann (1874–1952), first president of the State of Israel, was born in Motol, Belorussia. He was educated in Pinsk and later in Western Europe where he received a doctorate in chemistry. He was influential in persuading the British government to issue the Balfour Declaration in 1917, and was for many years the leader of the world Zionist movement.

We used to freely express our conviction that Jewish culture could contribute to the culture of mankind and surely also to Russian culture."[21]

It was difficult to keep faith in such high ideals in the face of successive waves of anti-Jewish acts by the government and attacks by the population. The world was shocked in 1903 when the 50,000 Jews in the Bessarabian city of Kishinev were attacked at the instigation of P. A. Krushevan, editor of a local newspaper, a former official, and a notorious Jew-hater. In the course of two days in April, 45 Jews were slain, 86 others seriously wounded, and several hundred others injured. More than 1,500 shops and houses were destroyed or plundered. Mass protests followed in England and the United States, and some prominent Russian intellectuals, including the great writer Leo Tolstoy, also voiced their disgust and blamed the government for its complicity. The government was forced to bring some of the rioters to trial. Those whose guilt could not be denied received only light sentences. The government refused to accept any responsibility for making material amends, and the real organizers of the massacre went not only unpunished but unidentified. Some leading tsarist officials expressed the opinion that the Jews had gotten what they deserved, for were they not for the most part revolutionaries and rebels against the natural order of things?

Victims of the Kishinev pogrom, 1903. CREDIT: David Mowshowitch.

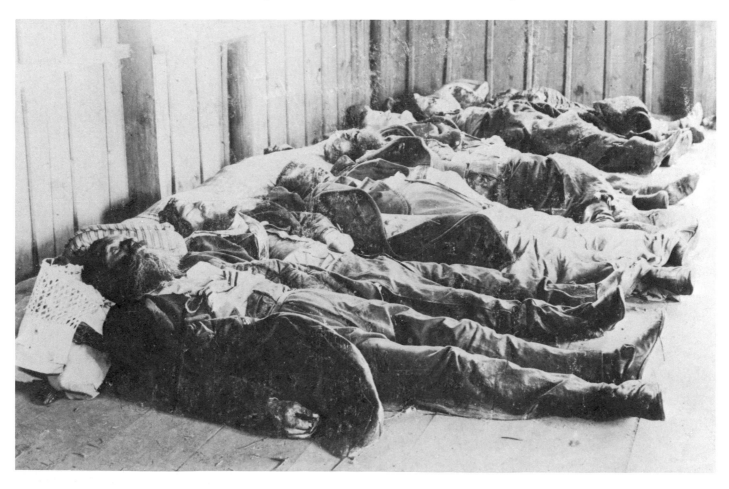

ABOVE: Wounded victims of the pogrom. CREDIT: Mrs. E. G. Greenberg.

BELOW: Victims of the Kishinev pogrom, 1903. CREDIT: David Mowshowitch.

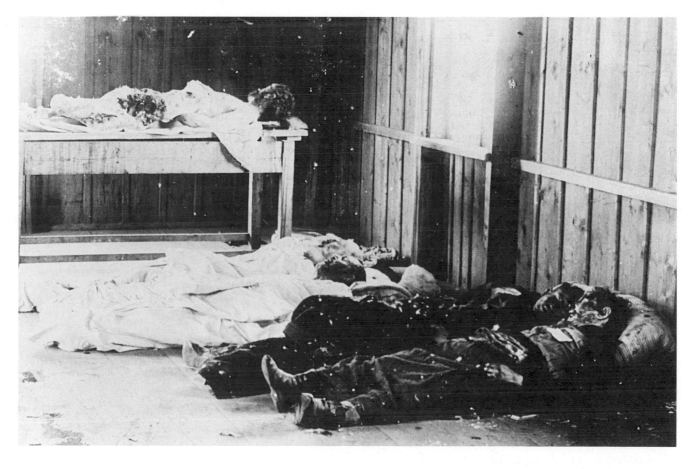

ABOVE: Vandalized homes in Kishinev. CREDIT: Elias Tcherikower.

BELOW: Burying Torah scrolls torn apart during the Kishinev pogrom, 1903.

גניזת ספרי התורה הנקרעים

Kishinev was but a prelude to the events of 1905. In the first week of October in that year a general strike was declared against the government. This was the culmination of several months of protests, initiated by the "Bloody Sunday" in January, when troops had fired on many thousands of demonstrators who had marched on the Winter Palace to petition the tsar. The October strikes brought the country to a halt. Yielding reluctantly to the advice of his more pragmatic ministers, Tsar Nicholas II stunned the country

Vandalized homes of wealthy Jews, Kishinev. CREDIT: Raphael Abramovitch.

Pogrom victims in Ekaterinoslav (now Dnepropetrovsk), Ukraine. These pictures were on postcards published by the self-defense organization of the Poalai Zion. CREDIT: Charles Zunzer.

Grausam hingeschlachtete jüdische Kinder in Jekaterinoslaw

on October 17 by declaring a Manifesto which granted the people a constitutional government. The parliament, or Duma, was to have legislative, not merely consultative, power, though the tsar would continue to rule. Within less than a year this concession was watered down by political maneuvering. Nevertheless, anti-Semitic organizations used the October Manifesto as an excuse for launching pogroms against the Jews, blaming them for undermining the autocracy and promoting the "anarchy" that the reactionaries equated with democratization. One day after the Manifesto was issued, amid general unrest, pogroms broke out in over 300 cities, and in most places lasted a full week. The historian Simon Dubnow wrote that this week, "in its horrors, finds no parallel in the entire history of humanity." He could not have foreseen the greater horrors perpetrated by the Nazis, who murdered him in Riga in 1941. He described "the customary procedure" of these pogroms:

> In connection with the manifesto of October 17, the progressive elements would arrange a street procession, frequently adorned by the red flags of the left parties. . . . Simultaneously, the participants in the "patriotic demonstration"—consisting mostly of the scum of society, of detectives and police officials in plain clothes—would emerge . . . carrying the portrait of the Tzar under the shadow of the national flag, singing the national hymn and shouting, "Hurrah, beat the Zhyds! [Jews] The Zhyds are eager for liberty. They go against our Tzar to put a Zhyd in his place." These "patriotic" demonstrators would be accompanied by police and Cossack patrols (or soldiers), ostensibly to preserve order, but in reality to enable the hooligans to attack and maltreat the Jews and prevent the victims from defending themselves. As soon as the Jews assembled for self-defense, they would be driven off by the police and troops. Thereupon, the "patriotic" demonstrators . . . would break up into small bands and disperse all over the city, invading Jewish houses and stores, ruin, plunder, beat, and sometimes slaughter entire families.[22]

In Odessa, where perhaps the worst pogrom took place, over 300 died. Thousands were wounded, nearly 600 children were orphaned, and about 40,000 Jews were "materially ruined."

The twelve Jewish deputies to the first Duma tried to use the new legislature to stop the terror, and the Duma did adopt a resolution condemning pogroms and demanding punishment of the guilty. But the Duma was soon disbanded, as the tsar and his supporters regrouped to fight against liberalization. The Second Duma, two of whose Jewish deputies were assassinated, was also dismissed. The Third Duma, elected by a much narrower franchise, was dominated by the supporters of the tsar and enemies of the Jews.

The world's attention was again drawn to Russian anti-Semitism in 1911, this time not by the murder of large numbers of Jews but by a blood libel against a solitary, humble man, Mendel Beilis. A Christian boy had been murdered by a gang of thieves because he had incriminating evidence on the gang's activities. When the body was found in the Dnieper River, the reactionary press leaped to the conclusion that the boy had been murdered by Jews for ritual purposes, a charge harking back to the Middle Ages. The Jews supposedly had a "horrible commandment" to murder Christian children, else their religious obligations would not be fulfilled. High officials conspired to suppress evidence turned up by the police that Beilis was in no way involved in the murder. They protected the true murderers, whose identity had become known. Beilis remained in prison for two years while the officials tried to build their case against him. In Western Europe and the United States leading personalities protested against the blood libel charge, but to no avail.

Mendel Beilis lived in this house in the "Podol" section of Kiev, an area inhabited by Jews for hundreds of years. CREDIT: Boris Feldblyum.

БЕЙЛИСЪ и его ЗАЩИТНИКИ.

О. О. Грузенбергъ.

В. М. Маклаковъ.

Н. П. Карабчевскій.

М. Бейлисъ.

А. С. Зарудный.

Григоровичъ-Барскій.

Тип. М. Шайняка въ Лодзи. — Изд. М. Крышекъ.

Russian liberals and radicals joined in the protest with equal futility. In September 1913 Beilis was brought to trial. The trial itself, like that of Dreyfus in France some two decades earlier, aroused much controversy, split the attentive public, and brought the issue of anti-Semitism into clear focus. Against the machinations of officialdom and the "experts" marshalled to support the claim that Jews had to kill Christians for ritual purposes, the defense mobilized the best legal minds of the day and the services of leading Russian scientists and scholars. Though the judge tried to sway the jury and hamper the defense, the twelve peasants sitting on it—all intelligentsia had been struck from the jury by the prosecuting attorney—declared a verdict of "not guilty." As Oskar Gruzenberg, the leading defense attorney, remarked: "The plain peasants proved to be higher in their moral sensitivity than many representatives of the . . . judiciary."[23]

The trial ended in victory for Beilis and the Jews and ignominious defeat for the government and the camp of anti-Semites. Up to the eve of the 1917 revolution the government was still trying to "prove" its case against Beilis and the Jewish people as a whole. That a government facing economic and political difficulties so great that they were shortly to bring it down could devote so much effort to libeling one Jew testifies eloquently both to its bankruptcy and its obsessions.

Mendel Beilis and his family after his acquittal.

OPPOSITE: Poster entitled "Beilis and His Defenders." In the center is Beilis. Clockwise, from top left, are O. O. Gruzenberg, V. M. Maklakov, N. P. Karabchevsky, Grigorovich-Barsky, and A. S. Zarudnyi.

Jewish Life and Culture in the Tsarist Empire

Against the dismal background of oppression, and official and social intolerance, the lights of Jewish culture shone brightly. Perhaps because the world around them was so hostile, the Jews of the Russian Empire developed a dynamic internal life and a self-contained, but multifaceted, culture. Enormous stores of creative energy that could not easily find an outlet in the larger society were channeled into specifically Jewish creativity. They found expression in music, literature, religious and cultural scholarship and thought, art, drama, and a rich folk culture which permeated even the most remote areas of Jewish settlement. In the late nineteenth century this culture became more pluralistic, touched as it was by new political, social, and cultural ideas. Even when resisted, these ideas left their imprint on the changing Jewish way of life.

A "Mountain Jew" of the Caucasus, early in this century.

Young "Mountain Jews," ca. 1900.

Jews could expect nothing from the government or society in the way of welfare and educational functions. Moreover, as an oppressed minority, they felt keenly the need to protect themselves and preserve their values, as had Jews in Western Europe in the Middle Ages. Therefore Jews developed a complex network of institutions to take care of their own and to guard their cherished values and beliefs.

By 1897 there were 5.2 million Jews in the Russian Empire. All but 300,000 of them resided within the Pale of Settlement. Those outside the Pale included 60,000 Georgian and "Mountain" Jews living in the Caucasus, as well as 50,000 residents of Central Asia and Siberia. Within the Pale, Jews constituted over 11 percent of the population, though they were but 4 percent of the empire's total population. They were especially concentrated in the urban areas, so that they made up more than half the population of the cities of Belorussia and Lithuania and 30 percent of the Ukraine's city population. By the end of the century more Jews were living in cities than in the *shtetlekh*, those largely Jewish hamlets which occupied a position midway between the vast expanses of rural Russia and her growing cities.

In both cities and *shtetlekh* Jews lived in self-contained environments. Restricted severely in their political, cultural, and economic opportunities, the Jews concentrated on creating a comprehensive communal structure which performed many of the functions of the modern welfare state. Russian Jewry produced two modern literatures, regulated their lives by the tenets of their faith, and began to create new political ideologies and movements. Jewish communities were very dense concentrations. In most *shtetlekh* and in many smaller cities Jews constituted the great majority of the population. This gave people a strong feeling of communal solidarity. It also produced social and religious conformity. Many welcomed the warmth and security of an all-embracing community, but some found it stifling and confining. The latter either tried to reach out beyond the Jewish community, or, by the end of the century, to create alternatives within it, and to turn a homogeneously traditional community into a more pluralistic "modern" one.

Until 1844 the authorities had formally recognized the *kahals*, the local Jewish communal bodies whose authority extended beyond religious matters to the regulation of commerce, licensing of professions, regulation of education, and the provision of services in the areas of health, education, and general welfare. Though the tsar abolished the *kahals* in 1844, the communities continued to regulate their own affairs much as before. Every community, no matter how small, had its *khevra kadisha* (holy society) which took care of burying the dead and maintaining cemeteries. Every community also had its mechanism for collecting alms for the poor and providing dowries for indigent brides. This did not prevent some from adopting begging as a more or less permanent occupation, but it did signal the communal commitment to taking care of the poor. The often-humorous confrontations between supplicants and potential donors provided much of the material for the folklore of Eastern Europe. Communities also erected a *hekdesh*, a primitive hospital or infirmary, which, because of the miserable condition of most such institutions, came to be a synonym for filth and disarray. Another institution that evoked ambivalent feelings was the orphanage, usually a last resort for the poor. The great majority of the aged lived with their extended families, but there were *moshavei zkeinim*—literally, old-age homes—for those who could or would not.

In a country where 80 percent of the population was illiterate as late as the eve of World War I, almost all Jewish boys, and most of the girls, learned to read and write their own language. By the twentieth century over 30 percent of Jewish men and 16 percent of the women could also read Russian, and by 1911, 126,000 Jews were enrolled in Russian schools. But the dominant forms of education remained the traditional ones right up to the revolutions of 1917. The best known was the *kheyder*—literally, room—where boys

Old-age home in Khmelnik, Ukraine. CREDIT: Sholom Vasilevsky.

Old-age home in Kiev, administered by KEBO (Society for Relief of the Poor and the Sick). CREDIT: Joseph Rosen.

The KEBO home. CREDIT:
Joint Distribution Committee.

would start their studies as early as the age of three and no later than five. Usually, boys of different ages would be in the same classroom, presided over by a *melamed*, or teacher. He was often looked down upon by the community as someone who could not succeed at any other profession and had become a teacher by default. Indeed the *melamdim* had no pedagogical training, though some had great innate abilities, and their miserable incomes signalled their lowly status. Educational materials usually consisted of no more than the prayer book, the Bible, the Talmud, and rabbinic writings, almost none of which was adapted for use by young students. The *kheyder* was often simply a room in the *melamed*'s modest home. Despite these disadvantages, it seems that a substantial number of *kheyder* pupils mastered impressive amounts of traditional lore and developed outstanding powers of reasoning as well as a lifelong commitment to the study of the Torah. Increasingly, the products of the *khadorim* directed their intellectual curiosity beyond the world of Torah study, some to other branches of Judaica, others to secular studies, and many to a combination of both.

Mazepa is our *rebbe*. His name is really Boruch Moshe, but since he's come down recently from Mazepevka, the town calls him the Mazepevker, and we *cheder* [*kheyder*] boys have shortened it and turned it into Mazepa—"dark and ugly." Generally, when students crown their *rebbe* with a lovely name like that, he has earned it. Let me present him to you.

Short, shrivelled and skinny—a creep. Without a trace of a beard, mustache, or eyebrows. Not, God forbid, because he shaves, but just because they don't care to grow. They talked themselves out of it. But to compensate, he has a pair of lips on him, and oh, my! a nose! A braided loaf, a horn, a *shofar*! And a voice like a bell, a lion's roar. How did a creature like him get such a terrifying voice? And where did he get his strength? When he grabs your arm with his skinny, cold fingers, you can see the world to come. And when he slaps you, you feel it for the next three days. He hates lengthy discussions. For the least thing, guilty or not guilty, he has one law: Lie down!

"*Rebbe*! Yossel Yankev Yossel's hit me."

"Lie down!"

"*Rebbe*, it's a lie! He kicked me in the side first."

"Lie down!"

"*Rebbe*! Chaim Berl Lappes stuck his tongue out at me."

"Lie down!"

"*Rebbe*, lies and falsehood! It was just the opposite. He gave me the high sign."

"Lie down!"

And you have to lie down. Nothing helps. Even redheaded Eli, who is already *Bar Mitzvah* and betrothed and wears a silver pocketwatch—you think he isn't beaten? Oh my, isn't he! Eli says that he'll regret those beatings. He says he'll pay Mazepa back with interest; he says he'll give him something to remember him by until he has grandchildren. That's what Eli always says after a whipping, and we answer:

"Amen. Hope so. From your mouth to God's ears."[24]

From Sholem Aleichem's "Bandits."

The *kheyder* and Talmud Torah constituted the elementary rung on the educational ladder. The next step up was the *yeshiva*, attended by post–Bar Mitzvah young men and emphasizing Talmudic studies. Only a tiny minority of the students became professional rabbis; most became *yeshiva* instructors themselves, or merchants, bookkeepers, professionals, clerks—or life-long students supported either by wives who would run a shop or by wealthy fathers-in-law proud to have scholars in the family. The *yeshivas* started as local institutions, and it was a matter of considerable prestige for a town and its rabbi to have such an institution. But by the mid–nineteenth century a few national institutions had

Graduating class of the Hebrew-
language Moriah school in
Zhvanietz, Ukraine, 1910.

A *melamed* and his pupils,
Satanov, Ukraine. CREDIT:
Sol Liptzin.

Reb Shmuel Mende, a teacher in Lithuania, 1911. CREDIT: Isaac Levitas.

School in Demievka, 1911, where Hebrew was the language of instruction. CREDIT: Abraham Shulman.

emerged, such as the academies at Volozhin and Mir. Though such great cities as Vilna, Minsk, and Warsaw had several *yeshivas*, some of the most famous *yeshivas* were in tiny towns. As with any school system, the *yeshivas* produced their own folklore, centering around the different methods employed, the reputations of the faculty, the caliber of students, and the individual emphases and intellectual styles that emerged. Brilliant young students were call *iluyim* (prodigies or geniuses) and their reputation often followed them through-

A school in Keidan, Lithuania, 1904. CREDIT: Yitzhak Edelman.

The inauguration of the first Yiddish school in Dvinsk (Daugavpils), Latvia, 1914. The guest of honor in the center is the writer Sholem Aleichem. CREDIT: I. Levin-Shatzkes.

out their lives, even those who "strayed from the straight path." Often students were known not by their actual family names but by the places they came from. Thus someone might be called "Avrom der Vilner," "Yisroel Slutzker," or "Shmuel Shklover," and this would become the man's name for life.

Because of intellectual or financial limitations, only a minority of the *kheyder* students ever rose to the heights of the *yeshiva*. But for the most of the rest Torah study did not end with the *kheyder* but continued on a part-time basis in the study groups that would meet every day, often twice daily, in the synagogue before or in between prayer services. Classes (*shiurim*) were conducted on several levels so that each person could find his niche. Few women were given much formal Jewish education, but there were Yiddish texts designed specifically for them containing popularized and heavily moralistic versions of the sacred texts.

Though there had been great resistance to the Russian schools in earlier decades, by 1900 significant numbers of Jews were attending such schools, often in combination with private religious instruction. Around the turn of the century, too, new types of schools began to appear. Nontraditional Yiddish and Hebrew schools, most of which had political tinges of one sort or another, came on the horizon. Bundists promoted the establishment of nonreligious Yiddish schools which would educate children in the spirit of socialism. A reformed type of *kheyder*, the *kheyder metukan* (improved), appeared around the turn of the century. Not only were the physical surroundings improved, but the curriculum included general studies, such as reading and writing Russian, mathematics, and some general history and geography. Hebrew was used not only as *loshn koidesh* (the holy tongue), but as the language of a modern literature and one with the potential to be used in daily life. The Zionists established schools that used Hebrew as the medium of instruction, even for subjects such as geography and chemistry. A network of such schools, called *Tarbut* (culture), was to spread to Poland and the Baltic. Partisans of Yiddish, on the other hand, dismissed Hebrew as a theological language only, and stressed that the vast majority of Russian Jews were Yiddish speakers. The great Yiddish writer who also wrote in Hebrew, I. L. Peretz, said at the 1908 conference in Chernovits called to resolve the *Kulturkampf* between Yiddish and Hebrew: "The Jews constitute one nation whose language is Yiddish. . . . In this culture we shall build up our national treasure, create our culture, awaken our spirit, and unite culturally in all lands and at all times."[25]

Delegates to the Chernovits Conference, 1908. Among them are, seated, from left: Nathan Birnbaum, social and political thinker and activist; Esther Frumkin; unidentified; Helena Peretz, and her husband, the writer I. L. Peretz. In the second row, first on the left is the writer Sholem Asch; third from left is the poet Abraham Reisin, and to his right is the writer H. D. Nomberg. On the extreme right in the same row is the Yiddishist and socialist, Khayim Zhitlovsky.

The spirit of change and reform even touched lightly on the world of the *yeshivas*. In Odessa, Khayim Tchernowitz, known as Rav Tsair, opened a *yeshiva* that introduced the scientific methods of *Wissenschaft des Judentums* developed in Western Europe. Among its faculty the *yeshiva* included Chaim Nachman Bialik, himself a former student at the Volozhin *yeshiva*, later known as the Hebrew national poet, and Joseph Klausner, later a literature and history professor at the Hebrew University in Jerusalem. Rabbi Isaac Jacob Reines had proposed a new plan for the study of Talmud along with general studies as early as 1880, but only in 1905 did he get the chance to establish a *yeshiva* along these lines in Lida. He argued that only the inclusion of secular studies in the *yeshiva* curriculum could prevent ever-larger numbers of students from abandoning religious studies altogether. "The world is changed now," he wrote in 1913. "To be employed nowadays, a man needs general education and training. . . . Now the Jewish community is being swayed by an alien voice; the Jewish voice has been silenced . . . A *yeshiva* . . . must at the same time prepare students in general subjects. Only this sort of *yeshiva* can rescue Judaism."[26] Rabbi Reines, among the founders of religious Zionism, declared himself "distressed and heartsick" by the absence of religious leadership in the Zionist ranks. Here, too, he argued that religious Jews should not shun new ideas and movements. As a result of his efforts, the Mizrachi movement of religious Zionism was created.

Neither the *yeshiva* in Odessa nor the one in Lida was widely imitated. Their importance lies not in their popularity but in their signalling changing times.

What had come to be known as Orthodoxy in Western Europe and America was the only form of religious Judaism in Russia. Reform Judaism, born of the European Enlightenment, was unknown, since the conditions that had created it—exposure to Western culture and ideas of scientific rationalism and progress, as well as of social and political equality—were kept out of the Russian Empire and did not penetrate the Pale until the late nineteenth century. Dissent and rebellion generally meant not changing religious practices and beliefs, but abandoning them altogether, or adopting new "secular religions" such as socialism. The great majority of Russian Jews continued to adhere to the principles of faith as they had evolved in the rabbinic tradition,

The grave of Rabbi Nachman of Bratslav in Uman, Ukraine, now in the yard of a peasant's home. Every year followers of the "Bratslaver Rebbe" make a pilgrimage to the grave. This photograph was taken in 1985. CREDIT: Gerald and Judith Teller.

and, in the smaller towns especially, even those who had doubts about those principles usually continued conforming in their outward behavior. The fact that the "town skeptic" or, in the larger cities, groups of "doubters," could be identified as such pointed out the dominance of the faithful. But the Haskalah had introduced questions and ideas that could not be ignored and that had penetrated even the most famous of the *yeshivas*. Some students were "infected" and left tradition for political and cultural activism; others left for new lands, dropping their religious and cultural baggage by the wayside; still others sought ways of synthesizing tradition with new ideas.

Within the traditional camp, too, there was a certain differentiation. The Hassidic movement, originating in the Ukraine but most popular in Polish Galicia and later in Romania and Hungary, was outlawed in the late eighteenth century by Rabbi Elijah, the Gaon (Genius) of Vilna, the acknowledged rabbinic authority of his day. Nevertheless, Hassidism made some headway even in the northwest area (Lithuania, Latvia, and Belorussia) where the Lubavitcher dynasty established itself. In the Ukraine, Chernobyl, Bratslav, and Ruzhin-Sadigora, Hassidic houses arose, and some outstanding Hassidic leaders, such as Levi Yitzhak of Berdichev, gained enormous reputations.

The Hassidim emphasized that one could attain spiritual fulfillment not only through learning and intellectual efforts, but through sincere prayer and behavior expressive of the joy of drawing closer to God. The *misnagdim* (opponents) suspected that this doctrine, with its emphasis on song and dance, often fueled by alcohol, could divert attention from the study of Torah, legitimate its neglect, and lead to licentious behavior. The Vilna Gaon, painfully aware of the tragedy of Sabbatai Zvi and the false messianic movement he had created in the mid–seventeenth century, foresaw the development of a cultic movement in Hassidism, wherein wonder-working *rebbes*, or Hassidic leaders, would become objects of adulation and near worship. Mutual hostility between Hassidism and *misnagdim* led them not only to pray in different synagogues and in slightly different forms, but to mutual accusations of heresy and even of disloyalty to the authorities. Thus, for example, an early leader of the Lubavitcher sect was jailed by tsarist officials on the basis of information supplied by *misnagdim*. In later years the controversy died down somewhat, though the breach was never completely healed. The Hassidim remained a distinct group within the religious community.

In the second half of the nineteenth century a new movement appeared in Lithuania. The *musar* movement, whose central figure was Rabbi Israel Lipkin—called Salanter after the town of Salanty in which he settled—advocated self-scrutiny and ethical behavior. Building on the prophetic tradition of condemning ritual that was not accompanied by personal morality, the *musarists* established their own *yeshivas* and tried to emphasize the ethical literature in Judaism without giving up any of the traditional Talmudic and rabbinic learning. Tales were told of the good deeds of the *musarists*, and of their constant self-examination. Some were said to stand in tubs of cold water in order to avoid the seductive effects of creature comforts. The following vignette, told of Rabbi Salanter, illustrates the outlook of the movement. On his way to the Kol Nidre service on Yom Kippur eve, the holiest time of the year, Rabbi Israel, as he was known, heard a child crying and saw that it was lying in its cradle with a bottle of milk just out of reach. The mother had left for the synagogue, expecting her six-year-old daughter to feed the baby, but the daughter had fallen asleep and did not hear the crying. Rabbi Israel fed the baby and put it to sleep, whereupon the daughter awoke and begged him not to leave for she was afraid of being left alone. Fearful of letting the children stay alone with low-burning candles, he stayed until the mother came home. His followers were amazed that the rabbi would have missed the Yom Kippur service just because of one child's crying and another's fears. The rabbi scolded them, reminding them that Jews were permitted to violate the Sabbath and even Yom Kippur if a life in jeopardy could be saved. Indeed, he rejoiced in having had the fortune to do a good deed at a time as holy as Yom Kippur.

Religion was not confined to the synagogue or school. Prayers were said at home, ritual objects and religious ceremonies in the home were an important part of the life cycle, and even in their dress and appearance Jews followed religious prescriptions. The government tried to limit the number of synagogues and Houses of Study (*batei midrash*) that could be established; it issued licenses for them, and held an executive board responsible for the personnel, decorum, and financial affairs of the synagogue, much as the Soviet government was to do later. Seventeen articles of an 1835 statute regulating the functioning of the rabbinate detailed the responsibilities of the rabbi, which included keeping the community's vital statistics, reporting them to the government, and seeing to it that all activities conformed to Russian

The synagogue in Tomsk, Siberia. The city, thousands of miles from the Pale of Settlement, had fewer than 4,000 Jews around the turn of the century. Most were descendants of the few Cantonists who had not converted.

OLD SYNAGOGUE of Tomsk, Siberia.

Siyum ha-Torah (completion of writing a Torah scroll) celebration in synagogue, Dubrovna, Belorussia. Dubrovna's main industry was textiles. Almost all the *taleisim* (prayer shawls) for the Russian Empire were made here. CREDIT: A. Litwin.

law. The rabbis proved unwilling or incompetent to perform many of these services, so the government created the official "Crown rabbis" (known as the *kazioner rabbiner*). Many people regarded them as government agents, and since most Crown rabbis had some secular education, they were further suspect of heretical leanings. In time, however, they came to be perceived as effective representatives of the communities to the authorities, leaving internal communal and religious matters in the hands of the old rabbinic leadership. Some Crown rabbis became prominent national spokesmen and leaders of the Zionist movement, such as Rabbi Jacob Mazeh of Moscow and the Zionist orator Shmaryah Levin in Ekaterinoslav.

The synagogues of the Russian Empire were usually not as grand as those in the cities of Western Europe or even Hungary—and neither were the cities. But by the turn of the century in a few of the larger cities—Saint Petersburg, Moscow, Odessa, and Kiev—grand edifices had been erected, perhaps more as showcases than as houses of intense worship. In the smaller cities and *shtetlekh* one could still find the wooden synagogues, sometimes elaborately decorated, of earlier centuries. There were also the small *batei midrash* and synagogues of the various trades and professions as the professional guilds usually established a house of worship for their membership. There were synagogues of the Hassidic groups and of the neighborhoods. In the cities there would often be a *groise shul* (large synagogue) as well. Need-

The synagogue in Mstislavl was built in the first half of the seventeenth century. In August 1708, according to the record book of the Jewish community, Tsar Peter the Great arrived in town with a military force which proceeded to carry out a pogrom. "And if God had not moved the Tsar to personally visit our synagogue there would have been bloodshed. Only with the help of God did the Tsar save us . . . and the land quieted down."

A synagogue in Belaia Tserkov, Ukraine. The nearly 20,000 Jews here in 1897 were mainly artisans and workers in light industry.

Elizavetgrad (now Kirovograd), Ukraine. In 1897 there were nearly 24,000 Jews in the city. There were pogroms in Elizavetgrad in 1881 and 1905. CREDIT: A. Litwin.

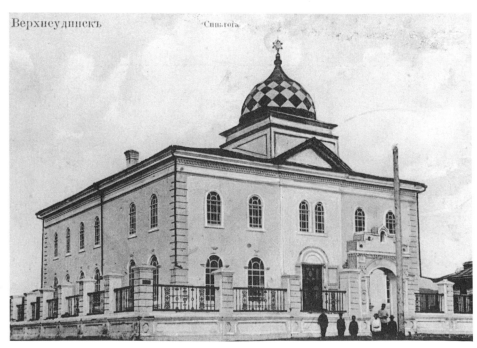

Synagogue in Verkhneudinsk, near Lake Baikal in what is now the Buriat-Mongol Autonomous Soviet Socialist Republic. This remote town had only 65 Jewish families in 1879, but by 1897 there were nearly 1,000 Jews there. CREDIT: Solomon Stedman.

Cantor Pinkhas Minkovsky and his choir in the "Brody" Synagogue in Odessa, probably around the turn of the century. The synagogue was built in the 1840s by people from the Galician town of Brody. Odessa was known as a city of outstanding cantors, some of whom had formal musical training, unusual in Russia. The Brody Synagogue was perhaps the only one in Russia that had an organ, installed in 1909. Today the synagogue is used as the Odessa municipal archive. CREDIT: Esther Schechter.

The "Great Synagogue" in Vitebsk, a center for Zionists and *misnagdim*. Jews are identified in Vitebsk for the first time in 1551. The 34,000 Jews in Vitebsk around 1900 represented over half the total population of the town. In 1904 Tsar Nicholas II passed through the city and was presented by the Jewish community with a 300-year-old Torah scroll.

A Passover seder in the Russian army, 1905. CREDIT: William Sriro.

The Great Synagogue in St. Petersburg (Leningrad). Jews had a very difficult time obtaining permission to build a synagogue in the capital of the Russian Empire. When permission was finally given, it was stipulated that the synagogue would have to be a specified distance away from churches and public buildings. This synagogue was opened in 1893 and has 1,200 seats. Popularly known as the "Baron Ginzburg Synagogue," it is today the only one in Leningrad, whose Jewish population was 162,600 in 1970. CREDIT: *The Day Morning Journal*.

At prayer in Vilkomir
(Ukmerge), Lithuania, ca. 1921.
CREDIT: S. Joshua Kohn.

Synagogue in Samara, built in
1908, which had 1,000 seats.
Samara is on the Volga River,
outside the former Pale.

The *aron kodesh* (Holy Ark) and *bimah* (reader's platform) of the main synagogue in Mariampol (Marijampole), Lithuania. CREDIT: Alte Sudarsky.

LEFT, BELOW: The *Magid* (popular preacher) of Minsk, Belorussia, Reb Binyamin Shukbitsky, 1865–1937. CREDIT: David Cohen.

RIGHT, BELOW: Portrait of Rabbi Yitzhak Elkhanan Spector (1817–1896), leading rabbinical authority of Russian Jewry, Kovno (Kaunas), Lithuania. CREDIT: Joint Distribution Committee.

Reciting the *Tashlikh* prayers (prayers said on Rosh Hashanah at a flowing body of water, symbolizing the casting-off of one's sins) in Lithuania. CREDIT: American Jewish Historical Society.

less to say, all were Orthodox in their ritual, though in a few places, such as Odessa—which was generally considered a haven for freethinkers—such "radical" innovations as a formally attired and conservatory-trained cantor and a professional choir were introduced.

THE EMERGENCE OF MODERN HEBREW AND YIDDISH LITERATURE

Out of the Haskalah came both a revival of Hebrew as a medium of nonreligious literary expression and a commitment to examine the Jewish way of life critically. Form and content were joined in Hebrew prose and poetry which began to appear in mid-century and gathered momentum sufficient to produce a respectable corpus by the time of World War I. At first rather primitive in its rationalist critique of tradition and stultified in its artificial, improvised language, Hebrew literature became linked to the Zionist movement, just as literary and linguistic revivals accompanied the romantic national movements in Eastern and Western Europe. Much of the literature displayed an ambivalence toward the Jewish tradition: appreciative of its spiritual and moral strength, but critical of its conservative effects. Thus the stories of Micha Yosef Berdichevsky simultaneously display an admiration of physical strength as well as a sympathy for Hassidic piety. Chaim Nachman Bialik synthesized his own

Writers and historians, Odessa, 1913. From right to left: Y. Kh. Ravnitsky, Mendele Mokher Sforim, Simon Dubnow, Chaim Nachman Bialik, A. Druyanov.

experience in the traditional *yeshiva* with the free-wheeling, and sometimes freethinking, spirit of Odessa where he lived for many years. His poems "Hamatmid" (The Scholar) and "Im yesh et nafshekha ladaat" (If You Would Like to Know) reflect an admiration for the world of Talmudic study and its inhabitants, but at the same time a fear that it would no longer do to retreat into the ivory tower of Torah learning. Bialik gave powerful expression to the pain of his people following the Kishinev pogrom, but held out the hope for a brighter future in the ancestral homeland of Palestine, to which he himself emigrated in the early 1920s. Most writers chose either Russian, Yiddish, or Hebrew, but Shimon Frug was one of the rare poets who wrote in all three. Ahad Haam (pen name of Asher Ginzburg) who was employed in the huge tea business owned by a Jew, Visotsky, became famous for his essays on contemporary Jewish questions which were models of clarity and style and important contributions to Zionist thought. The literature produced by these and many other Hebrew writers appeared not only in book form, but in the growing number of Hebrew journals which, in the tradition of the Russian "thick journal," included prose, po-

The writer Daniel Charney and his wife near the grave of Mikhail Lermontov, the Russian romantic poet, Piatigorsk, Caucasus Mountains, 1917. CREDIT: Daniel Charney.

Ahad Haam, second from left, with the writer Mordechai ben Hillel Hacohen, surrounded by admirers. CREDIT: Aryeh Tsentsifer, Central Zionist Archives.

etry, philosophical and social essays, and news reportage from the world over and from the Pale. These were devoured by the intelligentsia of the big cities as well as by the youth and provincial observers of the new cultural currents.

For several hundred years there had been a Yiddish literature, part folk tales, part religious homilies and legends. In the nineteenth century Yiddish novels and short stories were written, marking the emergence of a major literature. As in the parallel Hebrew literature, the first works in Yiddish were in a satirical reformist vein, though later this mellowed somewhat. Sholem Jacob Abramovich, better known by his pen name of Mendele Mokher Sforim (Mendele the Bookseller), is considered the father (or sometimes the *zaide*, or grandfather) of modern Yiddish literature, and he has a strong claim to paternity also in Hebrew literature. His novels display both satire and sympathy, as he captured the characters and landscapes of the Pale in mid-century. "I divided my literary work in three parts," he recalled. He translated scientific texts into Yiddish and Hebrew in order to enlighten the Jews of the Pale. He also wrote essays and stories in Hebrew. Yiddish, he observed, "in my time was an empty vessel, filled only with ridicule, nonsense, and the twaddle of fools. . . . The women and the commonest people

The writer Mendel Elkin (left) and the playwright Peretz Hirshbein, 1910. Life-long friends, they were active in the Yiddish theater in Russia, Poland, and the United States. In this photo they are dressed like typical "artistic" dandies of the time. CREDIT: Mendel Elkin.

The Okun family, ca. 1900, in Bobruisk, Belorussia. Standing on the left is Yisroel Okun, who became the first director of the ORT vocational high school in Vilna after World War I. To his left is Rivka Okun, who later married the writer Mendel Elkin. CREDIT: Mendel Elkin.

Bobruisk, 1913. Standing, from the right: publisher Boris Kletskin and writers Yaakov Dineson, I. L. Peretz, and Mendel Elkin. The writer A. Y. Paperno is seated. CREDIT: Mendel Elkin.

This airplane, en route from Berlin to St. Petersburg in 1913, made a landing in Taurage, Lithuania. The pilot, Mendele Mokher Sforim's grandson (with goggles, center), crashed and was killed on the next leg of the flight. CREDIT: Jacob Rabinowitz.

Mendele Mokher Sforim's grave, Odessa. PHOTO: Jacob Roth.

read this stuff, without understanding what it was they read. Other people, though they knew no other language, were ashamed to read Yiddish, not wanting to show their backwardness. . . . The Hebrew writers . . . despised Yiddish and mocked it. . . . This was my dilemma, for if I started writing in this 'unworthy' language my honor would be besmirched. . . . But my concern for utility conquered my vanity and I decided, come what may, I would have pity for Yiddish, that rejected daughter, for its was time to do something for our people." In 1864 he published his first short story in Yiddish. "I fell in love with Yiddish and wedded her forever."[27]

Aside from Mendele, the other two "classic" Yiddish writers were Isaac Leib Peretz and Sholem Aleichem. Peretz had written in Hebrew, as well as in Russian and Polish, but he is best known today for his Yiddish works. Far from religion himself, he wrote admiringly of Hassidic figures and

Sholem Aleichem and his family, New Year's card, 1889.

"Gitl di Bobeh," grandmother of Yiddish poet David Hofshtain, Korostyshev, Ukraine. CREDIT: Frieda Weiner.

Mani Leib's grandparents, Nezhin, Ukraine. Mani Leib (Brahinsky) grew up in a poor family, became a radical, and later settled in America where he became a well-known poet, associated with the group known as Di Yunge (The Young). CREDIT: Mani Leib.

of humble, religious Jews. Like Mendele, Peretz encouraged many younger writers to dedicate themselves to Yiddish literature, though he was himself a lawyer by training, secretary of the Warsaw Jewish community, and a civic activist. Sholem Aleichem is undoubtedly the best-known Yiddish writer. His works have been translated into most of the world's major languages, though he is perhaps the most difficult author of all to translate. His language is highly idiomatic and his ear for the speech of his contemporaries was an astoundingly sensitive instrument. In contrast to Mendele and many other writers with social and political agendas, Sholem Aleichem was, in Irving Howe and Eliezer Greenberg's words, "a man without didactic intentions or social ideology, one of those rare storytellers whose work sums up the outlook of a whole culture."[28] Often remembered as a humorist, Sholem Aleichem was a serious writer who could at once sympathize deeply with his subjects and yet hold up their pretensions for all to see. His marvelously inventive language is deeply embedded in the folklore of the people, in turn suffused with the traditional lore of centuries. It is a great tribute to his grasp of human nature that his so intensely Jewish writings should have such universal appeal.

The family of the American composer Aaron Copland. His grandparents were Zussman Alexander and Fayga, here posing with their three youngest daughters in Siaulai (Shavel), Lithuania, 1897. CREDIT: Irving Copland.

In the 1870s a Yiddish theater came on the Russian scene. With few serious works in the repertoire, the early years of the theater saw rather simplistic melodramas and musicals presented to wide and appreciative audiences. The government barred public performances in Yiddish at various times and the Yiddish theater did not become a stable and respected part of the cultural scene in Russia until after the revolution. But it was authors, directors, and actors of Russian origin who created the Yiddish theaters in North and South America and in Romania.

Jews became more involved with music and the arts in the two or three decades before the revolution. Earlier there had been composers, artists, and performers of Jewish origin, but they had to pay the price of conversion in order to gain recognition. By the early twentieth century some Jews were able to find their way into the arts and remain Jewish. The city of Odessa, more open to general culture than the rest of the Pale, was to be the nurturing ground for half a dozen world-famous violinists, including some who made their reputations in the United States.

A few of the wealthier Jews of Moscow and St. Petersburg supported organizations and societies whose aim

Itche Epshtain, proprietor of the Yiddish theater in Bobruisk, ca. 1900. CREDIT: Mendel Elkin.

A group of Jewish actors, Odessa, 1910. CREDIT: Misha Fishzon.

was to promote general education among Jews and also to sponsor modern scholarly research in Jewish fields. A Jewish Historical-Ethnographical Society was established, Russian-language journals were published, and distinguished scholars began to appear on the Russian scene. Lasting contributions were made in Semitics, ancient Jewish history, the ethnography of Jewish communities ranging from the Ukraine to the Caucasus and Central Asia, and of course, Russian Jewish history. Serious work was done on the social and economic structure of Russian Jewry, and it served as a basis for political and welfare activities. People such as Maxim Vinaver, Leon Bramson, and Julius Brutz-

Simeon Bellison, later the first clarinetist of the New York Philharmonic Orchestra, in his father's band in Yelna, Russia. He stands to the right of his father, the band leader. CREDIT: *Jewish Daily Forward*.

Sh. An-sky at the front, 1916. An-sky was the pseudonym of Shlomo-Zanvel Rappaport. He is best known as the author of the play *The Dybbuk*, and composer of the anthem of the Bund, "*Di Shvua*" (The Oath). He worked at many trades, lived among peasants and miners, was a Populist, and was forced to flee to Western Europe. At the turn of the century he began to direct his ethnographic interests toward Jewish matters. Baron Horace Ginzburg funded his ethnographic expedition, the first of its kind, which visited about seventy localities in Volhynia and Podolia, returning with 2,000 photographs, thousands of folk tales and folk songs, recordings, and important documents. Most of this material has remained in the Soviet Union.

Historian Simon Dubnow preparing to leave Soviet Russia for Berlin, 1922.

kus combined academic research with vigorous public activity. The great historian Simon Dubnow evolved a political ideology and founded a party to implement it. A Jewish literature in Russian was developing so that the Jewish intelligentsia had access to literature of Jewish interest in several languages. Sh. An-sky wrote plays, including the famous *Dybbuk*, but shortly before World War I also organized ethnographic expeditions which collected valuable information about a Jewish way of life that was soon to end.

Artisans, Workers, and Luftmentshn: Making a Living in the Pale

It was a cruel irony that one of the world's richest countries in resources had one of its poorest populations. The great majority of the peasantry, and that is to say of the population as a whole, lived in misery well into this century. In 1902 a committee investigating the peasantry in the Tula region, a relatively well-endowed area where the soil was rich and where the famous brass samovars were made, reported that the typical dwelling was a cottage of eighteen by twenty-one feet by seven feet high. "Cottages having no chimneys are still very common, the smoke being let out through a hole in the roof." Thatched roofs were the norm, and walls were covered with dung in the winter to keep the household warm. "Earth floors are the rule because in cold weather lambs, calves, pigs, and even cows are brought into the cottage. . . . Bathhouses are practically non-existent. . . . The peasants almost never use soap. . . . Meat, meal, lard, and vegetable oil appear on the family table only on rare occasions, perhaps two or three times a year. The normal fare consists of bread, kvass, and often cabbage and onions." Almost three-quarters of household income was spent on food. In Viatka province in 1900 the average outlay on schools, newspapers, and books was seven cents a year.[29] Anyone who has ever visited the Hermitage, the former palace of the tsars, with its hundreds of magnificent rooms and priceless art treasures, can immediately appreciate the enormous gulf separating the autocracy from its subjects and understand why a revolution was made in Russia.

Though the urban standard of living was generally higher than that in the countryside, the extremely rapid growth of the cities, beginning in the 1860s, outstripped the ability or willingness of the authorities to meet their needs. The eco-

Street scene in Vilkomir,
Lithuania. PHOTO: M. Levi.

After a fire in Telsiai (Telz,
Telshe), Lithuania. Fires were
quite common and spread
rapidly in the smaller towns
where thatched roofs and
flammable materials made even
the smallest fire a potential
catastrophe.

Market day, Rzhishchev.
CREDIT: A. Kanevsky.

The marketplace in Poltava, Ukraine. CREDIT: Abraham Cohen.

BELOW, LEFT: Street scene, Rzhishchev, Ukraine.
CREDIT: A. Kanevsky.

BELOW, RIGHT: Cinema in Jurbarkas.

nomic position of the Jews in the towns and cities was especially precarious because their confinement in the Pale meant that economic competition was fierce. In the Kiev area, for example, in mid-century the living space of Jews was a third that of Christians. At the end of the century in Kursk and Yaroslav provinces, where no Jew was allowed to reside, there was less than one artisan for every thousand inhabitants. But in Kiev province, inside the Pale, there were 2.6 artisans for the same number of inhabitants. Jewish artisans usually had little capital, equipment, raw materials, or access to credit. They often worked for middlemen, or acted as commission agents or suppliers for manufacturers and wholesalers. Many of them worked at home alongside

Street scene, Proskurov (now Khmelnitsky), Ukraine.

"Sonka of the Golden Hands," Jewish woman thief, being placed in irons, Sakhalin Island, 1915. CREDIT: Solomon Stedman.

The *shtot meshugener* (town fool) of Mozyr, Belorussia, 1912–1913. CREDIT: Vera Sheinin.

their families, including children. Little wonder that periodically artisans, petty traders, and shopkeepers would sink into the category of the unemployed, or *luftmentshn*—those who loitered about the market square hoping for the big deal that would bring them economic salvation, but that for most remained only a pipe dream. In many communities, it was calculated, 40 percent of the population fell into the *luftmentshn* category. In 1898 nearly 20 percent of the Jews

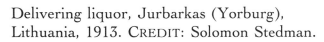

Munya the *shammes* (sexton) in Dubrovna.
CREDIT: *Jewish Daily Forward.*

Delivering liquor, Jurbarkas (Yorburg),
Lithuania, 1913. CREDIT: Solomon Stedman.

Making wine, Kishinev.
CREDIT: Federation of
Bessarabian Jews.

Knife grinders, Kishinev.
CREDIT: Federation of
Bessarabian Jews.

A *balegole*, or carriage driver, Belaia Tserkov. PHOTO: Louis Meyer; CREDIT: Bernard Meyer.

in the Pale applied for Passover charities. In 1900 an investigation in Odessa found that nearly two-thirds of the Jewish dead had to be buried at the community's expense. While the figure of the *kabtsn*, the poor man reduced to begging or living by his wits, enriched folk music, Yiddish and Hebrew literature, and popular drama, for millions it was a harsh reality, with no romance attached. It was estimated that at the turn of the century between 30 and 35 percent of the Jewish population depended on relief provided by Jewish welfare institutions.

Even in the face of formidable political and social barriers, some Jews managed to achieve positions of leadership in a few industries. Because they were so rare, these few very wealthy Jews became household words and the subjects of anecdotes and folklore. Izrail Brodsky was a pioneer in the sugar industry, introducing technology which transformed Russia into an exporter of this product. Samuil Poliakov and the ennobled Günzburg family played major roles in the building of Russia's railroads which many saw as the key to industrial development. Some Jews became prominent in the development of water transport, the oil industry, and banking. But these were exceptions. For most, it was a constant struggle to eke out a subsistence living. For many, this meant wandering from place to place trying to sell some items at a slightly higher price than what had been paid for them. It was not uncommon for men to leave home for the entire work week, or even for several weeks and months at a time, peddling their wares among the villages and hamlets. An early Yiddish novelist, Isaac Meier Dick, observed that "men spend the week until Friday in the country, they wander from village to village and from court to court with all sorts of notions, which they exchange against flax, linseed, rabbit and calf skins, pig bristles and feathers. They sell all that to . . . the rich men of the community. In the hamlet itself remain only women, children, communal officials, students of the academy and a few *batlonim* [unemployed men]."[30]

By the end of the century two new kinds of opportunities became available to the Jew seeking work. The expansion of workshops into factories allowed many to go from artisanry and cottage industry to industrial labor, and the massive emigration overseas was probably more an economic than a political one. It was on the foundations of unemployment, exploitation, and the lack of opportunity that the Zionist and socialist movement built their designs for better ways of life. Bitter realities induced utopian dreams.

The Schwab family of Libau (Liepaja), Latvia, ca. 1908. At the extreme right is Dr. Arkady (Jacob Aaron) Schwab. The oldest member of the family clearly adhered to Jewish tradition, but younger people are dressed as Russian *intelligenty* of the time. CREDIT: Dr. George Schwab.

LEFT, ABOVE: Selling seltzer, Proskurov. PHOTO: Louis Meyer; CREDIT: Bernard Meyer.

RIGHT, ABOVE: A peddler, the Ukraine, turn of the century. CREDIT: Dallas Memorial Center for Holocaust Studies.

A porter in Proskurov (now Khmelnitsky). PHOTO: Louis Meyer; CREDIT: Bernard Meyer.

When World War I broke out, the Jews, like the Russians, were baffled. What was the war all about? The machinations of great-power politics and the intrigues of the crowned heads of Europe were remote from their own worlds. Ordinary people did not understand the conflict. A Russian peasant was reported to have asked, "If our tsar is at war with the German kaiser, does that mean that we ordinary people will have to go fight?" The Jews similarly asked what could the fight between the *Fonye ganev* (an uncomplimentary term for the tsar and for all Russian non-Jews) and Kaiser Wilhelm have to do with them.

They soon found out. Jews, like others, rallied to the flag and delivered their full quota of reservists, and many volunteers, to the army. Well over half a million Jews served in the army, despite the fact that as of the summer of 1915 a great many were under German occupation. In July 1914

LEFT: A bagel peddler, Kishinev.

RIGHT: Selling *kvass*, a slightly fermented drink, Kishinev.
CREDIT: Federation of Bessarabian Jews.

a Jewish Russian-language periodical reflected the ambivalence felt by many when it declared: "We were born and grew up in Russia. . . . Russian Jews are . . . inseparably allied with our mother country where we have been living for centuries and from which there is no power that can separate us—neither persecution nor oppression." But the same journal went on to say two weeks later: "The Jews trust that with the vanishing of the mailed fist the German spirit of militarism . . . will also be destroyed and that humanity will come nearer to the ideals of the ancient prophets."[31]

Such hopes were dashed by the actions of the Russian government in the first months of the war. Jews were accused of disloyalty, and wholesale expulsions of Jews were ordered from towns in and near the war zones. Jewish hostages were taken and held responsible for the activities of all Jews. Acts of heroism by Jewish soldiers were not re-

Cutting lumber in the forest, near Kharkov, 1914. The owner of this property, Kalman Gottman (right) is standing with his employees. CREDIT: Kalman Gottman.

LEFT, BELOW: Wheelwright, Belaia Tserkov. PHOTO: Louis Meyer.

RIGHT, BELOW: A cobbler, Kishinev, Bessarabia.

A group of Jewish soldiers,
Troitskossovsk, December 1887.

ported or were reported with the nationality of the hero unmentioned. Wounded soldiers were sent back to the Pale for treatment rather than being treated where they were located at the time. In 1915 there was such a mass of expulsions of Jews from their homes—all told, over half a million were uprooted by the war and became refugees— that the government was forced to allow Jews to move into the interior, thus effectively abolishing the Pale of Settlement. It stressed that this was only a "temporary" measure. The irony that only an act of persecution led to the abolition of the hated Pale was not lost on the Jews. They were called on to fight for Russia while being accused of disloyalty to her. Some Russian intellectuals, including the writers Leonid Andreyev, Maxim Gorky, and Dmitri Merezhkovsky, the composer Rimsky-Korsakov, and Alexander Kerensky, later the head of the Provisional Government, issued an "Appeal for the Jews" in which they protested the government's policies: "Russian Jews have rendered honest service in all domains left open to them. They have given ample proof of their desire to offer supreme sacrifices for their country. Hence, the curtailment of their civil rights is not only a crying injustice but also . . . injurious to the best interests of the state. . . . Fellow Russians! Remember that the Russian Jew has no fatherland other than Russia and that nothing is more precious to a man than his native soil. . . . the welfare of Russia is inseparable from the welfare and freedom of all its constituent nationalities."[32] Needless to say, the appeal had no effect on the government, though it demonstrated that at least part of the Russian intelligentsia was prepared to defend the Jews against the government.

Moshe Bliach (Amir) as a
yeshiva student in 1915 (above,
standing) and as a soldier a year
later (below, holding kettle).

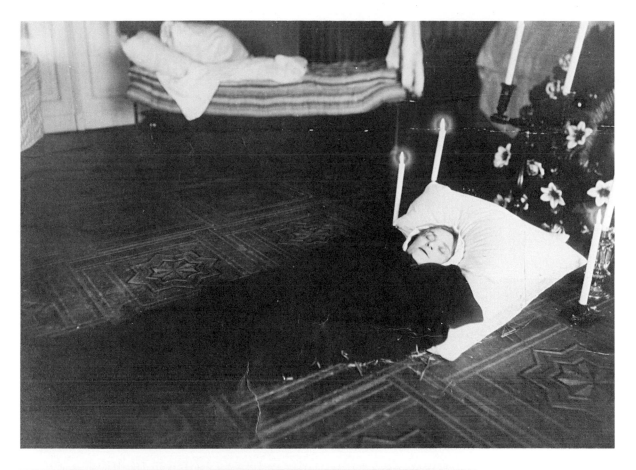

Maria Samsonovich, dead at the age of forty-eight, wife of Aron Samsonovich, a wealthy merchant of Chita, Siberia. Many Jews living outside the Pale combined Christian customs, such as the flowers and candles shown here, with their Jewish beliefs. CREDIT: Mary Eitigon, granddaughter.

Moshe Krupnik on a leave from the army to see his fiancée in Odessa, 1916. CREDIT: Roman Krupnik.

Main street of Telsiai (Telz, Telshe), Lithuania, 1915, with German soldiers visible.

World War I tore apart the fabric of almost all the societies that were directly involved in it. The social structure of Europe collapsed as the war laid bare the weakness of societies as different as France and Russia, England and Austria-Hungary. Authority was shattered under barrages of artillery fire. The senselessness of prolonged trench warfare impressed itself on increasingly cynical soldiers who were being used as cannon fodder. The same men who had marched off enthusiastically under their national flags in 1914 now questioned the purpose of their fighting. Among the Jews of Russia, who had less reason to support the old order than most others, it was not only the tsarist order that was revealed as hopelessly weak and corrupt, but the Jewish community itself which came under increasingly critical scrutiny. For one thing, the war had changed the social status of many—rich became poor, pillars of the community became refugees, and the helplessness of the old undermined their authority in the eyes of the young. Large numbers of Jews found themselves fighting at the front against Jews who marched under a different flag. The struggle of Jew against Jew in the name of distant and perhaps alien authorities made little sense to many of the combatants. *Shtetlekh* lay in ruins, cities were starving, families were torn apart, the world seemed to be in chaos, and life itself appeared to hang by a thread. The traditional way of life could not survive the war intact.

An unintended consequence of the war was the breakup of the empires of Europe and the emergence of two of the most powerful forces of the twentieth century, nationalism and communism. Nationalism forced the redrawing of the map of Europe and the creation and re-creation of states which were to separate defeated Germany and Austria from shrunken and radicalized Russia. Within the collapsed Russian Empire the war opened the way for revolution, civil war, and social upheaval. All these were to change the Jewish way of life forever.

CHAPTER TWO

REVOLUTION AND THE AMBIGUITIES OF LIBERATION

On March 8, 1917, almost exactly thirty-six years after the assassination of Tsar Alexander II, some women standing on line in Petrograd (the name had been changed during the war from the German-sounding St. Petersburg) waiting to buy bread became increasingly exasperated. Their mutterings soon became shouts of "Give us some bread!" and these were followed by more audacious shouts of "Down with autocracy!" and "End the imperialist war!" There had been such demonstrations before, just as there had been lockouts of workers at some of the main plants and factories of the capital. Though this time workers joined the women in their shouts of frustration, the British ambassador cabled his government that "Some disorders occurred today, but nothing serious." The Council of Ministers of Tsar Nicholas II, meeting the following day, did not bother to discuss the demonstrations, and the tsarina cabled her husband at his military headquarters that "This is a hooligan movement. . . . but all this will pass."

A week later the tsar was forced to abdicate. His resignation surprised not only his retinue and foreign diplomats, but even revolutionaries—the Bolsheviks among them—many of whom believed that Russia was not yet ripe for revolution, certainly not of a proletarian variety. A Provisional Government was established, pending the convening of a constituent assembly which would draw up the new type of political system. The Provisional Government had to deal simultaneously with an economic crisis, an increasingly unpopular war, and the resentments accumulated over years against the high-handed rule of the country's aristocrats and autocrats. Seizing the unexpected opportunity, Lenin and the Bolsheviks pushed up their revolutionary timetable. They labeled the Provisional Government a "bourgeois" one, the kind which, according to Marx's theory, was to precede a socialist revolution. Brushing aside the arguments of the Mensheviks, his socialist rivals who believed that the Russian proletariat was too small and weak to make a genuinely proletarian revolution, Lenin was determined to establish Bolshevik power before the Constituent Assembly could meet. In early November (October, according to the Julian calendar, which prevailed in Russia until 1918), a Bolshevik Military-Revolutionary Committee, led by Lev Davidovich Trotsky, mounted a successful coup d'état against the Provisional Government and seized power in the name of the soviets, the workers–peasants–soldiers councils which had been operating independently of the government. During the next three years a civil war pitted the Bolsheviks against several armies that sought to restore tsarist rule. The Bolsheviks had to fight as well against groups of Ukrainian nationalists demanding independence from Russia, the newly formed Polish state which had territorial claims on Russia, and the Georgians, Armenians, and Baltic and Central Asian peoples who tried to wrest independence for themselves. In this seeming "war of all against all," a diverse range of bandit groups and political organizations pursued their own aims. A confusing array of flags, uniforms, and armies dotted the landscape of the old Russian Empire. By 1921 some semblance of order had been restored, and the Bolsheviks set about consolidating their rule, planning the transformation of neofeudal Russia into a socialist Soviet state.

The Jews greeted the downfall of tsarism enthusiastically. "It is impossible," said a recent arrival from the United States, "to describe the exhilaration and holiday atmosphere in the Jewish world. . . . Jews supported the Provisional Government to the hilt. . . . There were no differences of opinion in the Jewish world. Class interest disappeared."[1] In April the Provisional Government lifted all restrictions imposed

Conference of Zionist soldiers at the Minsk front, 1918. CREDIT: David Cohen.

אונטערשריפט: יעדע קינדער אין טעלז לעבען צו קומען אין בית הספר און זיין אויסגאבע
...טעלז די שמחה "צו גיבען ישראל".

Children in Telsiai (Telz, Telshe), Lithuania, lined up to celebrate the Balfour Declaration. The caption reads: "Demonstration to celebrate announcement of the giving of the Land of Israel to our nation, and an outing of our school, sponsored by the Union of Young Israel, Lag Ba'omer, 1919–20." CREDIT: Isaac Sherman.

on national and religious groups, spurring Jews and others to plan for a free, active cultural and political life in the new Russia. The Jewish community burst into unparalleled activity. A tremendous number of publications, in Russian, Hebrew, and Yiddish, reflected the pent-up literary, political, and social energy suppressed under tsarism. Schools, musical and dramatic societies, theaters, and religious activities were hastily organized, some emerging from a shadowy underground existence.

Several major political groups dominated. Though the revolution seemed to promise a better future for Jews in Russia, it was the Zionist movement that claimed the largest membership, 300,000 members in 1,200 localities. Membership was simply a matter of paying a symbolic "shekel," but the numbers reflect widespread sympathy for the Zionist ideal. The biggest boost to Zionist aspirations came in November 1917 when the British Lord Balfour wrote his famous letter to Lord Rothschild, expressing His Majesty's support for a Jewish homeland in Palestine. No longer could the critics of Zionism deride the idea of a return to Zion as an illusion; the power which was replacing the Ottomans in the Middle East seemed to have given official sanction to the Jewish aspiration for a homeland in Palestine. Curiously, part of the British government's motivation was to curry favor with Jews, who they saw as politically powerful in revolutionary Russia, so that the Provisional Government would keep Russia in the war against the Central Powers. Of course, the Bolsheviks seized power very soon after. The Jewish Bolsheviks were highly antagonistic to Zionism, and in any case, the Bolshevik government made a separate peace with the Germans at Brest-Litovsk.

The Bund, with a membership of nearly 34,000 in 1917, was more intensely involved in Russian politics than the Zionists, whose gaze was directed elsewhere. Most Bundists shared the Menshevik view of the revolution: the tsars had

I. N. Steinberg was an observant Jew and a lawyer by profession. Yet he represented the Left Socialist Revolutionary Party, and served as commissar for justice in the 1917–1918 coalition government dominated by the Bolsheviks. He later lived in Europe and America, where he died in 1957 after a long career as an essayist and editor. He tried to combine socialism and the principles of Judaism, and sought to promote territories other than Palestine for Jewish colonization. CREDIT: I. N. Steinberg.

presided over a semi-feudal social order; Russia was only in the early stages of capitalism, and true Marxists would support the development of a bourgeois order which would only later give way to a socialist one. Taking power prematurely in the name of the proletariat would hasten the downfall of the socialist revolution, for it lacked a social and economic base. Borrowing ideas developed by Parvus-Helphand and Trotsky, both revolutionaries of Jewish origin, Lenin waved away the Mensheviks' hesitations and argued that Russia's circumstances were special since the bourgeoisie, always heavily dependent on the state, was weaker than in Western capitalist societies. That allowed for the "telescoping" of the bourgeois and proletarian revolutions. The few months between the downfall of the tsarism and the Bolshevik seizure of power would suffice for the "bourgeois" stage. To reject power on doctrinal grounds after it had fallen into the hands of the socialists would be absurd and irresponsible. These arguments began to make more sense to Bundists and others in 1918 when a series of strikes and political uprisings in Germany seemed to signal the spread of the revolution into areas where capitalism was highly developed and where Marxists had expected socialist revolutions to occur first. Revolution in the capitalist states would guarantee the success of the Russian socialist revolution, it was argued, because larger and more powerful working classes would come to the aid of less developed ones. This persuaded part of the Bundist intelligentsia to take a more sympathetic view of the Bolshevik position. "Left" factions began to appear in many Bundist organizations, advocating cooperation with the Bolshevik-dominated government.

Between the Zionists and the Bund stood the United Jewish Socialist Workers Party, formed in 1917 by a merger of two parties, one of which had been a basically Marxist party whose "Zionism" consisted of advocating the establishment of an autonomous Jewish territory, not necessarily in Palestine. The other party to the merger was known as the SERP, or "Sejmists," and advocated national-cultural autonomy with a parliament, or *sejm*, for each nationality in the state. Largely an intelligentsia party, it, too, began to split over the question of support for the Bolsheviks. The same occurred in the ranks of the Poalai Zion Party, one which reflected the ideas of Ber Borochov. Thus in all the Jewish socialist parties, Zionist or not, whether or not to support the Bolshevik revolution became the main issue.

This issue did not agitate Simon Dubnow's Folkspartai which advocated national-cultural autonomy in the diaspora,

Five young women, members of the "Sejmist" Party, Polotsk, Belorussia, 1906.

nor did it affect the various religious parties that had been organized with the end of tsarism. These groups had no sympathy with the atheism, "internationalism," or socialism of the Marxist parties, least of all with the Bolsheviks, who had never made inroads among the Jewish masses. Neither was there a debate on the revolution in the Folksgruppe, a small association of distinguished jurists and intellectuals associated with the Russian middle-class Kadet Party which had played a prominent role in the Provisional Government. People such as Henrik Sliozberg, Maxim Vinaver, and Oskar Gruzenberg, leaders of the Folksgruppe, urged full civil rights and independent religious bodies for the Jews. In contrast to Dubnow's Folkspartai, the Folksgruppe made no demands for national autonomy.

All over the country elections were held to the newly formed *kehillas* (local Jewish self-governing bodies). There were also elections to an all-Russian Jewish congress which was supposed to set policy for the entire community, and to the aborted Constituent Assembly. In all these elections the Zionists emerged as the largest vote-getters. The popularity of Zionism derived, no doubt, from age-old yearnings for a return to Zion and from disillusion with oppressive regimes and hostile societies, given new impetus by the Balfour Declaration. One witness recalled:

הציונות שואפת לרכוש בשביל עם ישראל בארץ
ישראל מקלט בטוח

First Conference of Siberian Zionists, Irkutsk, October 1917. The banner reads: "Zionism aims to acquire a safe haven for the people of Israel in the land of Israel." CREDIT: Aryeh Tsentsifer, Central Zionist Archives.

It is impossible to describe the joy which seized the Jewish masses all over the country. . . . On November 6 there was an unparalleled Jewish demonstration in Kiev. . . . From early morning thousands of Jews, dressed in their holiday clothes and Zionist emblems, streamed to the university campus. . . . All balconies of Jewish homes were decorated in blue and white. . . . Professor Hrushevsky, president of the Rada, [Ukrainian independent government], greeted us. Even many Bundists and sworn anti-Zionists were swept along in the general Jewish celebration.[2]

A British officer stationed in Siberia was amazed by the hopes the Jews put in the Declaration. "Many of those I talked with spoke with pathetic hope of the day when a Jewish state would be established in Palestine. Not that they all wished to go there—many . . . felt that their *real* home was in Russia—but they harbored the strange hope that the future Ambassador or Consul from such a State would be able to secure them better treatment from the Russian government. . . . Apart from the large number who hope for such benefits, there are many, especially among the younger men, who are anxious to emigrate to Palestine, and a still more numerous class, who do not mind where they go, so long as they get out of Russia."[3] These perceptions and sentiments were to be repeated with remarkable parallelism more than half a century later.

The Bolsheviks were aware of their weakness among the Jews. Before the revolution they had far fewer Jewish members than the Mensheviks and, of course, the Bund. The 1922 census of the party revealed that there were only 958 Jewish members who had joined before 1917, about 4 percent of the party membership on the eve of the collapse of tsarism, and only 1,175 joined in 1917. In the Yiddish newspaper the Bolsheviks managed to publish in 1918 only by using Jewish emigrés who had returned to Russia, one observer wrote: "So you want to know what's doing on the Jewish street [among the Jewish population]? Better not to ask. . . . Some kind of revolution took place, first in February, then in October . . . some business with socialism, decrees, dictatorship of the proletariat, and the like. The Jews couldn't care less. Let 'them' tear each other to pieces. It doesn't matter to us."[4] But to most Jews the difference between the two revolutions was clear. "Who can ever forget with what great enthusiasm, what deep spiritual wonder, what ecstatic joy and heavenly pleasure . . . the first Russian revolution aroused in the very depth of our hearts? The soul itself sang the Marseillaise. . . . The essence of the February Revolution was freedom; the essence of the October Revolution was dictatorship . . . the premature dictatorship of the minority over the majority."[5]

Zionist conference in western Siberia, 1917. Note the variety of uniforms and the presence of both religious and nonreligious delegates. CREDIT: Aryeh Tsentsifer, Central Zionist Archives.

POGROMS AND THE DILEMMA
OF THE ONE ALTERNATIVE

Initially Jews had little reason to welcome the Bolshevik revolution. The Provisional Government had treated them as well as could be expected, whereas the Bolsheviks were avowed atheists and were also opposed to private trade. But Jewish hostility toward the Bolsheviks soon gave way to more ambivalent feelings. As the White forces opposing the Red Bolsheviks were quick to point out, many of the prominent leaders of the Bolsheviks were of Jewish origin: not only Trotsky, widely perceived as being second only to Lenin, but the first head of the Soviet state, Yakov Sverdlov, and party leaders Kamenev and Zinoviev, among others. Jews even quipped that the real meaning of VTsIK (Vserosiiskii Tsentral'nyi Ispolnitel'nyi Komitet, or All-Russian Central Executive Committee) was *"vu tsen idn komandeven"* (where ten Jews give the orders). Very soon they learned that this was a mixed blessing, for these Bolsheviks were quite unsympathetic to Jewish concerns; on the other hand, the Whites rallied anti-Bolshevik feelings by playing on anti-Semitic sentiments. Because much of the Russian intelligentsia had fled in fear of the Bolsheviks, there were great opportunities for literate Jews. The Bolsheviks could hardly suspect them of pro-White leanings, and the Jews were permitted to occupy posts that they could only dream about before 1917. Lenin himself commented that the Jews had saved the revolution by filling the vacuum created by the "deserters and saboteurs" of the old regime. Yet most of the Jewish Bolsheviks were reluctant to create Jewish sections within the party and barely tolerated the Commissariat for Jewish Affairs, part of the People's Commissariat for Nationality Affairs headed by Joseph Stalin. They feared that such organs would resemble the Bund too closely in its insistence on a specifically Jewish apparatus to serve the Jewish masses. But since such bodies had been created for other nationalities, the Jews were ultimately allowed them as well, though in their first few years they attracted few people knowledgeable about Jewish affairs. The exception was the first commissar for Jewish affairs, Semën Dimanshtain, born in 1888 in Sebezh, Vitebsk province. Dimanshtain had been expelled from the Telshe, (Telz, Telsai) *yeshiva* for leading a student demonstration, but continued his studies in the Slobodka *yeshiva*, where he became a follower of the *musar* movement. He later studied in the Lubavitcher *yeshiva*, having been attracted to Hassidism. He received rabbinical

Leon Trotsky (Lev Davidovich Bronshtain), 1879–1940.

ordination from none other than Chaim Oyzer Grodzensky of Vilna, one of the greatest authorities of the day. But the young rabbi was not at peace with himself and began to pursue a general education. He was drawn into illegal social circles in Vilna, was arrested in 1906, escaped, and was rearrested in 1908 at a Bolshevik conference. Sentenced to Siberia, he served five years and then escaped abroad, studying in Paris where he remained active in Bolshevik circles. Throughout his career Dimanshtain maintained a reputation as a fair and reasonable man, less fanatic than those who entered the party later and who seemed to have a compulsion to prove their "true Bolshevism."

Neither the Jewish Commissariat nor the Jewish Sections in the party, known as *Evsektsii*, had much success in attracting the Jewish masses. The latter were driven reluctantly into the hands of the Bolsheviks by the pogroms mounted by just about every other armed group in the country: the White armies of Generals Denikin, Wrangel, Kolchak, and others; the anarchists under Nestor Makhno; the Ukrainian national army commanded by Semën Petliura; and a long list of bandit groups often led by *atamans*, or chieftains. Beginning in March 1919, soldiers of the independent Ukrainian government, based in Kiev, carried out the greatest massacre of Jews in Eastern Europe since 1648, when Bohdan Khmielnitsky had led the Ukrainians in a revolt

Trotsky, seated in the middle of the second row, surrounded by young military men, including several Jews, 1924. Jews were prominent in the Soviet military until the late 1930s.

Trotsky, in the center, wearing glasses, with Bolshevik military and political leaders. To his right stands Klementi Voroshilov, later a marshal of the Soviet Union and close ally of Joseph Stalin. To his left stands Mikhail Kalinin, later ceremonial head of the Soviet state and an advocate of Jewish agricultural settlement; M. V. Frunze, a top military leader; Klara Zetkin, a leader of the German Communist movement and a well-known figure in international Communism. In the background above Frunze is Semën Budënny, hero of the civil war, marshal of the Soviet Union, and a figurehead politician in his later years.

against the Poles, killing tens of thousands of Jews in the process. In 1918–1919 over 1,200 pogroms took place in the Ukraine, over a third of them attributed to the Ukrainian nationalist military. The White armies identified the Jews with disloyalty to tsarism and support for the Bolsheviks, so they, too, pogromized Jews who came under their occupation. They were supported by many Russian Orthodox clergymen who saw the White struggle as a holy war against the godless Jews who had usurped power in Holy Mother Russia. Dean Vostorgov sent a message to the clergy for obligatory reading to their parishioners, offering this pithy message for the salvation of Russia: "Bless yourselves, beat the Jews, overthrow the People's Commissars."[6]

The pogroms were marked by indescribable cruelty and face-to-face brutality. Men were buried up to their necks and then killed by the hooves of horses driven over them, or were literally pulled apart by horses driven in opposite directions. Children were smashed against walls in view of their parents; pregnant women were a favorite target, their unborn children killed in their mothers' sight. Thousands of women were raped and hundreds were left insane by their experiences. Hundreds of *shtetlekh* were pillaged, and Jewish neighborhoods of cities were left in ruins. It is estimated that

LEFT: Semën Dimanshtain (1888–1938), commissar for Jewish affairs. CREDIT: A. Nadel.

RIGHT: In this poster published by anti-Bolshevik Whites, Trotsky rules over the Kremlin. The title reads: "Peace and Freedom in Sovdepya" (Soviet Republic). CREDIT: David King.

Jewish self-defense force in Chernobyl, 1919. CREDIT: Elias Tcherikower.

Members of Ataman Struk's band, one of many Ukrainian armed groups that carried out pogroms, posing with a hobby horse. In April 1919 Struk's forces started a pogrom in Chernobyl, then populated by about 10,000 Jews. The pogrom went on for twenty-five days. Struk's bands are said to have carried out forty pogroms in the Chernobyl area. CREDIT: Elias Tcherikower.

Teenagers looking at a deranged woman, victim of a pogrom, in Durashna, Ukraine, 1929. PHOTO: Louis Meyer; CREDIT: Bernard Meyer.

Pogrom victims from Khodorkovtsy in Alexandrov Hospital, Kiev. The man on the left was shot twice. His wife was killed before his eyes. CREDIT: Elias Tcherikower.

Members of the anarchist Nestor Makhno's forces with their banner which reads, in Ukrainian: "Death to anyone who stands in the way of working people winning their freedom." CREDIT: Elias Tcherikower.

Reciting prayers over the victims of a pogrom in Proskurov, February 1919. CREDIT: Elias Tcherikower.

Children wounded in pogroms near Kiev. CREDIT: Elias Tcherikower.

Self-defense unit in Odessa, April 1918. This unit was very well equipped compared to most, as its members had uniforms and even a machine gun.

A family victimized by the pogroms, the Ukraine. CREDIT: Elias Tcherikower.

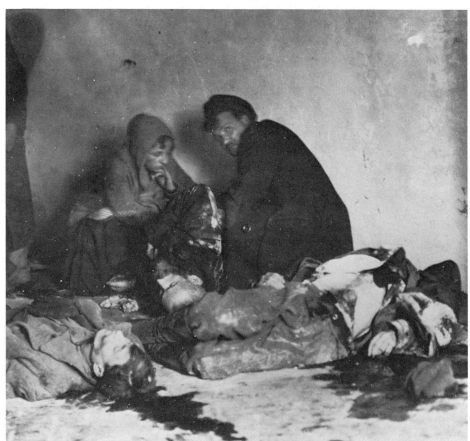

In the Kurenevka police station, near Kiev, children are examining the body of their father, killed in a pogrom, April 1919. CREDIT: Elias Tcherikower.

Pogrom victims from Glubokovich being buried in Bobruisk, Belorussia. CREDIT: Elias Tcherikower.

Synagogue in Demievka, Ukraine, wrecked by Polish forces that had invaded the Ukraine, in May-June 1919. CREDIT: Elias Tcherikower.

These refugees from Ukrainian pogroms, in Kishinev, Romania, 1922, were members of the Hashomer (The Guardian) Scout group. CREDIT: Judith Slobin.

in 1918–1921 more than 2,000 pogroms took place, most of them in the Ukraine; half a million Jews were left homeless; 30,000 Jews were killed directly, and together with those who died of wounds or as a result of illnesses contracted during the pogroms, a total of about 150,000 Jews died.

The only armed force that did not systematically terrorize the Jews was the Red Army of the Bolsheviks. Though over 700 Jews were killed in pogroms mounted by Red Army detachments, the Red Army command condemned these actions and punished them. Jews came to regard the Red Army as their protector, and young Jews joined it in order to avenge the crimes against their families and people. A Jewish Red Army soldier was seen executing wounded Ukrainians left behind by their retreating forces. The "Jewish soldier from Berdichev ran amok. He would wipe his bayonet in the grass to remove the blood and with every head he cut off he screamed, 'This is my payment for my murdered sister, this is my retribution for my murdered mother!' The Jewish crowd . . . held its breath and kept silent."[7] The organizer of the Red Army, Trotsky, recognized the motivations driving Jews into the Red Army and warned that "these are not the best Communists" and that they needed intensive political education. Indeed, ideological opponents of Bolshevism were joining the Red Army out of Jewish national motivations. "In the Klinovka station I was surprised to see a Red Army company composed entirely of Jews and even including some wearing earlocks. These were *yeshiva* students from Proskurov who joined the Red Army after Petliura's riots in order to take revenge . . . and I, the Zionist opponent of Communism [which] I saw . . . as a fatal danger to Judaism—I was filled with pride seeing those Jewish fellows. . . ."[8]

Coming on the heels of World War I and the revolution, the pogroms left many communities totally devastated. Economic life in the *shtetlekh* of the Ukraine and Belorussia did not recover until the 1930s. Thousands of orphaned and homeless children roamed the cities and countryside. "You see them

Isaak Babel. Born in the Moldavanka neighborhood of Odessa in 1894, Babel was the son of a shopkeeper who saw to it that he received an intensive religious education. He was a soldier in the Russian army in 1917–1918 and during the civil war he served in the Red cavalry commanded by Semën Budënny. He also claimed to have served in the Cheka, the secret police, in the section responsible for fighting counter-revolutionaries. Babel began to publish short stories, including the collection *Red Cavalry*, in the mid-1920s. He also wrote about the Jewish gangster Benya Krik. Babel's attachment to both Jewish culture and Communism is reflected in many of his stories.

Babel was arrested in 1939 and sentenced in 1940. He died in an unknown place in 1941. In 1954 the Military College of the Supreme Court of the USSR issued a document declaring that Babel's sentence "is revoked on the basis of newly discovered circumstances and the case against him is terminated in the absence of elements of a crime" (quoted in Nathalie Babel, *Isaac Babel: The Lonely Years, 1925–1939* [New York: Farrar, Straus, 1964], p. xxviii).
PHOTO: Moisei Nappelbaum;
CREDIT: Ilya Rudiak.

all over the cities and towns, in the villages, in the railroad stations, hungry, sick, naked, shoeless. . . . They wander about first with a bewildered, forlorn expression, then with a hand stretched forth for a handout, and finally in a camp of little criminals . . . embittered, degenerate. . . . In Kiev there are about five thousand such children and in Kharkov, three thousand."[9] An official of the American Relief Administration—Jews joked that ARA stood for *"Amerike ratevet alemen"* (America rescues everyone)—visited a Ukrainian town where he found one-third destitute, among them 2,500 children. There were twenty-five to thirty deaths a day, half of them children, in a total population of 15,000. "Families were known as cat, dog or horse families, the title indicating the character of their food."[10] Small wonder that while the overall population of the Ukraine increased by 36 percent from 1897 to 1926, the Jewish population declined by 5 percent. In 1926 there were 80,000 fewer Jews in the Ukraine than there had been in 1897.

The Jewish population of the old empire was reduced also by the newly won independence of the Baltic states—Estonia, Latvia, and Lithuania—which they managed to keep until 1940. Similarly, Polish independence meant that large numbers of Jews in eastern Poland were no longer under Russian rule, nor were the Jews of Bessarabia, now part of an expanded Romania. The Jews of Georgia and Central Asia were in areas that tried to become independent after 1917 but were quickly reabsorbed into the Soviet Russian state.

"REVOLUTION ON THE JEWISH STREET"

Just as society as a whole was not suddenly transformed by the Bolshevik ascension to power but had to be "revolutionized" by intensive efforts over many years, so, too, did the revolution among the Jewish population come "from above." Aside from the welcome opening of vocational and educational opportunities, there was little in Bolshevism that attracted the "broad Jewish masses." Even the members of the Jewish socialist parties were initially opposed to the Bolsheviks, though the mistaken belief that revolution was about to sweep the industrialized West and the realization that the only significant force not attacking the Jews was the Bolsheviks moved many toward greater sympathy with the latter. As some of the "Left Bundists" put it, "The social

revolution has come and we have to reorient our-selves. . . . Within each party member there is a real battle between two ideologies . . . the old ideology is retreating bit by bit. . . ."[11] Another Bundist asked, "To whom can we turn? . . . To civilized Europe which signs treaties with the anti-Semitic Directory [the Ukrainian government]?" The Bolsheviks, "the armed carriers of socialism, are now the only force which can oppose the pogroms. . . . For us there is no other way."[12] In 1919, when the Kiev organization of the Bund split, the majority voting to found a "Jewish Com-munist Workers Bund," the two wings adjourned to separate rooms where the left wing sang the "Internationale" and the others sang the traditional Bund hymn, "Di Shvua" (The Oath).

The Bolsheviks did not sit back and let the Bundists find their own political way, but repressed Bundist organizations where they could and undermined others from within. All non-Bolshevik parties came under increasing pressure as the Bolsheviks were determined to establish a monopoly of power. Until 1921 even those Bundists who urged cooperation with the Bolsheviks and adoption of the Communist program insisted that Jewish Communists must have their indepen-dent organizations, not the despised *Evsektsii* (Jewish Sec-

Conference of Jewish commissars and cultural activists, October 23, 1918. In the first seated row, just to the right of the center, the man wearing a suit and tie is Samuil ("Sam") Agursky, at one time active in the Bund and later in the anarchist movement. Fleeing the tsarist police, Agursky wound up in the American Midwest but returned to Russia when the revolution broke out. He volunteered his services to the new regime and became an important cultural and political figure until pushed aside by the more experienced activists who joined the Communist Party from the Bund. Eventually he was purged. His son, Mikhail, became a dissident and a Zionist and emigrated to Israel in the early 1970s.

tions of the Communist Party) but a Bundist Communist organization. As late as 1921 Left Bundists were demanding that they enter the Russian Communist Party on the same basis as the Bund had entered the Russian Social Democratic Labor Party in 1898—as a Jewish organization exercising autonomy in matters concerning the Jewish proletariat. Having rejected this idea in 1903, the Bolsheviks were not about to adopt it now that they held state power. Esther Frumkin, the firebrand Bundist leader who was about to join the Communist Party, declared defiantly, "Let it be said clearly and precisely at this, the last moment, that whatever happens to the name of the Bund . . . Bundism will live as long as the Jewish proletariat lives, Bundism will live—and will be triumphant." Under pressure from the Bolsheviks to merge the remnants of the Left Bund into the Communist Party, Frumkin claimed she was joining the Communist Party "in order to save the idea of the Bund, in order to at least preserve the Bund as an *apparat* until the inevitable moment (I believe in it even now) when the Russian Communist Party will recognize our organizational principle, in order to preserve the great treasure smeared with the blood and tears of the Jewish proletariat, soaked with the hopes and sufferings of generations of fighters, with memories of superhuman achievements."[13] Of course the Communist Party never "recognized the organizational principle of the Bund," and the "great treasure" of Bundism, rather than being preserved, has always been criticized and reviled in Communist historiography. In the official Soviet view, the Bund stood for Jewish separatism and "petit bourgeois nationalism." Even more than sixty years after the Bund was dissolved and its left wing forced to merge with the Communist Party, the Bund is still attacked in Soviet publications as a "petit bourgeois, nationalist" and even "Zionist" (!) organization. Esther Frumkin played a leading role in the *Evsektsii* after she became a Communist, but was arrested as a "deviationist" in January 1938 and sentenced to eight years imprisonment. She died in a Soviet labor camp in 1943.

Along with the Bund, the left wings of the United Jewish Socialist Workers Party and of the Poalai Zion were forced to dissolve themselves into the Communist Party. Those who refused to do so were barred from political activity or arrested. The liquidation of the socialist parties meant that the Communist Party and its *Evsektsii* now had a monopoly "on the Jewish street." Ironically, the *Evsektsii* came to life as a result of the influx of former socialists, people with close ties to the Jewish masses, vast political experience, and a willingness to try and build a new Jewish life within the parameters of Soviet socialism. The Communists believed that to build socialism one first had to clear away the "debris" of a civilization whose day had passed.

The Communist Party and its Jewish Sections regarded the values and institutions of the Jewish community as so alien to Marxist ideology and to the new society that was to be based on it that they were determined to eradicate them as soon as possible. Bolshevism brooked no pluralism even within the socialist camp. Its intolerance was exaggerated in Jewish affairs because the *Evsektsii*, insecure in their small numbers, "late arrival" to Bolshevism, and dependence on former Bundists, were determined to prove themselves "more Bolshevik than Lenin" and fully qualified to carry out the "revolution on the Jewish street." Local organizations and institutions were taken over by the *Evsektsii*, acting for a while through the Jewish Commissariat. Welfare organizations were maintained, partly because they were receiving funds from abroad, but under Communist control. The local *kehillas*, which were the agency for Jewish local self-government, were abolished in 1919 and their assets taken over by the local branches of the Jewish Commissariat.

The *Evsektsii* saw the main enemy as the "bourgeois-clerical-Zionist" camp. Moishe Rafes, a former Bundist, boasted that the struggle against the Zionists, among others, was initiated by Jewish Communists and "This means that we are dealing with a manifestation of *Jewish civil war*. . . . This concretizes the dictatorship of the Jewish proletariat on the Jewish street."[14] The *Evsektsii* targeted for elimination not only the Zionist movement and the Jewish religion, but even

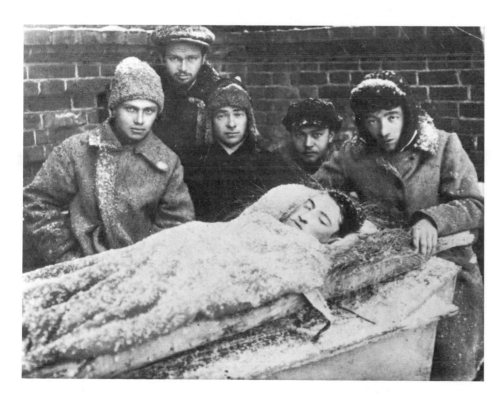

Yaakov Moiseev, member of Hashomer HaTsair HaAmlani-HaLeumi (National-Labor Young Guardian), a Zionist organization, dead at the age of twenty-one in exile, Kirghizia (Central Asia), 1921. CREDIT: Aryeh Tsentsifer, Central Zionist Archives.

Zionist exiles in Narym, Siberia, December 1928. CREDIT: Aryeh Tsentsifer, Central Zionist Archives.

the Hebrew language. Some Jewish Communists saw this drive as preparatory to the reconstruction of Jewish culture and community on a secular, Yiddish, socialist basis, while others saw it as a prerequisite for the assimilation of Jews into Russian culture and Soviet society as a whole. In both instances the Jewish Communists were spurred by utopian visions of a new society, unparalleled in all of history, which would once and for all solve the "Jewish problem."

THE BATTLE AGAINST ZIONISM AND HEBREW

Most Zionists opposed the Bolsheviks, though a handful dreamed of constructing a Communist society in Palestine. Hekhalutz (The Pioneer), an organization of Zionists who established agricultural communes, was tolerated by the government in Belorussia and the Ukraine, and explicitly legalized in 1923. However, after the *Evsektsii* had launched a campaign to settle Jews on the land, Hekhalutz, which claimed a membership of 3,000, was liquidated. The Zionist Central Office was closed in September 1919, and in April 1920 the delegates to an All-Russian Zionist Conference were arrested. In the following years thousands of Zionists were arrested as "counter-revolutionaries." Many were sent into exile in Central Asia and Siberia, and some more fortunate ones were "exiled" to Palestine or other countries. Zionist youth organizations stubbornly continued their activities, operating at great risk. They took part in public meetings where they pointed out the failure of the new regime to solve the economic problems of the Jews; they continued to study Hebrew and Zionist literature secretly;

they even got themselves elected to local soviets so that they could influence community affairs. Sometimes they joined state-sponsored agricultural colonies, calculating that they would gain agricultural experience which could someday be applied in Palestine. In the colonies they would also be further removed from the eyes of the authorities. By 1928 what was left of the Zionist movement was forced underground. Under the extreme pressures of the purges in the 1930s Zionist activity became almost impossible, but the Zionist dream never disappeared.

Exiles of the twenties recall that the only live and militant party [in the camps] at that time was the Zionist Socialist Party with its vigorous youth organization, Hashomer, and its illegal "Hekhalutz" organization, which existed to establish Jewish agrarian communes in the Crimea. In 1926 the whole Central Committee was jailed, and in 1927 indomitably cheerful boys and girls of fifteen, sixteen, and under were taken from the Crimea and exiled. They were sent to Turktul and other strict places. This really was a party—close-knit, determined, sure that its cause was just. Their aim, however, was not one which all could share, but private and particular: to live as a nation, in a Palestine of their own. The Communist Party, which had voluntarily disowned its fatherland, could not tolerate narrow nationalism in others.[15]

From Aleksandr I. Solzhenitsyn,
The Gulag Archipelago, Three.

The Zionists saw Hebrew as part of the renewal of the Jewish spirit that would come by ending the unnatural situation of exile. As the diaspora disappeared, so, too, would its backward economy, peculiar social structure, and ridiculous mores. Yiddish, a language based on German but with

LEFT: Zionist agricultural cooperative near Odessa, 1924. CREDIT: Aryeh Tsentsifer, Central Zionist Archives.

RIGHT: Zionist exiles at work in the village of Parabeli, 1927. CREDIT: Aryeh Tsentsifer, Central Zionist Archives.

Rabbi Jacob Mazeh (1860–1925), rabbi of Moscow and Zionist leader.

Slavic, Aramaic, and Hebrew elements, was a borrowed language, in the view of the Zionists. It would have to be replaced by the biblical language, Hebrew, which not only was the original language of the Jewish people, but was also the one language that the widely dispersed communities— from Yemen to Russia to North America—had in common. Most Jewish socialists were hostile to Hebrew, which they saw as a language of the rabbis and the wealthy, and they refused to abandon Yiddish, which they regarded as the "language of the masses." The Hebrew–Yiddish struggle thus became enmeshed in political differences, but even the most radical Yiddishists could not match the Jewish Communists in the fury with which they attacked Hebrew. The Russian Communists did not quite understand the *Evsektsii*'s animus against Hebrew. The commissar of education (literally, "enlightenment"), Anatoly V. Lunacharsky, admitted to the Zionist leader Rabbi Jacob Mazeh, "I do not know who would doubt the value of Hebrew, except for the Jewish Communists. And they, after all, are our allies and we can hardly disbelieve them when they say that Hebrew is the language of the bourgeoisie and not of the people. . . . "[16] The *Evsektsii* contended that the conflict between Hebrew and Yiddish was a class struggle: since Hebrew was the "language of the bourgeoisie," it was a "bourgeois language," and since Yiddish was the language of the Jewish proletariat, it was obviously a "proletarian language." For a Marxist, what followed was obvious: just as the bourgeoisie had to be eliminated, so would its language. Later on Jewish Communists, like some Yiddishists in Poland, went further and attempted to "purify" Yiddish by eliminating some of its Hebraic features. Words of Hebrew origin, heretofore spelled in the Hebrew orthography, were now transcribed into a phonetic Yiddish spelling, rendering them well nigh incomprehensible to the traditional Yiddish reader. Final letters, written differently from when they appear in the middle of a word, were dropped altogether. Some linguists urged that classic idioms, derived mainly from religious literature, be purged from the language.

All Hebrew schools were closed and Hebrew publication virtually ceased. Hebrew writers and poets were hounded by the *Evsektsii*. The Russian writer Maxim Gorky, long an associate of Lenin and one of the culture heroes of the Soviet Union, tried to secure permission for prominent Hebrew writers to leave the country, but the *Evsektsii* barred the way. Only the intervention of Feliks Dzerzhinsky, the chief of the secret police (the Cheka), enabled such luminaries as Bialik, Saul Tshernikhovsky, B. Z. Dinaburg, and ten other Hebrew writers to leave Soviet Russia in 1921. The famous Hebrew theatrical troupe, Habimah, though much admired by some Bolshevik leaders, decided not to return to Soviet Russia after a foreign tour. Devoted Hebraists, who had given so much energy to reviving and disseminating the language, felt increasingly isolated and threatened. Barukh Shpilberg, a writer in the Ukraine, wrote to a friend, "I look around and I see that I have no one to leave the few books to, that I am the last. . . . You write something in Hebrew, you come up with a new idea—there is no one to whom you can show it, there is no 'learned man' [*yodaia sefer*] in Berdichev. . . . "[17] Shlomo Yaakov Niepomniashchi, a former *yeshiva* student who became enthusiastic about the Soviet experiment, nevertheless could not tear himself away from Hebrew. "I will say, in Gordon's words, 'I am a slave to Hebrew forever.' No one will be able to uproot 'Khumash-and-Rashi' from my soul. I gave my best years to these old writings. But here I stop and go no further. I return the Torah to Mount Sinai, even though I know we remain naked without it. But that's all right! . . . We have to begin to write Genesis again. The old stuff—let it rot!"[18] Niepomniashchi nevertheless spent all his money on books, and constantly begged his friends abroad to send him Yiddish and Hebrew books. Apparently he wrote a large number of works in Hebrew, but none could be published before his death in 1930 at the age of thirty-three.

The *Evsektsii* attacks on religion were, like the assault on Zionism and Hebrew, an extension and exaggeration of pre-revolutionary socialist positions. The Bund rarely attacked faith or customs, concentrating its criticism on the rabbinate who upheld the established order. The Bundists were convinced that in an enlightened socialist society religion would die a natural death, but there was no sense in alienating part of the Jewish masses by a direct attack on things they held sacred. In 1917 a Bundist pamphlet stated, "We do not at all wish to uproot the Jewish religion. Religion, in its pure form, is an intimate feeling . . . like love—and we do not oppose it. We fight only against religion having the social power to force someone into doing something."[19]

In 1921–1922 the *Evsektsii* devoted a large part of their efforts to the anti-religious campaign. The editor-in-chief of the main Yiddish Communist newspaper, *Der emes*, was Moishe Litvakov, himself a former socialist and a student of Hebrew as well as Yiddish literature. He was chagrined to discover that the typesetters of his "revolutionary" newspaper refused to work on the High Holidays. He lamented that "this is almost a mass phenomenon. The Jewish worker remains mired in the old Judaistic garbage; he sends his children to *kheyder*, observes the Sabbath and holidays, and often trembles over the most minute religious detail."[20] *Der emes* thereafter became a forum for much anti-religious writing.

In contrast to the anti-Judaism campaigns that were launched in the 1950s and 1960s, the efforts of the 1920s were made almost exclusively by Jews in the Yiddish language. To a considerable extent this seemed to be an internal Jewish affair. In the 1920s campaign against religion, three main methods were used: agitation and propaganda, feigned accession to the "demands of the toiling masses," and outright coercion. While Jews participated, often enthusiastically and out of proportion to their numbers, in the general party campaign against other religions, non-Jews did not take part in the anti-Judaism campaign. Any taint of anti-Semitism was thus avoided. Maxim Gorky regretted both the *Evsektsii* attacks on Hebrew culture and the tactlessness of Jewish Communists in participating in anti-Christian activities. He noted cases where "Jewish Communists were purposely put in the ranks of those persecuting the Russian church and priests in order that the Russian

Torahs piled up in Vitebsk, 1921, before they were taken away by the authorities. CREDIT: Aryeh Tsentsifer, Central Zionist Archives.

A synagogue in Vitebsk, wrecked by the Communists. CREDIT: Aryeh Tsentsifer, Central Zionist Archives.

Synagogue in Vitebsk which has been turned into a worker's club. The signs on the wall in Yiddish say, "Education is the path to Communism" and, quoting Lenin, "Soviet power sets the goal of learning to work for the entire people." CREDIT: Yosel Mlotek.

peasants should see with their own eyes that the Jews are desecrating their holy places."[21]

The propaganda effort included meetings and lectures, often at the workplace, a torrent of articles in the Yiddish and Russian press, and public debates much like the medieval disputations that the Catholic church had forced on the Jews. There were theatrical "show trials," not only of religious functionaries, but even of institutions and customs. For example, on Rosh Hashanah, 1921, the Jewish religion was "tried" in Kiev, ironically, in the same auditorium where the Beilis trial had been held. The "judges" saw a strange array of "witnesses": a "rabbi" testified solemnly that he taught religion in order to keep the masses ignorant and subservient; an obese "bourgeois," bedecked in glittering jewelry, testified to the alliance between the exploiters and Judaism. The "prosecutor," summarizing the case against religion, demanded a "sentence of death for the Jewish religion." A Hebrew teacher who rose from the audience to defend Judaism was arrested on the spot. The "judges" returned from their chambers and, to no one's surprise, announced a death verdict. In other places, the *yeshiva*, the *kheyder*, and circumcision were "put on trial." Borrowing from the repertoire of the anarchists, the Jewish Communists organized dances, torchlight parades, and entertain-

Scene from an anti-religious play, *Kheyder*, performed at the Belorussian State Yiddish Theater, M. F. Rafalsky, director. The letters on the backsides of the actors spell "kosher."

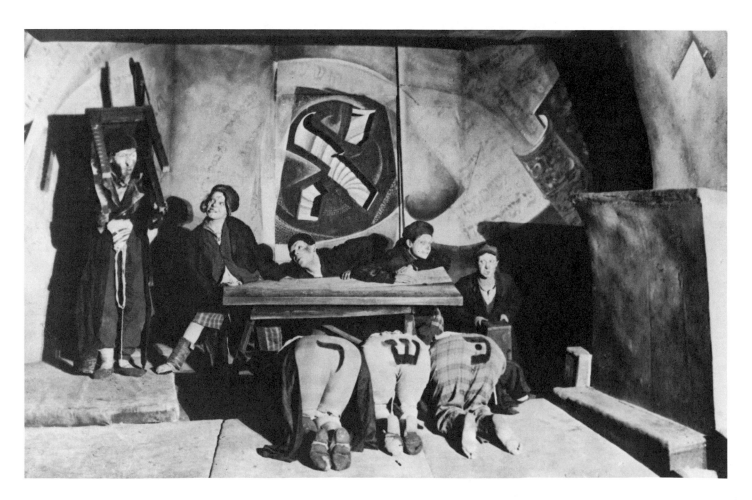

ment by clowns on Yom Kippur, the most solemn of Jewish holy days, and sometimes a free lunch would be served on this fast day.

Much of the anti-religious effort was masked by the pretense of fulfilling the wishes of the Jewish masses. Meetings would be carefully prepared so that they were controlled by *Evsektsii*, and resolutions were adopted turning a synagogue into a workers' club, closing a *kheyder*, or turning over the gold and silver ornaments of the synagogue to the campaign for the poor. When opposition was expressed at such meetings it was usually quickly suppressed, though in smaller localities the Communists were sometimes temporarily defeated, as they had little support among the populace.

SO WHAT IF I'VE BEEN CIRCUMCISED

So what if I've been circumcised
With rituals, as among the Jews?
Field winds have tanned my middle-sized,
Pale, dreaming feet to darker hues.

Some Jews long for *tsimmis* yet —
We toughs, for smoke, and flame in motion;
Eight years' embattled meadows, set
Underneath the sky's blue ocean.

I'm a quiet guy and hardly a villain;
My honesty has no great appeal;
I'm never known to put on *tefillin*,
I'm never known to wheel and deal.

So what if I've been circumcised
With rituals, as among the Jews?
Field winds have tanned my middle-sized,
Pale, dreaming feet to darker hues."

Itsik Feffer

The law was mobilized in the effort to "liberate" people from "superstition and cant." All religious associations were required to submit membership lists to the authorities and register with them. Religious instruction for anyone under the age of eighteen became illegal. Religious functionaries were deprived of the right to vote, and their families were classified as *lishentsy*, or people without civil rights. They had a hard time finding employment or admission to schools. Religious publications could no longer appear. In some cases the military was used to aid in the seizure of religious premises, and in Minsk and Odessa some people were killed in the struggle over synagogues.

Rabbi Yehoshua Tsimbelist ("Reb Shiye Horotzner") of the water carriers' synagogue in Minsk, who organized religious resistance against the Communists. CREDIT: David Cohen.

Former synagogue turned into a worker's club. CREDIT: Yosel Mlotek.

The *Evsektsii* reported that between January 1923 and March 1924, 303 campaigns were mounted, of which 120 were directed against religion. Moishe Litvakov boasted that this "was not the cantankerous atheism of the small-town anarchists against the small-town 'important Jews' . . . but a revolutionary demonstration of the entire Jewish working class . . . against the tarnished Assembly of Israel."[23] Indeed, in 1922–1923 over 1,000 *kheyders* were closed. It is estimated that nearly 650 synagogues were closed in the 1920s. So great was the frenzy with which the campaign was conducted that a non-Jewish Communist was prompted to note, "It would be nice to see the Russian Communists tear into the monasteries and the holy days as the Jewish Communists do to Yom Kippur."[24] Esther Frumkin, at one time married to a rabbi, defended the anti-religious zeal of the *Evsektsii*:

> The danger is that the masses may think that Judaism is exempt from anti-religious propaganda and, therefore, it rests with the Jewish Communists to be even more ruthless with rabbis than non-Jewish Communists are with priests.[25]

Once again, the insecurity of the Jewish Communists drove them to prove their fidelity to the cause and their ability to transcend kinship in order to serve ideology. By the 1950s and 1960s these considerations were irrelevant. The anti-Judaism campaigns included non-Jews and were carried out in languages accessible to the general public (Russian, Ukrainian). The messages were carried in the pages of popular magazines, thus exposing a large non-Jewish audience to anti-Judaism propaganda. As it turned out, neither the campaign of the 1920s nor the later ones were as effective in diminishing the influence of religion as the larger shifts that took place in the 1930s from the *shtetlekh* to the cities, from crafts and trade to industry. It was those changes that truly revolutionized the lives of Soviet Jews.

I'VE NEVER BEEN LOST

In all my short, happy life, I've never
Been lost, nor forgotten the way I came.
I laugh to myself when I remember
That I carry some famous rabbi's name.

The name that my grandfather wanted for me
was the Holy Reb Itzikel of Skvira's
That I might lay *tefillin* and wear a *tallis*
And do my singing of prayers and *zmires*,

That I might be the richest man in town,
And my wife's housekeeping be the best,
So days and nights gave way to each other,
And each year came to follow the rest.

The sun has blessedly bronzed my body,
My life is all battles and songs of fame;
It really breaks me up to remember
That I carry some famous rabbi's name.[26]

Itsik Feffer

American relief officials, in uniform, posing with some leading cultural figures at a Jewish art exhibition in Kiev, 1919. Seated, right to left: Zelig Kalmanovich, Nokhum Shtif, Volf Latski-Bartoldi, Dovid Bergelson, two Americans, Baal Makhshoves (Isidore Eliashev), Elias Tcherikower. Standing, right to left: Epstein, Baruch Aronson, Yissachar Ber Rybak, Leib Kvitko, Yosef Chaikov.

RUINATION AND RECONSTRUCTION IN THE SHTETLEKH

World war, revolution, civil war, and pogroms had left the economic life of the Jews in shambles. Aside from the considerable physical destruction, the economic life of the *shtetl* in particular was seriously upset. It has been estimated that between 70 and 80 percent of the Jewish population was without a regular income in 1918–1921. All trade was considered "speculation" by the government, but for many, "speculation" was the only way to avoid starvation. Even the Jewish farming colonies, normally self-sufficient, were so badly damaged that nearly half the farmsteads were abandoned in Ekaterinoslav province between 1919 and 1921. Thousands emigrated to neighboring Poland, Latvia, Lithuania, and Romania, sometimes continuing on to Western Europe and the Americas. Relief organizations established before or during World War I were permitted to continue

Children aided by the Joint Distribution Committee.
CREDIT: Joint Distribution Committee.

their operations, although the Communists attempted to control them. They were tolerated mainly because they attracted foreign capital. In 1921–1923 the American Joint Distribution Committee spent over eight million dollars for Russian relief, more than one-third of it through the American Relief Administration for nonsectarian purposes. An additional ten million dollars was collected in remittance of food to individuals, mostly those who had relatives in America. In 1924 alone the JDC allocated nearly ten million dollars for relief and reconstruction. It also supplied tractors, livestock, agricultural implements, and horses to Jewish agriculturalists, who received an infusion of new blood as desperate *shtetl* and city dwellers tried their luck at farming in order to avoid total ruination.

The *shtetl*, often satirized by prerevolutionary social reformers and critics, was regarded by the Jewish Bolsheviks almost as a leper colony, for it was there that Jewish traditional life seemed to hang on most tenaciously and where the least desirable social elements—traders, *luftmentshn*, clerics—seemed to dominate. Having seized control of the "Jewish street" by 1923, the *Evsektsii* announced a kind of "Jewish New Economic Policy" which they termed "face to the *shtetl*." Paralleling the general New Economic Policy, which in-

Homeless children in the Crimea.

Jewish orphans of the civil war.

volved a partial retreat from socialist principles, this was to be a partial reconciliation with the "petit bourgeois" elements. It was designed to persuade them to adjust to the new economic realities and take active part in "socialist construction." Indeed, there was much work to be done. Many of the most productive people had left for the cities or abroad, leaving behind a disproportionate number of widows, dependents, and charity cases. The new economic system rendered at least partially superfluous the traditional role of the *shtetl* as the economic link between the countryside and the cities. One study concluded that the *shtetlekh* were in worse shape than they had been before 1914 or even during the war. A 1924 survey of 43 *shtetlekh* in Belorussia concluded that only one-quarter of the more than 90,000 inhabitants could claim a profession or a business. In Monastyrshchina, said to be typical of Ukrainian *shtetlekh*, nearly half the loans made by the local bank could not be paid back. Fully one-third of Monastyrshchina's population was categorized as "half-beggars," including 115 widows. Since about one-third of the Jewish population in the

A typical *shtetl* Jew, Zev (Velvel) Moiseevich Kipnis of Korostyn, Ukraine. He was born in 1855 and died in 1937, never having changed his religious way of life. CREDIT: Elia Kipnis.

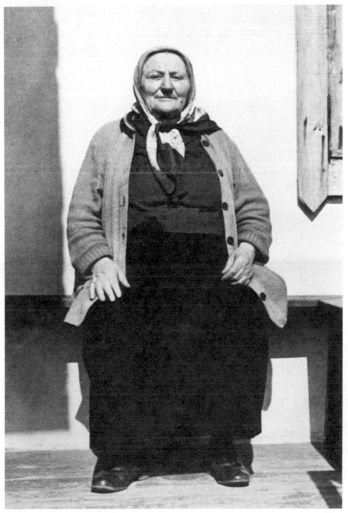

Risl Kipnis, born in Olevsk, Ukraine, wife of Zev Kipnis. This picture was taken in the 1930s when she was in her eighties. CREDIT: Elia Kipnis.

A *shtetl* Jew in the 1920s.
PHOTO: Louis Meyer; CREDIT: Bernard Meyer.

Ukraine was still living in *shtetlekh* as late as 1929, the devastation of these hamlets was a major social and economic problem. In the *Evsektsii*'s view, this was also a political problem, because a poor economic situation could be exploited by the enemies of Communism. Indeed, of nearly 600 Jews in Nezhin, there were only 24 party members and 86 members of the Komsomol (Communist Youth League).

The situation in Belorussia was no better. A survey of thirteen *shtetlekh* discovered that the population had declined 20 percent between 1897 and 1931, but over half of that decline had occurred between 1926 and 1931. From 17,476 Jews living in these *shtetlekh*, the population declined to 11,722. The proportion of women grew, but only one-fourth of them were economically self-sufficient, compared to one-half of the men. It was precisely the age groups who would typically dominate the labor force that had fled the *shtetlekh*, leaving behind the very young and the aged. At least half the Jewish population in thirteen Belorussian *shtetlekh* surveyed in 1931 was either too young or too old to enter the labor force even had

A Jewish woman at a well in Fastov, Ukraine.
PHOTO: Louis Meyer; CREDIT: Bernard Meyer.

Children surrounding the coffin of their father,
Potchep, 1924. CREDIT: Sorell Skolnick.

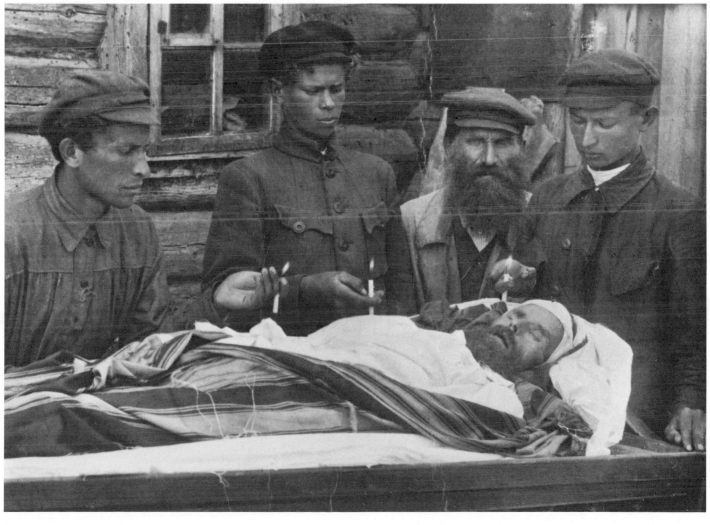

ABOVE: The marketplace in Shklov, Belorussia, is deserted because of the Bolsheviks' prohibition on private trade. CREDIT: Raphael Abramovitch.

BELOW: Homeless refugees from the Ukraine in Grivita, Romania (1920), who were forced back over the border. CREDIT: Elias Tcherikower.

employment opportunities existed. Of course, many people under the age of eighteen could be employed.

The structure of the working population also did not give much satisfaction to the Communists. More than a decade after Soviet power had been consolidated, distinct traces of the prerevolutionary economy remained, as many were still working in cottage industries, though the massive industrialization and collectivization of agriculture begun under the first Five Year Plan in 1928 were beginning to make their mark.

It was claimed that by 1931 there were no longer any unemployed or traders in any of the *shtetlekh*. The decline in the number of peasants in the *shtetlekh* was explained partially by the migration of Jewish peasants to the new agricultural colonies in Belorussia, the Ukraine, the Crimea, and Birobidzhan, and by the transfer of a few to industrial work. The researchers found that 1,872 people had left the *shtetlekh*, the largest number (982) of whom had remained in Belorussia but had moved to cities; over 500 moved to the Russian republic,

The grandfather of Abraham Rechtman, a folklorist, dictating his memoirs, Brailov, Ukraine.

The Lazar Davidovich family, 1925. CREDIT: Berta Rostinina.

where even greater industrial opportunities existed, nearly 200 went to the Ukraine, and twenty-four to the Crimea, presumably to the new colonies. Smaller numbers went to other parts of the USSR, seven emigrated to America and sixteen to other lands.[27]

The *Evsektsii* and the party as a whole perceived political advantages in the "reconstruction" of the *shtetl* and bringing it into "socialist construction." "These achievements are a result of the successful socialist attack on the capitalist, parasitical elements in the *shtetl* who exploited the difficulties of socialist construction to spread nationalism and Zionism among certain strata of the population. With the help of the right opportunists, they would worm their way into Soviet cooperatives and institutions where they would try to poison the atmosphere with the Zionist spirit. This shows that the class enemy does not yield his position without a struggle and that the fight against them must be stepped up."[28] Religion, too, was dealt a serious blow by the new efforts in the *shtetl*, it was claimed: "A crisis hit the religious-traditional way of life of the *shtetl*, with its outmoded customs. In almost all the cooperatives Sabbath as the day off was eliminated, with a few small exceptions. The rabbis left many of the *shtetlekh* and no new ones replaced them. The new way of life is becoming more and more accepted among the working class of the *shtetl*."[29] Nevertheless it was admitted that "hostile elements" were still at work. In a brick factory in Turov, "thanks to the activity of a hostile person," both Saturday and Sunday were given as days off "so as not to offend anyone's God." In the collective farms people did not go into the fields on religious holidays. A "mixed funeral" was described: first, the *khevra kadisha* (burial society) conducted a religious ceremony at home with the proper Psalms recited, and then the public funeral, organized by the trade union, took place on the street to the accompaniment of funeral music. Such phenomena were attributed to the older generation's influence and its overrepresentation in the *shtetl*.

The Communists were confident that the future belonged to them. After all, in less than a decade they had eliminated

Residents of the *shtetl* Durashna, 1929. PHOTO: Louis Meyer; CREDIT: Bernard Meyer.

B. Lerman, police chief of Vitebsk, 1927. CREDIT: P. Frumer.

the Jewish political parties, suppressed Zionism and Hebrew, driven religion into the remote corners of Soviet life or underground, and gained a monopoly of power "on the Jewish street." The question was now whether the destruction of the traditional community need be followed by the construction of a unique and wholly new Jewish subculture based on secularism and socialist internationalism. Or had the decline of the traditional way of life brought the Jews so close to the Leninist vision of their integration into the larger society that there was no need for "Jewish work"? Many Jewish members of the party believed that assimilation was at hand. Therefore programs designed specifically to address Jewish issues and problems were unnecessary and would artificially impede the natural process of assimilation. On the other hand many *Evsektsii* activists, coming out of the Jewish socialist (and in some cases, even Zionist) movements and having a vested interest in the maintenance of "Jewish work," advocated programs that would address the specific economic and cultural problems of the Jews. For some, an important by-product of such programs would be the preservation of Jewish self-consciousness, albeit based on a new kind of Jewish identity which could be part of the socialist society now in the making throughout the Soviet Union. Their vision of a socialist future was shared by Jews in other countries, some of whom—poets, workers, writers, and would-be farmers—were even moved to immigrate to the land of socialism.

CHAPTER THREE

REACHING FOR UTOPIA:
BUILDING SOCIALISM AND
A NEW JEWISH CULTURE

ТОКАРНЫЙ ЦЕХ ФЗУ. МРЗ АГРОДЖОЙНТ

Subtly and without fanfare the *Evsektsii* and the party as a whole began to adjust their ideology to undeniable realities. Defining the tasks of the *Evsektsii* in 1918, Semën Dimanshtain asserted that, "as internationalists, we do not set any special national tasks for ourselves. . . . We are not . . . fanatics of the Yiddish language. There is no 'Holy Yiddish' (*Yiddish hakoidesh*) for us. . . . It is entirely possible that in the near future the richer languages of the stronger and more developed peoples will push aside the Yiddish language. . . . We Communists will shed no tears over this, nor will we do anything to obstruct this development."[1]

By the mid-1920s most *Evsektsii* activists were singing a different tune, one called by the Communist Party. The party was encouraging the "flowering of the nationality cultures" and even inventing national alphabets for the Asian peoples who, until that point, had no written languages. The party and the state were investing in schools, theaters, newspapers, and magazines in non-Russian languages, including Yiddish. They insisted that governmental and even party activities be carried on in the languages of the ethnic groups involved. Stalin sanctioned the new policy with his famous definition of proletarian culture as "socialist in content, national in form." For the Jews this meant the promotion of Yiddish, and new cultural and economic progress. *Evsektsii* activists who envisioned a secular, socialist Yiddish future eagerly welcomed the chance to translate their dreams into reality. Now they had the backing of the party line and they hastened to take advantage of the funds, personnel, buildings, and other resources put at their disposal.

The new policy resulted in a rapid expansion of publication in Yiddish, all of it paid for by the state. In 1924 only 76 Yiddish books and pamphlets had been published; by 1930 there were 531. In 1923–1925 there were twenty-one Yiddish newspapers published; in 1927 there were forty. State funding of Yiddish culture and the opportunity to create a modern Yiddish culture free of commercial calculations attracted some prominent cultural figures from abroad. The writers Dovid Bergelson, Peretz Markish, and Der Nister, and scholars such as Maks Erik and Meir Viener, immigrated to the USSR from Eastern and Western Europe. They hoped to participate in a Yiddish cultural renaissance in which their talents could find full expression. But they probably misjudged their audience. In 1928 the total circulation of the three main Yiddish dailies reached only 32,000, whereas the potential readership was in the hundreds of thousands. A survey taken in 1928 revealed that Yiddish book readers preferred the Yiddish classics, then Yiddish translations of European classics, and only in third place, new Soviet Yiddish literature. Clearly the Yiddish readership was drawn disproportionately from the older, more traditional generation. Younger Jews had every opportunity to learn Russian, and it had become their preferred language, as Dimanshtain had predicted. Moreover, many Soviet Jews were singularly unenthusiastic about the attempt to create a secular, socialist Yiddish culture, rejecting it either because they clung to Jewish tradition or because they would rather embrace the "higher" Russian culture.

The history of the secular, state-run Yiddish schools, the only legal Jewish schools, illustrates the point. The *kheyders*

First All-Union Conference of Yiddish Writers, August 5, 1934. Among the writers are: bottom row (left to right): Joseph Opatoshu (fifth from left), Peretz Markish (6), Leib Kvitko (7), Itsik Feffer (8), Note Lurie (9), Avrom Veviorka (11), Aron Kushnirov (12). Second row: Moishe Teitch (1), Izi Kharik (7), Moishe Litvakov (9), Naftali Hertz Kon (13), Shmuel Halkin (15). Third row: A. Abtchuk (5), Noah Lurie (6), Nokhum Oislender (8). Fourth row: Rokhl Boimvol (2), Moishe Khashtchevatsky (10), Zelig Akselrod (11). Fifth row: Motl Grubian (2), Khayim Maltinsky (5). CREDIT: Joseph Opatoshu.

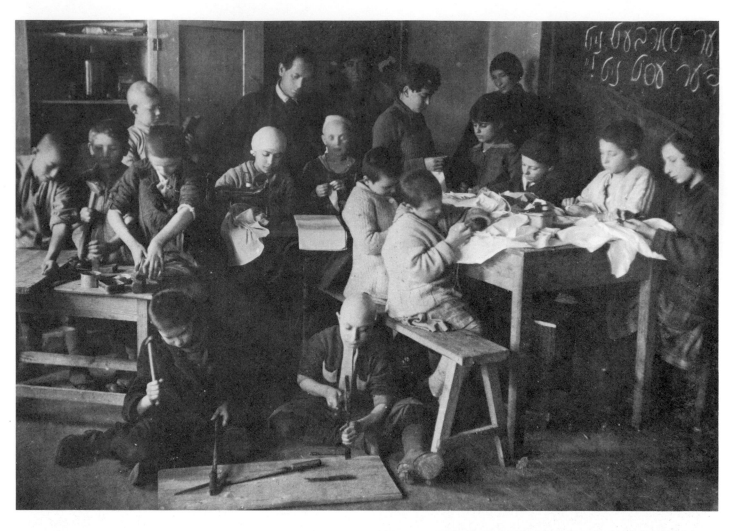

OPPOSITE, ABOVE: Yiddish school in Kharkov, Ukraine. On the board, in Yiddish, is the slogan "He who does not work, does not eat."

OPPOSITE, BELOW: A "general assembly" of the school with the agenda on the board. The agenda items include: (1) general holiday of Jewish children's homes; (2) comradely relations; (3) current issues. The banner reads: "Children's home: The home of Communist culture." CREDIT: Joint Distribution Committee.

The Ratmansky school in Kiev, built originally as a trade school by the sugar magnate Brodsky. In the 1930s there were about 350 students in this school, supported by "Agro-Joint." "Shock worker" [outstanding] students are posing in front of a banner which reads (in the Communist orthography): "Long live the Komsomol tribe — the powerful reserve force and reliable helper of the Communist Party." The Komsomol is the youth organization of the party. CREDIT: Joseph Rosen.

Marc Chagall (front row, first on the right) with teachers and children at the children's colony Malakhovka, near Moscow, 1923. In the second row, second from right, is the writer Der Nister. The literary critic Yekhezkel Dobrushin is third from right. CREDIT: Joint Distribution Committee.

were destroyed or driven underground, and any other religious or even Hebrew instruction was made illegal, leaving the secular Yiddish school as the only alternative. The number of such schools, increased dramatically in the mid-1920s, from 366 in 1923–1924 to 1,100 in 1929–1930. Student enrollment jumped from 54,173 to 130,000 in that same period. Indeed, while well over a quarter of the Jewish children in Belorussia and the Ukraine, areas of the old Pale, were not attending school at all, almost half the Jewish children who were enrolled were attending Yiddish schools. Yet in the Russian Republic, which had few Jews before the revolution but which was now attracting upwardly mobile workers, white-collar workers, and professionals, less than 17 percent of Jewish students were in Yiddish schools. The most ambitious Soviet Jews were convinced that they could leave Jewish culture behind and find their place in the larger

Russian society which now offered them great, and equal, opportunities.

Despite the high proportion of Jewish children enrolled in Yiddish schools, many Jewish parents were not attracted to them because the schools were Jewish in language only. As one Jewish Communist noted approvingly, "The very concept of 'Jewish history' is excluded from the school." Only general courses in the history of class struggles could include "elements describing the struggle of the Jewish artisans against their employers and of Jewish workers against the Jewish or any other bourgeoisie."[2] Religious Jews preferred to send their children to Russian-, Belorussian-, or Ukrainian-language schools because the latter did not single out Judaism for criticism but condemned all religions, whereas the Yiddish school naturally focused its antireligious messages on Judaism, such as warnings against "nonhygienic customs such as kissing the Torah," and comparisons between Jewish agriculture in the USSR and in Palestine in order to show the "utopianism and harmfulness" of Zionism.[3]

Perhaps most important, the Yiddish schools existed mainly at the elementary level. A graduate who wished to go on to secondary school and to higher education was at a disadvantage because all entrance examinations as well as instruc-

The second graduating class of the Yiddish Professional-Technical School in Cherkassy, Ukraine. The only non-Jew on the staff is the instructor in Ukrainian. Among the staff is the party secretary of the school.

The Jewish Children's Home in Krivoi Rog, Ukraine, "funded by the Soviet power." The Yiddish sign reads "Long live Comrade Lenin, the guide to Communism." The children's heads may have been shaved to prevent the spread of lice. CREDIT: Joint Distribution Committee.

tion in the higher schools, were in Russian. Jewish parents, anxious for their children to go to high school and beyond, sent them to Russian schools from the start if they could. The *Evsektsii* functionaries, well aware of this, pressured parents to enroll their children in Yiddish schools, either because they believed that the future of Yiddish culture depended on Yiddish education, or because they simply wanted to justify the existence of their own organization and activities. They went so far that they were publicly reprimanded by higher authorities in the *Evsektsii* who criticized the "tendency to drag all Jewish children into Yiddish schools by force, taking no account of the language they use or the wishes of their parents. . . ."[4] Even children in Yiddish schools were attracted to Russian. An American visitor to a Yiddish school in the Ukraine observed the children carrying Russian textbooks. He was assured that Yiddish texts existed, "but we like to read the Russian texts better than the Yiddish."[5]

Local and regional soviets, trade unions, and even law courts and Communist Party cells were encouraged to conduct their affairs in Yiddish in places where Jews constituted a majority. By 1930, 169 Jewish soviets had been created. In the Ukraine they embraced nearly 12 percent of the Jewish population. However, many Jews could not participate in their affairs or even vote in soviet elections because they were classified as *lishentsy*, people deprived of civil rights because of their class origin, vocation, or religious beliefs. It was enough to be the child of a former rabbi or even a sexton to be put in this category. Over 40 percent of *shtetl*

inhabitants were barred from voting in the 1927 elections in the Ukraine. In 1926–1927 nearly a third of the Jews in all of the Ukraine were ineligible to vote.

The Yiddish courts never amounted to much because Jewish legal terminology was derived from rabbinic law and, as such, was inadmissible and impractical. Moreover, there were no appeals courts operating in Yiddish, Yiddish-speaking lawyers were scarce, and non-Jewish litigants obviously preferred other courts.

Yiddish party cells and trade unions were also not very popular, not so much because they were impractical but because Yiddish could not compete in prestige and utility with Russian. Until 1924 there was not a single party cell operating in Yiddish, but by the end of the 1920s there were nearly a hundred. However, they included only about 2,000 of the 45,000 Jewish party members, of whom 18,000 had declared Yiddish their mother tongue. The *Evsektsii*, anxious to promote the use of Yiddish and fearful that its absence in party work would erode its own *raison d'être*, complained that "Some believe that in the street and workshop you are *allowed* to speak Yiddish, but party work *must* be conducted in Russian."[6]

Resistance to using Yiddish was even stronger in the trade unions. In nearly 1,700 union cells with Jewish majorities, which included more than 35,000 workers, only 57 cells

Dr. Joseph A. Rosen and Joseph C. Hyman of the Joint Distribution Committee in America, both in suits, visiting the IKOR colony in 1928. The contrast between the "bourgeois" visitors and the residents is striking. CREDIT: Joseph Rosen.

conducted their affairs in Yiddish. The reason was clear. Before the revolution, when Jews had little opportunity to educate themselves in Russian culture and to be accepted by Russian society, Yiddish held its own. But now that the doors were open to both Russian society and culture, many Jews were only too happy to abandon Yiddish culture. They associated it with the *shtetl* and a way of life that they were being taught to regard as backward. Jews were eager to "graduate" to Russian and take their place in the forefront of general society, escaping the narrow confines of the Jewish Pale. A Yiddish newspaper published in Minsk lamented the fact that "The Jewish worker does not want to read a [Yiddish] newspaper. He will break his teeth, he will not understand a word, but give him Russian. A Jewish comrade begins to speak in Yiddish at a workers' meeting—they don't want to listen. And when she finishes, they translate, even though you can't find a non-Jew here for love or money."[7]

Resistance to Yiddish and insistence on Russian stemmed from the conviction that Russian was a "higher" culture and that it was the key to opening the doors to advancement. "A meeting of the transport workers. One comrade, a porter, takes the floor and comes out categorically against any work in Yiddish. When challenged, he answered: The matter is quite simple. . . . For many years I have carried hundreds of pounds on my back day in and day out. Now I want to learn some Russian and become an office worker."[8]

SETTLING JEWS ON THE LAND

Jews did indeed use the new opportunities to escape to the cities and move up the social scale. But until the massive industrialization of the 1930s, many, especially middle-aged and elderly people, remained in the *shtetlekh*. Their economic situation was difficult and their desire or ability to move out of their Jewish environments was limited. The Communist Party decided that they could be helped by turning them toward agriculture. The *Evsektsii*, in turn, found a way of "productivizing the Jewish masses" and at the same time keeping them culturally Jewish. In 1924 the Central Committee of the Communist Party created a Commission for the Rural Settlement of Jewish Toilers (KOMZET in Russian, and KOMERD in Yiddish). Two years later KOMERD announced plans to settle 100,000 Jews on the land within a few years. The *Evsektsii* welcomed these plans, believing that mass agricultural settlement would give Jews the means to subsist and would provide a social base for Yiddish institutions.

The directorate of the Hashakhar cooperative (possibly a Zionist one), Telmansky district, Ukraine, 1925. Chairman Rubenchik is the first on the right. CREDIT: Joseph Rosen.

Getting around in one of the
colonies. CREDIT: Joint
Distribution Committee.

Temporary barracks of new
colonists, Kherson province,
Ukraine. CREDIT: Joseph
Rosen.

Moshe and Dina Freedman
praying or studying at the
Peretzfeld collective farm
(kolkhoz), Crimea, 1935.

Exchanging news in the Poltavtsy colony, Ukraine. CREDIT: Joseph Rosen.

A sixteen-year-old driver of a John Deere tractor. CREDIT: Joseph Rosen.

Children tending pigs. A special point was made in the Jewish agricultural colonies about raising pigs in order to emphasize that the colonists had broken with religion. CREDIT: ORT.

Settlers in the Crimea, 1929.

A *sukkah* set up against the wall
of a colonist's home. CREDIT:
Joseph Rosen.

Elderly colonists returning from the synagogue, *taleisim* (prayer shawls) under their arms. CREDIT: Joseph Rosen.

Cooperative forms of agriculture would conform to socialist principles, and would be easier to institute among Jews coming onto the land than among non-Jewish peasants who were firmly committed to the individual farming that they and their ancestors had practiced for so long. Moreover, Jewish agricultural colonies would steal the thunder from the Zionists who boasted about their communal settlements in Palestine, and they would populate and secure border regions in the Crimea, the Ukraine, Belorussia—and later the Far East.

Ever since the nineteenth century, agricultural labor held a sort of mystique for the Jews of Eastern Europe. Many of the *maskilim* were stirred by visions of Jews abandoning their economically shaky and socially repulsive occupations for healthy, ennobling farm labor. Influenced by Romantic ideas of the "noble savage," and by their own ambivalence toward the peasants around them—they were pogromists, true, but they were also *gezunte goyim* (healthy Gentiles) in contrast to the weak Jews of the Pale—reformers devised schemes to create Jewish agricultural settlements in Argentina, North America, and Palestine. At the end of the nineteenth and beginning of the twentieth centuries, Baron DeHirsch, the Am Olam movement, and of course the Zi-

Colonists eating breakfast in the fields in the Nai-haim (New Home) colony, Kherson province, Ukraine, 1925. CREDIT: Joseph Rosen.

onists all tried to encourage Jews to become farmers. Now it was the Communists' turn. Foreign Jewish organizations, familiar with the idea of agricultural settlement, were attracted to support the effort because they were interested in the economic rehabilitation and physical survival of their coreligionists. The American Joint Distribution Committee, a thoroughly "bourgeois" organization backed by some of the most prominent bankers and financiers in the American Jewish establishment, supported agricultural colonies in the Ukraine. ORT, which had originated as a Jewish vocational training organization in Russia, but which now had an organization in the United States, supported colonies in the Odessa region and Belorussia. The Jewish Colonization Association was involved as well. IKOR and PROKOR, American leftist organizations, raised funds for tractors and other machinery. Settlers received free land, machines and livestock could be purchased on credit, and tax concessions were made. By 1928 there were nearly 220,000 Jewish farmers. Already by 1926 the JDC had supplied $2.3 million and had set up "Agro-Joint," an organization specifically designed to assist the colonization efforts in the USSR. By the mid-1930s the JDC had expended $13.8 million on agricultural work and an additional $10.3 million on other assistance.

The foreign "bourgeois" organizations aided colonization primarily because they were committed to relieving Jewish poverty and unemployment, but some of the *Evsektsii* activists had an additional agenda. Esther Frumkin, so active in

Proud colonist father with his twins. CREDIT: Joseph Rosen.

Mass meeting of the colonists in winter. Note the unplastered walls. The streamer on the wall reads "Dictatorship of the proletariat is the only form of national liberation." CREDIT: Joseph Rosen.

Mikhail Kalinin addressing the GEZERD Conference. This non-Jewish veteran Bolshevik created a sensation at the conference when he warned that Jews were marrying non-Jews and losing their culture. He urged them to settle on the land in compact masses in order simultaneously to solve their economic problems and to preserve their identity and culture. CREDIT: Joseph Rosen.

the destruction of the old order, now proclaimed that "New processes have started in Jewish life. Under the dictatorship of the proletariat, there is an opportunity for the Jewish people *to consolidate itself as a nation.* . . . The agricultural settlement of large Jewish masses in one territory. . . . "[9] At the first convention of the Association for Rural Settlement of Jewish Toilers (OZET in Russian, GEZERD in Yiddish), none other than Mikhail Kalinin, a Russian and the ceremonial head of the Soviet state, deplored Jewish assimilation and marriage to non-Jews(!): "The Jewish people faces the great task of preserving its own nationality, and to this end a large part of the Jewish population must be transformed into an economically stable, agriculturally compact group which should number at least hundreds of thousands. Only under such conditions can the Jewish masses hope for the future existence of their nationality."[10] The party line had apparently changed—temporarily, as it turned out—to permit contemplation of the idea of a Jewish nation, an idea so decisively rejected by Lenin and Stalin before the revolution.

The promise of agricultural settlement was never fulfilled. Colonization failed to attract those elements for whom it had

First national conference of GEZERD (Association for Rural Settlement of Jewish Toilers), 1926. Fourth from the right in the front row is Esther Frumkin. CREDIT: Joseph Rosen.

been designed. A majority of the colonists had already been employed before they came onto the land, though they could bring almost no capital with them. In the colonies political and cultural life hardly existed. The party complained that there was not enough political activity and the settlers complained that there weren't enough books, newspapers, and entertainment. Schools were few and far between. The Soviet press complained that the colonies were being used as "hiding places" for religious and even Zionist elements who felt that they could more easily maintain their beliefs and practices in a homogenously Jewish environment, far from the eyes of the political authorities. In their anxiety to recruit colonists and "fulfill the plan," the authorities were not overly fussy. Moreover, the religious and traditional elements were precisely those who were most likely to be without work and hence the logical candidates for settling on the land.

In several places, especially in the Ukraine, local peasants were hostile to the idea of Jews coming onto the land. The head of the Ukrainian Council of Peoples' Commissars, Vlas Chubar, found it necessary to reassure peasants that Jews would not take their land, nor were they being given special privileges. "Hooligans" were said to be spreading rumors

Two mothers with their children in a colony. CREDIT: Joint Distribution Committee.

At prayer in the home of a colonist, Tagancha, Krivoi Rog district, Ukraine. CREDIT: Joseph Rosen.

BELOW: Mountain Jewish women and a baby in a colony, 1929. CREDIT: Joseph Rosen.

The *shokhet* (ritual slaughterer) of the IKOR colony. CREDIT: Joseph Rosen.

that "the Yids will take over power on the steppes," and priests in some places were accused in the press of praying to God to "Save us from the Jewish nemesis."[11]

Despite foreign assistance, farm implements were very scarce in many colonies and livestock was rare. Almost all the colonies were collectivized in 1925–1926, but by the following year collectivization was abandoned. It resumed gradually until 1928, when Stalin launched a national collectivization campaign. Then nearly all Jewish colonies were forced to become collective farms, rather than colonies where each farmer had his own piece of land. The results of the collectivization drive were similar to those in agriculture generally. Many Jewish farmers refused to work or to bring in the harvest, knowing that most of it would go to the state in any case. Livestock was slaughtered rather than being turned over to the collective farm (*kolkhoz*). There was a substantial migration from the colonies, all of which had now become collective farms.

Simultaneous with collectivization came "internationalization." Jewish and non-Jewish collectives were forcibly merged: non-Jews were encouraged to settle in formerly Jewish colonies and vice versa. These steps were taken on the grounds that the larger *kolkhozy* would be more efficient, but they made the urgings of Kalinin and the vision of Esther Frumkin and some of her comrades sound hollow indeed.

ABOVE: Collective farmers from the Frayveg (Free Way) *kolkhoz* in the Larindorf district of the Crimea on their way to a pre-election meeting in 1938. The larger picture on the wagon is that of Vyacheslav Molotov, later a foreign minister of the USSR. CREDIT: Joseph Rosen.

BELOW: Children of Mountain Jewish Colony Number 36 near Evpatoria, Crimea. CREDIT: Joseph Rosen.

May Day celebration in the Roiter Poier (Red Peasant) collective farm. CREDIT: *Jewish Daily Forward.*

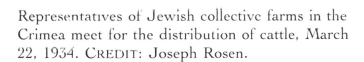

Representatives of Jewish collective farms in the Crimea meet for the distribution of cattle, March 22, 1934. CREDIT: Joseph Rosen.

Children in a Crimean colony. CREDIT: Joseph Rosen.

Little wonder that by February 1930 it was reported that 70 percent of all the settlers who had come to the Crimea had left the farms.

These changes were but a small part of a major shift in the party's policies in 1928–1929 following Stalin's defeat of the "Left Opposition" headed by Trotsky, Zinoviev, and Kamenev, and the "Right Opposition" led by Nikolai Bukharin. By 1928 Stalin emerged as the party leader. He then launched a tremendously ambitious "Five Year Plan" through which collectivization of agriculture and extremely rapid industrialization were supposed to propel the country from capitalism to socialism, from backwardness to modernity. As between agriculture and industry there was no mistaking Stalin's priority. Industry, and heavy industry at that, was to be the priority sector, and so it was to remain for the next sixty years. In 1926, when they were promoting Jewish agriculture, some Jewish Communists already saw the handwriting on the wall. Agriculture was to be the solution for the *luftmentshn*, the low road to socialism. The high road was industry. As Esther Frumkin pointed out, "Jewish workers should not go into farming" nor should productive artisans.

LEFT: The synagogue in the old Jewish agricultural colony, Starokonstantinovka, 1928. CREDIT: Joseph Rosen.

RIGHT: Bogatshevka, a colony supported by ORT (Organization for Rehabilitation and Training).

"Their road to socialism is the direct one. For them to become farmers would be going backward."[12] The number of Jewish family units on the farms declined from 38,100 in 1926 to 25,000 in 1939. It is impossible to know the decline in the number of farmers with any exactitude, but a reasonable estimate is that from a peak of 220,000 Jewish peasants in 1928, the number was down to less than half that on the eve of World War II. By 1938 ORT and Agro-Joint had ceased their operations in the USSR.

Shearing sheep, near Odessa.
CREDIT: Joseph Rosen.

BIROBIDZHAN: "THE LAND OF ISRAEL IN OUR OWN COUNTRY"

The last and most publicized effort to settle Jews on land came at the instigation not of the *Evsektsii* but, according to some undocumented reports, of Stalin himself. In 1927 a mission was sent to survey the area of Birobidzhan in the southern region of the Soviet Far East, bordering on China. This immense territory, larger than Belgium, had a population of only about 32,000 in the early 1930s. It was therefore vulnerable to infiltration by Chinese settlers, and later on by the Japanese, who were taking over Manchuria. Against the covert opposition of many in the *Evsektsii*—who feared that the idea was unfeasible and would draw off energies, funds, and people from agricultural settlements closer to traditionally Jewish areas—the Soviet government in 1928

,,J'estime que la nationalité juive de Birobidjan
ne possèdera pas les traits des Juifs des bour-
gades de Pologne, de Lithuanie, de Russie Blanche
et voire même d'Ukraine parce qu'elle donne
naissance aujourd'hui à des ,,colonisateurs"
socialistes d'un sol libre et riche, tous pourvus
de poings de taille et de dents solides, qui
seront la souche d'une nationalité régénérée et
forte dans la famille des peuples soviétiques".

(Extrait d'un entretien de M. I. KALININE
avec une délégation d'ouvriers à Moscou).

Composite of "heroic types" in
Birobidzhan, with a quote from
Mikhail Kalinin, resembling
Zionist posters of the time. Note
the boy holding a pig.

publicly assigned the area to Jewish colonization. The first
settlers, recruited by a massive propaganda campaign and
including young idealists, were rushed out. The campaign
to encourage settlement was conducted under the slogan "To
a Jewish land!" which, some pointed out, seemed to smack of
Zionism. Mass meetings were held to enlist potential settlers.
At one of them a Jewish woman, gripped by enthusiasm, ex-
claimed excitedly, "This is the Land of Israel in our own
country." The authorities did nothing to discourage such illusions. In line with Leninist-Stalinist dogma, the Jews were
told that if they were to settle Birobidzhan in large numbers,
they would acquire the element needed to make the Jews into
a full-fledged nation, a territory of their own. There was even
talk of creating a "Jewish republic" in the area.

Many of the settlers admitted discouragement in the face of the primitive conditions encountered in Birobidzhan, but others declared themselves more than satisfied with their new lives. Khaia Braterman, who arrived in Birobidzhan in April 1932, told her story to a visiting journalist. Born in 1892 in Uman (Ukraine), she was three years old when her mother died. Her father, a metalworker, barely eked out an existence. "In wintertime only one child at a time could leave the house, because we had only one pair of boots—my father's torn old ones—for a big family." She did not go to school but worked as a maid from the age of eight, and then moved on to a tobacco factory. The revolution, she said, "gave Jews the chance to be equal to others and to work the land, and now I'm one of the kolkhoz's Stakhanovites [leading workers]. I live in a bright room. On the wall hang pictures of party and government leaders. The radio plays a cheerful concert. The postman brings fresh newspapers." She was well satisfied with her income, supplemented by earnings from the cow and two pigs she owned. "I live well. What I used to be able only to dream about is now a reality. . . . We all live a happy, comfortable life, and we thank our party, our friend and leader Comrade Stalin. Recently I was accepted as a candidate member of the All Union Communist Party (Bolsheviks)."[13]

This kind of rhetoric could not mask what most saw as the harsh realities of Birobidzhan. The pioneering settlers found that they had to build their own houses from the materials of local forests. There was little machinery, and horses had to be brought from far away. Swarms of insects, heavy rains, and a disease that killed hundreds of horses made the life of the settlers quite miserable. Of the 654 settlers who arrived in the spring of 1928, only about 325 were left by the first of October. By the spring of 1929, 60 percent of the original settlers had gone. The population grew slowly, reaching only 8,200 at the end of 1933, whereas the plan was to have almost 50,000 Jews there by that date. Nevertheless, on May 7, 1934, the area was declared a "Jewish autonomous *oblast* [province]" despite the fact that the Jewish population was far less than 20 percent of the total. In subsequent years settlers were actively recruited—some say they were pressed into migration—irrespective of their social situation and economic status. The Soviet government boasted of its plan for the Jews, hoping to win foreign Jewish political sympathy and financial assistance. The government tried hard to appeal to national sentiment. It proclaimed that "For the first time in the history of the Jewish people its burning desire for the creation of a homeland of its own, for the achievement of its own national statehood, has been fulfilled."[14] Such rhetoric appeared to impress foreign audiences more than domestic ones. While the pace of migration continued to be slow, foreign assistance was once again mobilized. In America, ORT again lent a hand, though Agro-Joint and the Jewish Colonization Association were less enthusiastic. The pro-Soviet organizations, on the other hand, IKOR and the new AMBIJAN among them, waxed lyrical over the possibilities presented by Birobidzhan. An IKOR leader wrote, "The Jewish masses are getting a large and beautiful land. . . . They will become its masters and use their language in it. . . . The Jewish people will be members of the great family of nations building a new world for themselves, without exploitation and without national and racial oppression. . . ."[15] Some enthusiasts were so moved by the Birobidzhan idea that they migrated to the area from Poland, Argentina, the United States, and other countries. Most of the settlers, whether from the USSR or not, settled in the cities and towns. In 1939 there were only 18 Jewish *kolkhozy* in the entire area, in which no more than 3,000 Jews lived. This was apparently less than 15 percent of the Jewish population of the Birobidzhan Jewish Autonomous Region.

As many of the Jewish activists had foreseen, Birobidzhan did not attract the Jewish masses. It remains moot whether that was ever its true purpose, but there can be little doubt about the project's results: it diverted scarce resources from agricultural colonization efforts more likely to succeed, but it did establish a nominally Jewish territorial entity. Although it attracted a few who were already sympathetic to the Soviet experiment, it did not displace Zionism in the affections of foreign Jews, nor, apparently among Soviet Jews.

The Jewish Sections of the Communist Party could take little satisfaction in the results of their efforts to reconstruct Jewish life on a secular, socialist Yiddish basis. The Yiddishization campaign, supported for a time by the authorities, was defeated by the Jewish thirst for acculturation, and economic and social mobility. The agricultural colonization effort was vitiated by collectivization and finished off by Birobidzhan. The impressive network of Yiddish cultural institutions did not succeed in replacing the traditional institutions in the hearts of the Jews because much of the older generation remained loyal to prerevolutionary values, while only a part of the postrevolutionary generations saw any reason to partake of a Yiddish socialist culture rather than a Russian one. The Jewish Communists had succeeded in destroying much of the old Jewish way of life, but they

Rolling logs on a raft, Birobidzhan. CREDIT: ORT

A fisherman with his nets, Birobidzhan.
CREDIT: ORT

were not very successful in converting the masses to the new faith. In both their successes and failures they did not act alone, of course; they were mere tools in the hands of the larger party which most of them had entered only after the revolution, suffering from a political inferiority complex ever after.

In early 1930 the Jewish Sections of the party were dissolved. The leading Yiddish newspaper explained that rapid industrialization and collectivization of agriculture rendered "some forms of party leadership . . . obsolete . . . Bolsheviks have never made a fetish of *given* forms. . . . The so-called Jewish work must find its new forms. . . . "[16] By 1932 when the party line had changed and no longer encouraged the "flowering of the nationalities," the former *Evsektsii* were being accused of having had "nationalistic tendencies." As the purges initiated in 1934 gathered momentum, most of the leading officials of the former *Evsektsii* were arrested. Esther Frumkin, as mentioned earlier, died in a labor camp; her former Bundist comrade, Rakhmiel Veinshtain, de-

Moishe Litvakov (1875–1937), editor-in-chief of the main Yiddish Party newspaper *Der emes* (Truth), was born in Cherkassy, Ukraine. He received a traditional Jewish education and was regarded as an outstanding Talmudist. Later he attended the Sorbonne in Paris, became a socialist Zionist, and wrote for Yiddish and Russian journals. By 1919 he had moved close to the Bolsheviks and in 1921 he entered the party along with other former members of socialist and Zionist-socialist parties. Litvakov, who had a large personal Hebrew library and had published in Hebrew, was active in the campaigns against Hebrew and Judaism. He exerted great influence on Yiddish literary life and was involved in many literary and political disputes. In 1937 he was arrested as an "enemy of the people." He died in prison that year.

fended her in 1937 and was accused of "anti-party, Bundist hostile belching" for his trouble. He committed suicide in prison. Leading officials in Birobidzhan were accused of "bourgeois nationalism" and arrested. The editor-in-chief of the main Yiddish newspaper, Moishe Litvakov, was removed from his post in 1937 and died in prison. Even the Old Bolshevik, Semën Dimanshtain, Stalin's former subordinate in the Commissariat of Nationalities, fell victim to the purges. As early as 1931 he was accused of ideas that were "profoundly revisionist and hateful to Leninism." He survived until 1938, when he was shot, almost twenty years to the day after his appointment as Jewish commissar, in the bloodbath known as the *Ezhovshchina*, (named for Ezhov, then head of the secret police). Neither the *Evsektsii*, nor their leaders, nor the alternative culture they had tried to develop, survived Stalin.

THE IMPACT OF INDUSTRIALIZATION

The first Five Year Plan, covering 1928 to 1933, called for a quarter to a third of the national income to be invested in the economy, a proportion two and a half times that in Russia before 1914. About a third of the whole was to be invested in industry, and three-quarters of that amount in heavy industry. As if this were not ambitious enough, the figures were soon revised so that actual investment in industry was higher by nearly a half. Obviously, such rapid growth required large new inputs of labor and industrial training on a massive scale. Belorussian, Russian, and Ukrainian peasants, driven off the farms by collectivization, streamed into the cities. They were joined by the Jews of the *shtetlekh* and the smaller cities who saw new educational and employment opportunities in the rapidly expanding urban industrial centers. Often leaving the older generation behind, young Jews abandoned the traditional way of life for the exciting new Soviet industrial cities. Small wonder that between 1926 and 1935 the number of Jewish wage and salary earners nearly tripled. By the latter year there were more than 1,100,000 Jewish wage and salary earners, with slightly more wage earners (manual workers) than salaried employees. The *luftmentshn* had been indeed "productivized." By 1939 there were about 364,000 Jewish white-collar employees, a third of them bookkeepers and the rest mainly technicians, teachers, "cultural and artistic workers," and engineers. The overwhelmingly urban Jewish population was in a good position to take advantage of the vocational and educational opportunities the new economic program had opened up. Already in 1927 Jews made up 14 percent of all students in higher education, and in the 1934–1935 academic year they constituted 18 percent of the graduate student population. In contrast to the tsarist era, Jews could enter higher education and the professions freely. Moreover, as new hands came in from the countryside, workers with any education were being promoted into white-collar positions. As a result, the number of Jewish administrators rose and the number of manual workers declined. By the late 1930s Jews were well established in the proletariat and in the managerial and professional groups.

Once again foreign organizations came to the aid of the Soviet economic program. The same organizations that had

The fifth graduating class of the "Young Proletarian" vocational school going off to Stalingrad (now Volgograd) to build tractors, 1930.

Textile workers in a factory named for Yakov Sverdlov, the first head of the Soviet government, Kolai, Crimea, 1937. CREDIT: Joseph Rosen.

קורס אין אימבערקוואַליפיצירן בײַ דעם 6 טער פּראַפשׁול "מעטאַל"

Girls working on lathes in a vocational school, Odessa. CREDIT: Joseph Rosen.

supported agricultural work among the Jews helped them in the industrial sector as well, and for the same reasons: they were committed to helping Jews attain economic self-sufficiency. Vocational training courses were organized and entire vocational schools were funded, or at least partially subsidized, by ORT and the Joint Distribution Committee. Financial assistance was also rendered to enterprises directly. Agronomists and technical experts were dispatched not only to advise the nascent industries and farms, but to work there for extended periods of time.

Industrialization was probably a greater "revolution" for the Jewish population than the publicized agricultural schemes. Hundreds of thousands of people of all ages migrated to new cities and republics. In 1926, 23 percent of the Jewish population lived in the Russian republic; by 1939, one-third of the Jews lived there. The migrants left behind not only their homes, but in many cases their families, friends, traditions, and even their language. In 1926 only a quarter of the Jews listed Russian as their "native language"; by 1939, 55 percent did so. Many of the mobile Jews came into social contact with non-Jews for the first time. They quickly realized that Yiddish would not carry them very far,

A group of students in an Agro-Joint workshop for training metal workers. A portrait of Stalin is on the wall. CREDIT: Joseph Rosen.

Two young men going off to the city to work in industry. CREDIT: Dora Gelman.

and that there was a new world beyond that of the *shtetl*. Most felt they had to make up for the time lost when they were isolated in their Jewish environment and they eagerly seized upon the cultural, educational, vocational, and political opportunities that presented themselves. Jews became avid followers of Russian theater, devotees of classical music, voracious readers of literature—in Russian primarily, but also in Ukrainian and Belorussian. Among the writers in those languages there were significant numbers of Jews, and their presence was felt in cinematography, art, and music as well. Editorial boards of leading magazines, research institutes, universities, hospital staffs, and the ranks of the Soviet officer corps were populated by higher proportions of Jews than their numbers in the population would warrant.

Of course there was a price to be paid for this. Just as their relatives who had migrated overseas had often shed

The Jewish State Theater in Minsk, 1934. The building appears to be a former synagogue.

Students and faculty of the Institute for Jewish Proletarian Culture, Kiev, 1934. Prof. Yosef Liberberg is sitting in the first row, tenth from right. Alexander Pomerantz, a student from the U.S.A., is standing in the top row, second from the right. CREDIT: Kalman Marmor.

not only their culture but even their identities when entering their new worlds, so, too, did Soviet Jews abandon them. The Soviet sociologist Yankl Kantor pointed out that among urban Jews in the Ukraine the smallest percentage of Yiddish speakers was to be found in the five-to-nine-year-old group. Parents were trying to bring their children up in Russian, as proved by the fact that more children under the age of four spoke Yiddish than those who were slightly older, of nursery-school age. "That is, the mother speaks Yiddish, but when he is of nursery age she breaks her teeth and speaks Russian to him to make him equal to the others." Kantor noted that the "large city creates certain conditions for assimilatory processes and certain segments of the Jewish population become assimilated."[17]

By 1939 almost 40 percent of the Jews had left the former Pale areas. Leaving those areas, Jews seemed to feel released from many of the social bonds and taboos that once held the community together. For example, in the 1920s in the Ukraine and Belorussia, both formerly in the Pale, the percentage of Jews entering marriages with non-Jews rose only slightly. Less than 10 percent of the Jews there had intermarried as late as 1927. In the Russian Republic (RSFSR), by contrast, by 1927 nearly a third of the Jewish marriages were with non-Jews. In the 1930s the proportion of intermarriages in Belorussia and the Ukraine rose rapidly, nearly to the levels in the RSFSR.

פראזידיום

אינסטיטוט פאר ייד פראלעט קולטור — אמ"ררעף

As a recent Soviet emigré put it, "In those years we really believed in 'internationalism.' We thought there would no longer be any differences between Jews and others and we were proud to have friends from all the nationalities."[18] A demographer who had argued for industrialization rather than agricultural work as the solution to Jewish economic problems noted that assimilation had become "a massive development of the postwar period." He pointed out that the Jewish birth rate was declining as well.[19]

What appeared to be good for most individuals — the opportunity to move freely into new, multinational environments — was not beneficial to the Jewish collectivity. Yiddish schools began to close, newspapers declined in number and in circulation, and it seemed that only some of those who had come to maturity before the revolution were preserving the religious traditions. They found it increasingly difficult to do so, not only because of repression and the constant ridicule of the "League of the Godless," but also because their own children often regarded them as relics of an age that had passed. Even those who respected their elders and their ways rarely followed them. How could one keep the Sabbath and the holidays when these were workdays and the penalties for absence were severe? In the 1930s even being late to work could mean punishment and laying oneself open to suspicion of being a "Menshevik wrecker" (or a "Trotskyite" one, depending on

Presidium of the Institute for Jewish Proletarian Culture. Seated first from right is Osher Margulis, a historian; third from right is Kalman Marmor, a visiting scholar from America, a member of the American Communist Party for a time; fourth from right is Prof. Yosef Liberberg, later a leading personality in Birobidzhan before his arrest as a "Trotskyite" in 1936; in the second row, third from right is the philologist Elie Spivak; fifth from right is Maks Erik, a literary historian who immigrated to the Soviet Union from Poland in 1929. In 1932 he publicly admitted to "Yiddishist deviations" and a "mechanical-empirical approach to literature." He was arrested in 1936 and sent to the Gulag, where he died in 1937. CREDIT: Kalman Marmor.

the prevailing political winds). Technically, socially, politically, and economically it had become quite difficult to be an observant Jew in the Soviet Union.

The 1930s were a time of terrible tension for everyone, as the massive purges and general atmosphere of terror made every activity, expression, and even thought potentially dangerous, even life-threatening. The urban intelligentsia, and especially the party members, were particularly vulnerable to charges of ideological and political deviation because they were active in the most politically sensitive areas. Insofar as Jews were overrepresented in those groups, they were especially vulnerable. Moreover, as members of a national minority, and as people with many ties abroad, Jews were particularly susceptible to charges of "petit bourgeois nationalism" and disloyalty to the socialist fatherland. Soviet Jews were becoming increasingly isolated from Jews abroad. Contact with Poland and the Baltic states was highly risky, for these were considered "reactionary, fascist" states, part of the "capitalist encirclement" of the Soviet Union. A postcard from abroad could serve a "proof" that the recipient was a foreign

The *shokhet* (ritual slaughterer) Moshe Genkin in the *shtetl* Seredina-Buda, Chernigov district, the Ukraine, in the 1930s. Genkin also served as a *mohel* (ritual circumciser) and cantor. He is posing with his grandson, Lev Losev, now a professor of Russian literature at Dartmouth College. Moshe Genkin later joined his daughter, Basia, mother of the little boy, and a son who was also working in a factory in Leningrad. He found work as a bookkeeper in a factory where sympathetic Jews arranged things so that he would not have to work on the Sabbath. Increasingly, however, he became the butt of anti-Semitic remarks and several times on the tram his *yarmulke* was pulled off and thrown out the window. He was caught in the wartime siege of Leningrad. By the time he was evacuated to Siberia in 1942, he was so weakened by starvation that he died. CREDIT: Basia Genkina.

Naftali Hertz Kon (1910–1971), a Yiddish poet, was born in Bukovina, Romania. A Communist sympathizer, he fled to Poland, was imprisoned there, and released in 1932 to the Soviet Union in a prisoner exchange. Kon was arrested in 1937 during the Stalinist purges, and served four years. In 1948, at the height of mass arrests, he received a twenty-five-year sentence. Rehabilitated in 1956, Kon left three years later for Poland, where he was arrested again. In 1964 he emigrated to Israel, where he died in 1971. CREDIT: Ina Lancman.

agent. In fact, even having relatives abroad could be adduced as evidence. A visible interest in Jewish culture, even in its purely Soviet version, could lay one open to charges of "petit bourgeois nationalism" or worse.

The Great Purge of 1934–1939 was not directed specifically at Jews. Indeed, a high proportion of the purgers—most of whom were eventually purged themselves—were Jews, employees of the dreaded secret police. As members of a highly urbanized, educated nationality, Jews were overrepresented in the party, government, military, academia, and police, all of which were much more thoroughly purged than the general population. For every Genrikh Yagoda, the Jewish head of the secret police from 1934 until he himself was purged in 1936, there were countless former Zionists, clerics, *Evsektsii* activists, or highly assimilated Jews who were purged. To take only two examples among many, Boris Berman was an interrogator in the case against Zinoviev, but was himself shot in 1938; his brother, Matvei Berman, head of the GULAG (Chief

Mikhail Isaakovich Gershoyg, born in Odessa in 1907, served in the military, became a metalworker, and was elected to a local soviet. In 1935 he was sent to Kamchatka in the Far East to direct a large enterprise. In 1938 he was arrested on charges of selling secrets to the Japanese. In September 1940 he was freed, reentered the armed forces, and became an air force officer. He fought at Stalingrad, was decorated, and retired as a captain in 1955. CREDIT: Mikhail Gershoyg.

Administration of Corrective Labor Camps), was also shot in 1939. Jews were prominent among both victimizers and victims, but most of them were involved not as Jews but as party members or members of other elites. Generals Yan Gamarnik and Yona Yakir were among many high-ranking Jewish officers purged, and thousands of factory directors and engineers met similar fates. It is impossible to say how many Jews fell to the purges, but it is certain that the terror had a chilling effect on Jewish institutions and activities. The Institute of Jewish Proletarian Culture attached to the Ukrainian Academy of Sciences, as well as the Jewish Sector of the Belorussian Academy, were charged with the task of "unmasking" the history of the Bund and the "pseudo-scientific" work of foreign scholars, especially those at the "notorious" YIVO Institute in neighboring Poland. Soviet Jewish institutions were criticized for errors and "distortions," and were told to concentrate their attention on self-criticism, "their work being guided chiefly by Bolshevik intransigence toward all deviations from the general line of the Party and from the correct

Marxist-Leninist position."[20] Ultimately these institutions were abolished or reduced in jurisdiction and activity, and their staffs purged.

The pages of the Yiddish press were full of stories "unmasking traitors" among those who had just yesterday been leading Yiddish cultural figures, not a few of whom had themselves recently "unmasked" other "deviationists." Writers, scholars, politicians, and officials were "exposed" as "enemies of the people" or "deviationists." The lucky ones were those who had merely made "errors" and could confess them profusely, hoping thereby to escape the fate that had overtaken so many millions. The fear that pervaded the entire society paralyzed Yiddish cultural activity. In 1933–1934 there were eighteen Yiddish theaters active in the country; by 1937–1938 only 12 remained. In 1935 there were eighteen Yiddish newspapers, a decline from the previous decade, but only seven remained in 1939. The combination of acculturation and assimilation on one hand, and of the terror on the other, had reduced official Jewish activities to their lowest levels since the revolution. The hopes and joys of "socialist construction" were more than tempered by the terror that had descended upon all the peoples of the Soviet Union.

CHAPTER FOUR

THE HOLOCAUST

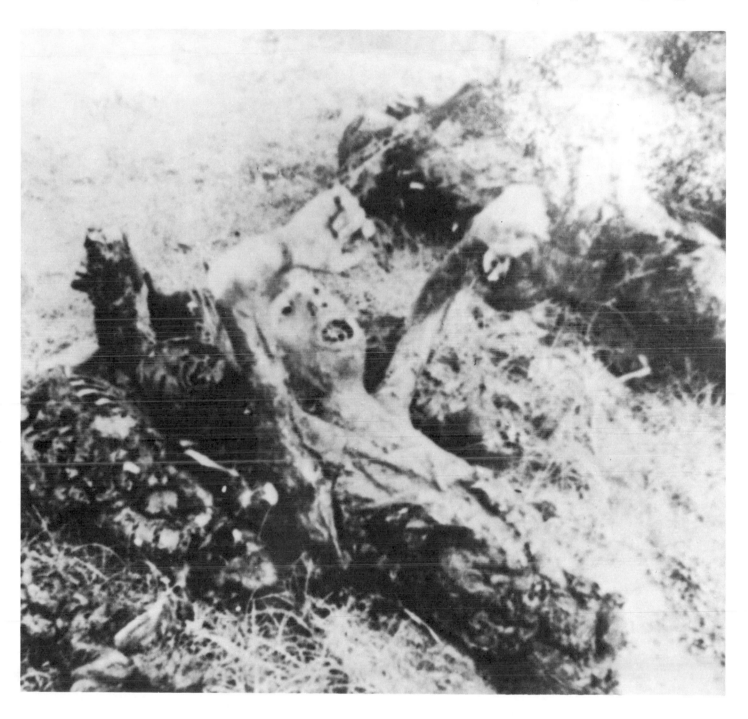

By 1939 the purges seemed to be winding down. The dreaded Ezhov had been replaced by Lavrentii Beria as head of the secret police and that institution was purged once again. Mass arrests waned as the country was completely subjugated. But the respite was an illusion, and new dangers appeared from without. The Soviet Union had attempted to mobilize a united front against fascism with the capitalist democracies of Western Europe since they shared a common fear of Nazi Germany and her allies. In August 1939 Stalin stunned his own people, as well as the anti-fascist front, by signing a nonaggression pact with Hitler's Germany. He had dismissed his Jewish foreign minister, Maxim Litvinov, in order not to offend Nazi sensibilities. Whether the pact was designed simply to buy time to prepare for a likely German attack on the USSR (as most Soviet historians would have it) or whether it was Stalin's attempt to divert Hitler's aggression toward Western Europe (as Western historians see it), the agreement was not taken seriously by either party, but a series of secret agreements accompanying it were to have far greater consequences. Those agreements provided that the Baltic republics—Estonia, Latvia, and Lithuania—would come under Soviet influence, that eastern Poland would be annexed by the Soviet Union, and that the same would happen to Romanian-controlled Bessarabia. On September 17, 1939, at five o'clock in the morning, Soviet troops crossed the Polish frontier on the pretext that they were needed to protect "our brother Ukrainians and brother Belorussians who live in Poland." Having been invaded by Germany on September 1, Poland was now caught between her two more powerful neighbors, as so often in her history, and her resistance was soon crushed. The Soviet Union now controlled an additional population of nearly thirteen million people, including about a million Jews.

In October the long-disputed city of Vilna (Wilno in Poland, Vilnius to the Lithuanians) was transferred from Poland to Lithuania, in return for Lithuania's permitting

Soviet Foreign Minister Maxim Litvinov addressing the League of Nations, 1934. Litvinov was born Issei Meir Wallach.

Soviet troops to be stationed on her territory. In the summer of 1940 the USSR occupied the Romanian provinces of northern Bukovina, made part of the Ukrainian Soviet Socialist Republic, and Bessarabia, most of which was included in the Moldavian Soviet Socialist Republic. At the same time pretexts were invented for the Soviet military takeover of the three Baltic states. As a result of these moves, between 1.8 and 2 million Jews, formerly citizens of Romania, Poland, and the Baltic states, found themselves under Soviet jurisdiction.

All residents of eastern Poland as of November 1939 were forced to take Soviet citizenship. Refugees from German-occupied Poland could decide whether to accept Soviet citizenship or return to the German zone. Those who refused to do either or who registered to return to the German zone were arrested in 1940 and deported to Soviet Central Asia and the Komi republic in Siberia. There they were joined in exile by such "bourgeois" elements as religious functionaries, merchants, Zionists, and political activists, whose presence in the newly "liberated" areas of Poland, the Baltic, and the former Romanian territories was regarded by the Soviets as undesirable and dangerous. At least a quarter of a million Jews from these areas were inadvertently saved by the Soviet government from Nazi annihilation by being deported to the Soviet interior. After the German invasion of the USSR on June 22, 1941, many Polish Jews were released from Soviet prisons or allowed to move to Central Asia, where they worked on collective farms or in the cities. Conditions were generally harsh. Urban Jews from Eastern

Europe had to adjust to life in small towns and villages in some of the most backward areas of the USSR. The newcomers were constantly under the scrutiny of the secret police, and were sometimes regarded with hostility by the local populations. In 1943 Polish Jews were allowed to reclaim Polish citizenship and join a Polish army under General Berling which was to fight under Soviet command and help in the liberation of Poland.

The sudden, massive entry of so many East European Jews into the Soviet Union brought many Soviet Jews into renewed contact with Jewish people outside the USSR and with their own cultural and religious heritage. More than twenty years of Soviet socialization and repressive measures had made traditional Jewish culture a memory for most Soviet Jews. Now they met up with large numbers of religious, learned Jews, people who spoke Yiddish naturally and without self-consciousness, who had graduated from Hebrew and Yiddish schools, and who had participated in Jewish political movements, including Zionist ones, even under the dictatorships that had come to power by the mid-1930s in all the recently annexed countries. On the other hand, the sight of Jews among the officers of the Red Army which had taken over their countries, and of state-sponsored Yiddish writers and cultural activists who were sent into the new territories, impressed those whom Soviet Jews called Western Jews or "Zapadniki." Such phenomena were hard to imagine under the increasingly anti-Semitic regimes that the Soviets had displaced.

The perceptions and interests of Jews and non-Jews in most of the Soviet-occupied territories diverged, with tragic consequences. Romanian anti-Semitism, spurred by native fascist organizations like the Iron Guard, and the German persecution of Jews in Poland and in the Baltic territories later ceded to the USSR, alerted the Jews to the possible consequences of German rule, though no one could envision all the horrors of the "final solution." Therefore, despite misgivings about the Bolsheviks' militant atheism, their persecution of Zionism and nationalization of property, many Jews welcomed the Red Army as a liberator. One resident of eastern Poland remembered that when the Red Army entered, "There was a holiday atmosphere. Things changed overnight. . . . The Germans would not come in, and that was the most important thing."[1] On the other hand, Poles and Balts saw the Red Army as an invader, a menace to their hard-won national independence, wrested only two decades earlier from the ruins of the Russian Empire. Therefore when the Germans drove the Soviets out in June–July

1941, non-Jews greeted the Germans as liberators and attacked the Jews as traitors to the national cause because the Jews had collaborated with the hated Russians. As soon as the Red Army retreated from Kaunas (Kovno), the interwar capital of Lithuania, anti-Soviet and anti-Semitic Lithuanians began to attack Jews and torture them in public. Three days after the German forces began their attack nearly a thousand Jews were murdered by Lithuanian "partisans" in the suburb of Slobodka, famed for its *yeshiva*. In the first few days of the German occupation Lithuanian groups murdered between 7,000 and 8,000 Jews.

May Day, 1940, in Gluboka, Lithuania. Members of a tailors' cooperative. The banners celebrate the Soviet Union and Stalin. One of them reads: "Hail to our beloved teacher and friend, the leader of nations, Comrade Stalin." CREDIT: Dora Ferdman Finefter.

Owners of a Jewish tailor shop at a farewell gathering for their former workers in Kaunas, Lithuania, October 1940. Independent Lithuania became part of the Soviet Union in July 1940, and one of the new authorities' first decrees called for the "nationalization" of private enterprise. A picture of Marshal Voroshilov is on the wall. CREDIT: Khana Bederis.

Germans and Lithuanians beating Jews to death on the streets of Kaunas, 1941.

While the Soviets were in control of eastern Poland they had attempted to win over the local populations by encouraging the use of the Ukrainian and Belorussian languages, which had been repressed under the Poles. For a few months they followed a tolerant economic policy resembling the New Economic Policy of the 1920s, which permitted a measure of private enterprise. Jews were eager to fill administrative posts, but they were soon pushed aside in favor of more reliable cadres brought from the Soviet heartland. Moreover, the Soviets began to restrict the visibility of the Jews, realizing that a large Jewish presence in party and governmental posts would not sit well with the local population. In the March 1940 elections not a single Jew was elected to the Supreme Soviet from the new territories taken from Poland. The party and state hierarchies in the territories were staffed predominantly by non-Jews. Still, some low-level posts were available to Jews, and educational opportunities were far greater than under the Polish regime in these territories. But most of the newly minted Soviet citizens were not allowed to migrate to the interior of the USSR and thus found themselves at the mercy of the invading Germans in 1941.

The brief experience of the Zapadniki with Soviet rule seemed to be a replay of what Soviet Jews had experienced over several decades. Like Soviet Jews in the Civil War period, the Zapadniki had been caught between anti-Soviet regimes which pogromized the Jews and a Communist system which offered them formal equality and educational opportunity, but with the proviso that traditional culture and religion be abandoned. Once again Jews' ambivalent feelings toward the Communist regime were resolved by the virulent anti-Semitism that surrounded them. Having been forced to cast their lot with the Soviet system, all Jews were misperceived by the local population as enthusiastic supporters of Bolshevism, further aggravating the hostility toward them on the part of nationalists among the non-Russian peoples. Opportunities newly opened to the Jews in the western territories closed down after a few months, rather than after a few years. Moreover, in the Soviet heartland itself the Jews were no longer as prominent as they had been earlier. The first few months of "liberation" proved time enough for the authorities to attack and repress religious, cultural, and political institutions, just as they had done fifteen years earlier in eastern Belorussia and the Ukraine. Political, religious, and cultural leaders were arrested and sent to the Soviet interior, to prison, or to various forms of forced labor. Jewish schools were closed down and a small number of Sovietized Yiddish schools were given a monopoly. The number of Yiddish newspapers in the new territories was drastically reduced and only Soviet Yiddish newspapers were permitted. Though the newly Sovietized Jews were not nearly as acculturated to Russian as the Jews in the Soviet heartland, their Jewish cultural opportunities were sharply curtailed, as were their economic ones. In Soviet Lithuania, of 1,593 firms that were nationalized, 1,320 belonged to Jews; of 986 workshops taken over by the state, 560 had been in Jewish hands. The newly Sovietized Jews were in transition from one way of life to another when the Nazi attack on the USSR made life on any terms an unlikely prospect for millions of Jews, regardless of their political or religious beliefs, or their economic and social status.

THE GERMAN OCCUPATION

When three million German troops invaded the USSR along her recently expanded western borders, they quickly encircled a huge Jewish population. Two days after the fighting began such major Jewish centers as Vilnius, Kaunas, and Grodno were captured, to be followed quickly by Minsk, Lvov, and other concentrations of Jewish population. The Red Army hastily retreated and hundreds of thousands of Soviet soldiers, among them a large number of Jews, were captured. The Nazis had long made clear their consuming

Soviet Union, showing maximum Territory occupied by the Germans, 1941-1942.

hatred for both Bolshevism and the Jews, which they equated. In 1930 Hitler had written, "The Nordic race has a right to rule the world. . . . Any cooperation with Russia is out of the question, for there on a Slavic-Tatar body is set a Jewish head."[2] The commander of the German Sixth Army, General von Reichenau, issued an order in November 1941 which stated: "The most essential aim of war against the Jewish-Bolshevistic system is a complete destruction of their . . . power. . . . Therefore the soldier must have full understanding for the necessity of severe but just revenge on subhuman Jewry." General Von Manstein, commander of another army, wrote in an order of the same month: "More strongly than in Europe, [Jewry] holds all the key positions in the political leadership and administration. . . . The Jewish-Bolshevist system must be exterminated once and for all. The soldier must appreciate the necessity for harsh punishment of Jewry, the spiritual bearer of the Bolshevist terror."[3]

Though the Nazis could not have been more explicit, their intentions may not have been understood by Soviet Jews. After the Stalin-Hitler pact of 1939, the Soviet media draped a blanket of silence over Nazi atrocities. Therefore, some have suggested, Soviet Jews were unprepared for the policies the invaders were to pursue. On the other hand, those Jews in the western areas taken very quickly by the Germans had come in contact with refugees from Poland who undoubtedly told them about their experiences. Perhaps those stories were dismissed as exaggerated, especially by older people who remembered the Germans from World War I as "decent people." In any case, despite several warnings from intelligence sources, the attack caught even the Soviet leadership unaware. Not only the Jews but the Soviet population as a whole, including the armed forces, were quite unprepared to deal with the *blitzkrieg* invasion.

In areas not taken immediately Soviet authorities feverishly tried to evacuate people and matériel vital to the war effort. Later on, some Soviet spokesmen and their sympathizers claimed that the USSR had deliberately evacuated Jews to areas beyond the reach of the enemy, but there is no evidence of such a policy. The evacuation was understandably chaotic, but as a highly urbanized population, well represented among the technical intelligentsia, political cadres, and managerial personnel, Jews had a better chance of being moved eastward than many other segments of the population. Estimates on the number evacuated vary quite widely, but there may have been as many as 900,000.

THE ANNIHILATION OF SOVIET JEWRY

The German army was followed very closely by four *Einsatzgruppen*, mobile killing squads, with between 500 and 900 men in each. Most Soviet Jews were not deported to concentration or labor camps, but were liquidated in or near their hometowns. The *Einsatzgruppen*, capitalizing on the shock of the invasion and the Red Army's rapid disintegration, either killed the Jews immediately, in mass machine-gun executions outside the towns, or by starvation and disease in ghettos established in such cities as Vilnius, Minsk, Bialystok, Riga, Mogilev, Zhitomir, and others. Most of these ghettos were liquidated by 1941–1942, though a few remained until July 1943. Raul Hilberg observes that most of the *Einsatzgruppen* officers were professional people in civilian life—lawyers, physicians, even opera singers and a Protestant minister. "These men were in no sense hoodlums, delinquents, common criminals, or sex maniacs. Most were intellectuals. By and large, they were in their thirties. . . ."[4] Within five months of their appearance these "intellectuals" had killed about half a million Jews. They had the assistance

Red Army men and civilians at a mass grave of Jews killed near Zhitomir, Ukraine, Tisha B'Av, 1942. CREDIT: Yad Vashem.

of Ukrainian, Lithuanian, Latvian, and Estonian "militia," recruited to the Nazi cause. Some of the Germans' allies—Hungarians, and especially Romanians—joined in the mass murder of the Jews in those areas that they occupied. In Odessa the Romanian army shot 19,000 Jews in the harbor area on the single night of October 22–23, 1941. Another 40,000 Jews were dispatched to a nearby collective farm, where they were shot in antitank ditches. This the Romanians managed themselves, with no German assistance. In fact the brutality of the Romanians annoyed their German

Jewish men forced to watch executions in a marketplace, Zhitomir.

A monument in Utian, Lithuania, where 8,000 Jews were killed in July–August 1941. They lie in a mass grave. The monument specifically mentions the Jews as the victims, unlike monuments at larger extermination sites such as Rumbuli in Latvia or Babi Yar in the Ukraine. At these sites, non-Jewish victims of the Nazis were also killed. CREDIT: Aaron Muleris.

Monument with all Jewish names, carved by amateurs. Inscription reads: "These people were viciously murdered by the German fascists, August 30, 1941." CREDIT: Yad Vashem.

partners, who regarded it unseemly that these acts were carried out in the form of spontaneous atrocities rather than as methodical operations.

One of the most notorious acts of mass murder occurred in Kiev, capital of the Ukraine. Just before Rosh Hashanah—the Nazis often chose Jewish holidays for major "actions" against the Jews—notices went up around the city ordering the Jews to appear at a certain point so they could be sent for "resettlement." Many Jews of the older generation, remembering the Germans of World War I as relatively humane, reasoned that the Germans were sending the Jews out of the city in order to protect them from a pogrom that was being threatened by the Ukrainian population. Most of the Jewish population, aside from those who were in the Soviet armed forces or who had been evacuated, dutifully assembled and were taken to an outlying district of the city, Babi Yar. There, on September 29–30, 1941, over 30,000 Jews were massacred by a unit of 150 Germans aided by several hundred men from two Ukrainian "militia" regiments. For several days the ground heaved with the bodies of those buried only half-dead. Over the next few years additional victims fell at Babi Yar—Communists, surviving Jews, Russians, and Ukrainians who ran afoul of those initially welcomed by some as "liberators of the Ukraine." Ever

Jewish men rounded up in the Ukraine in the first days of the occupation. CREDIT: David Greisdorf.

since, Soviet authorities have deemphasized the specifically Jewish nature of the tragedy, refusing even to heed the stirring words of the Soviet poet Yevgenii Yevtushenko, whose poem on the subject, published amid controversy in 1961, begins with the words, "Over Babi Yar there are no monuments. . . ." The inscription on the monument that was finally erected makes no reference to Jews.

Ilya Ehrenburg, a highly assimilated Jew, was the best-known Soviet war correspondent. His dispatches played a great part in maintaining Soviet morale. He gathered many eyewitness accounts from Jews—civilians, soldiers, and partisans—which he intended to publish in Russian and in foreign languages. Only small parts of these materials were published in the USSR, in line with the Soviet policy of downplaying the Jewish tragedy that took place during the "Great Patriotic Fatherland War." The following descriptions, gathered by Ehrenburg, are representative of what happened in hundreds of places in the Soviet Union during the occupation.

The town of Khmelnik, in the Ukraine, had a Jewish population of over 10,000. On July 16, 1941, it was captured by the Germans, who forbade peasants to speak to Jews or enter a Jewish home. Jews were rounded up for forced labor. A month later the Gestapo arrived and gathered a group of 365 men and two women. According to eyewitness A. Bender,

> On the main street, where the Lenin monument stood, the beards of old men were cut off, and the young were forced to eat the hair. The Jews were beaten and forced to hold

Ilya Ehrenburg, at left, and the writers Leonid Pervomaisky and Vasily Grossman at the front, 1943. CREDIT: Yad Vashem.

Rabbi Grodzensky, head of the Slobodka *yeshiva*, after his beard was cut off in the Kaunas ghetto.

hands, dance and sing the Internationale . . . for two hours. Then they were driven to the district council, where boards with protruding nails were prepared. They were chased into a glass warehouse and ordered to dance barefoot on the broken glass and on the boards with nails, forced to stand facing the wall and to eat salt.[5]

In January 1942 the entire Jewish population, except for "specialists" useful to the Germans, was driven into the nearby pine forest.

At the pit the people were placed in rows, they were forced to strip and to strip their children, and to stand like that for fifteen to twenty minutes in a forty degree frost. The children cried: "Mother, why do you undress me, it is so cold." . . . Two German women stood near the pit and threw live little children into it. Every fifteen to twenty minutes wagons carried the clothes of the killed people away to a warehouse. . . . 6,800 Jews were killed. They lie buried in two pits.[6]

In Glubokoye, a small Belorussian town, the "actions" started in December 1941. The mass murders were carried out in Borki, a rural spot just outside of town which had been a recreation area before the war.

> In Borki, the Rayak brothers write, the Germans forced the young to dance at the edge of an open grave and the old to sing songs. . . . After this sadistic mockery they forced, the young and healthy to carry the feeble old people and cripples into the pit and lay them down. Only after this were they to lie down themselves, and then the Germans methodically and calmly shot everyone.
>
> The murders were preceded by unimaginable torture: people were cut in half, teeth were pulled, nails were driven into the victims' heads, people were kept naked in the freezing cold and soaked with cold water, beaten with sticks and rifle butts until they lost consciousness. . . .
>
> The Fascists tortured women and children with a special passion. . . . [7]

The laundry which washed the murdered people's clothing worked night and day. Naturally, the people working in the laundry (and other "restoration" shops as well) were Jews.

When clothes were sorted and washed, strange scenes were played out. People recognized the underwear and belongings of their murdered relatives. Raphael Gitlits recognized his murdered mother's underwear and dress. Manya Freidkin had to wash her husband Shimon's blood-stained shirt. The wife of the teacher, Milikhman, had to put the suit of her murdered husband into "decent order" with her own hands. [8]

A monument in Glubokoye, Belorussia, 1950. The inscription, misspelled in places, reads: "Eternal rest. Here lie those murdered by Hitlerite Fascists, August 20, 1943." CREDIT: Maria Khaytovich.

German executing a Jew at the site of a mass grave, Vinnitsa, Ukraine, as other Germans look on.

In the fall of 1942, groups of young people began to escape from the town to the woods where they joined partisan detachments. In August 1943 the ghetto was "liquidated" by murder and deportation. The German newspapers announced that they had destroyed a major partisan nest of 3,000, headed by a seventy-year-old rabbi.

How did the non-Jewish population react to the atrocities against the Jews? The official Soviet line has consistently been that, except for a few marginal elements such as Ukrainian "bourgeois nationalists," the population did the best it could to resist the invader and assist his victims. Baltic and Ukrainian emigrés have minimized the extent of collaboration with the Germans and excused it on the grounds that these peoples hoped to use the Germans to win their

A monument in Dunaevtsa, Kamenetz-Podolsk area, Ukraine, to 8,000 people, most of them Jews, who were driven naked into the mine behind the monument. The mine was then sealed up. Shika Kuperman, now living in Chicago, was working nearby and saw the people being driven into the mine. He was saved by a Ukrainian who hid him for twenty months. CREDIT: Shika Kuperman.

Nazis hanging Jewish partisans in Minsk, October 1941. The girl is Masha Bruskin, aged seventeen. CREDIT: David Cohen.

A Nazi firing squad in Drohobych, West Ukraine. This photo was taken surreptitiously through a window. CREDIT: Siegfried Krigler.

independence of the Soviet Union. Anti-Jewish actions are said to be understandable because of Jewish enthusiasm, however short-lived, for the Soviet occupation of the Baltic republics and West Ukraine. Most Jewish eyewitness memoirs point out that Gentile individuals of all nationalities risked their lives to aid and even hide Jews, but that a far greater number of Gentiles actively persecuted the Jews, either in the ranks of collaborating paramilitary formations, by turning Jews in to the Germans, or by killing and looting.

In general, the populations of the recently Sovietized territories were more enthusiastic about the Germans than the Slavic populations who had been in the Soviet Union since 1917–1921. Most historians agree that the Germans squandered a great opportunity to win over the Ukrainian population. Their racist commitment to the dogma that, as Slavs, the Ukrainians were less than human prevailed over the military/economic argument that Ukrainian cooperation could turn the tide in favor of Germany on the Eastern front.

Hilberg's assessment of the Slavic populations is that "If few were on the side of the Germans, fewer still were on the side of the Jews. . . . Neutrality is a zero quantity which helps the stronger party in an unequal struggle."[9] He suggests that in the Ukraine anti-Jewish outbursts were not truly spontaneous but were inspired by the *Einsatzgruppen*. The victims were unable to make such distinctions, since they had to worry about outcomes and not what exactly brought them about. The facts remain that in Lvov, two days after the Germans took over, a three-day pogrom by Ukrainians resulted in the killing of 6,000 Jews, mostly by uniformed Ukrainian "militia," in the Brygidky prison. July 25 was declared "Petliura Day," after the Ukrainian leader of the Civil War period who was assassinated by the son of Jewish pogrom victims. Over 5,000 Jews were hunted down and most of them killed in honor of the "celebration." Emigrés from the Ukraine and Ukrainians from Poland were in the Organization of Ukrainian Nationalists (OUN), which pledged Hitler its "most loyal obedience" in building a Eu-

Jews being hanged by Germans in Kharkov, 1942.

Rumbuli, Latvia. The monument says in Yiddish, Russian, and Latvian: "To the victims of fascism." In the fall of 1941, 38,000 Jews were killed here.

rope "free of Jews, Bolsheviks and plutocrats."[10] In 1943 a Galician (Ukrainian) SS division attracted almost 100,000 volunteers, though fewer than 30,000 were accepted.[11] It should be noted that many were prisoners of war and "volunteered" for the SS in order to save their own lives. Some Ukrainian scholars outside the USSR admit that "some" Ukrainian police participated in rounding up Jews, but that these were the "worst elements of society" and were "detested" by the population.[12] Memoirs of Jews who fled to the forests to join the partisans or to hide out emphasize that they feared Ukrainian nationalist bands as much as they did the Germans. Even after the war these bands assassinated not only surviving Jews but Gentiles, including Ukrainians, who had helped the Jews. On the other hand, an American scholar of Ukrainian origin claims that "Neither the Ukrainian underground nor any other organizations . . . cultivated anti-Semitic programs or policies. They readily accepted Jews into their ranks and sheltered them from Nazi persecution, despite the popular perception of Jews as promoters of Communism. This perception naturally encouraged anti-Semitic attitudes and played into the hands of the Nazis."[13] The published manifestoes of the

Maj. Izrail Lebedev, a war veteran (on the right) in 1948 with a friend near Ponary, where most of Vilna's Jews were killed. A statue of Stalin stands in the background. CREDIT: Izrail Lebedev.

Ukrainian organizations and the experiences of Jews in the Ukraine cast serious doubt on this assertion.[14]

The Germans succeeded in mobilizing large units of police from among the Baltic and Ukrainian populations. These were sent beyond their own territories, so that Latvian and Lithuanian police, for example, took part in anti-Jewish operations outside the Baltic. In Belorussia the population seemed less disposed to help the Germans. Nazi officials complained that "Because of the passivity and political stupidity of the Belorussians it has been virtually impossible to stage pogroms against the Jews." In fact, persecution of the Jews was reported to turn some Belorussians against the Germans.[15] Many instances of Belorussian assistance to Jews are reported by survivors, though, as elsewhere, the Nazis did succeed in finding Belorussians willing to cooperate, and a Belorussian puppet political organization was set up.

Anti-Semitic tendencies emerged among the Russian population as well. German propaganda constantly pounded away on the theme that the misfortunes of war had been brought on the heads of the Russians by the "Jewish commissars." Despite the fact that half a million Jews were serving in the armed forces, many of the Zapadniki among the evacuees were not accepted into the Soviet forces because they were not deemed trustworthy. Their presence in areas where there had hardly been any Jews previously (Siberia, Central Asian *kolkhozy*) gave rise to the saying that "the Jews fought the war in Tashkent," a city far from the front. (Tashkent is the capital of Uzbekistan, where many Jewish refugees lived.) This canard was devastating to Jewish servicemen, especially as they were becoming aware of the catastrophe that had befallen their families. Many of them had come to maturity in the 1930s, the heyday of "internationalism," and the accusations against the Jews shattered the illusions of many highly acculturated young servicemen. In the ranks themselves there was sufficient anti-Semitism to cause many to conceal their Jewish nationality and even to change their names. Former Red Army men report being told by their comrades in arms, "Why don't the Jews fight? We don't mean you, you are one of us, but where are the rest?"

The grave in Kiev of Khaia Lorman and her three sons, all of whom died in battle. CREDIT: Mera Gelfand.

Jewish Participation in the Military

"The rest" of the Jews, if they were not in ghettos, prison, or forced labor gangs, were either sharing the fate of non-Jews in the siege of Leningrad, in the defense industries or in whatever jobs they were assigned, in evacuation, or fighting in the ranks of the Soviet armed forces and partisans. Though the Soviet public generally was not informed by the media about German treatment of the Jews—those in the occupied territories saw this with their own eyes—Dovid Bergelson, one of the leading Yiddish writers, told Yiddish readers straight out in 1941 that Hitler wishes to "murder all Jews, old and young, men and women. He boasts every day that shortly not a single Jew will survive anywhere in the world." Bergelson described the instruments of Hitler's policies: ghettos, forced labor, starvation, shooting, sterilization. Bergelson explained collaboration on the part of the local populations not, of course, by referring to the anti-Semitism that persisted in spite of Soviet principles, but by the fact that "Petliurists, Denikinites, and other White Guardists" had accompanied the invaders, and that "pogromchiks and anti-Semites who have remained hidden in various holes" had surfaced. He called upon Jewish men to fight the invader, and to their mothers and wives to enlist themselves, or to encourage their menfolk to do so. "Carrying Stalin's name in our hearts, each one of us must be ready at any moment to sacrifice his life. . . . With Stalin's name, come to defend our fatherland. . . . It's an exalted name—Stalin!—he will save the world."[16]

Whether or not they were stirred by the "exalted name," Jews understood that in this war they would be defending themselves and their families directly. Opponents of the Soviet regime—religious people, Zionists, "bourgeois elements" from among the Zapadniki as well as their erstwhile political opponents from the socialist camp—all pitched in to the war effort. An estimated 500,000 Jews served in the Soviet armed forces. This figure represents an extraordinarily high percentage of the available manpower, considering that about two million Jews survived outside occupied territory and that roughly half were women. Thousands of other Jews served in the Polish armies and a Czechoslovak army that were in the USSR and fought alongside the Red Army. (The Polish army commanded by General Anders was allowed to leave the USSR because of political tension between the Soviet authorities and the Polish government-

A common grave of 870 Soviet soldiers, including Mark Davidovich Dubinsky of Odessa (inset photo), in the village of Bobrovo near the site of the battle of the Kursk-Orel salient. This was the largest tank battle of World War II. It is estimated that 6,000 tanks and 4,000 planes took part in the battle. German losses were put at 70,000 killed.
CREDIT: Berta Dubinskaya.

in-exile. About 4,000 Jews were in its ranks.) Of the half million Jews in the Red Army, Navy, and Air Force, perhaps as many as 200,000 fell in combat. Over one hundred Jews were awarded the highest military decoration, Hero of the Soviet Union.[17] Jews ranked fifth among the nationalities who received the award. Of the Jewish Heroes, fifty-two died in combat. All told, over 160,000 orders and medals were awarded to Jews, making them the fourth-most-decorated nationality.

With such a high proportion of the population in the ranks, it is not surprising that Jewish servicemen and women came from every walk of life. At least thirty-six Yiddish

LEFT: Maj. Gitlya Iskold, a physician, who served for four years during the war. CREDIT: Gitlya Iskold.

RIGHT: Captain Polina Gelman, Hero of the Soviet Union. She flew 860 night sorties as a bombardier. After the war she became an instructor in political economy.

Capt. Hirsh Abramovich, of the Sixteenth Lithuanian Division, and his aide, in the yard of the Jewish Museum in Vilnius, ca. 1946. CREDIT: Boris Feldblyum.

Charge by a Cossack unit. A member of this unit was the much-decorated Mikhail Shmigeisky, a Jew. CREDIT: Mikhail Shmigeisky.

Gen. Yakov Smushkevich with his family, 1940. Smushkevich was the leading Soviet air ace in the civil war in Spain. He was awarded the title Hero of the Soviet Union and was given the award again for his part in the battle of Khalkhin-Gol against the Japanese in 1939. Smushkevich was executed either in October 1941 or February 1942 for "treacherous activity." He was "rehabilitated" in 1953, almost immediately after Stalin's death.

writers and poets were killed in combat. Jews were prominent in the medical and engineering corps, in the artillery and tank forces, as well as in the infantry. At least three Jewish submarine commanders became Heroes of the Soviet Union. The commander of the Soviet air forces, Air Marshal Yakov Smushkevich, came from a poor, traditional family in Lithuania and survived the purges that took the lives of Jewish generals such as Yan Gamarnik, Yona Yakir, and others, but he, too, was murdered by Stalin shortly thereafter. Of course the great majority of Jews were in the lower ranks, and most of the Heroes among them were drawn from those ranks. Among those in the higher ranks was Gen. David Dragunsky, now a prominent member of the Soviet Anti-Zionist Public Committee and a major official spokesman on Jewish issues, who was twice decorated as a Hero. Two Heroes emigrated to Israel in the 1970s, Maj. Wolf Vilensky, who served in the Sixteenth Lithuanian Division—a unit so heavily Jewish that some orders were given in Yiddish—and Milya Felzenshtain. The latter was a seventeen-year-old machine gunner who, in the battle for Kras-

LEFT: Gen. David Dragunsky, twice Hero of the Soviet Union. Dragunsky entered the Red Army in 1933 and was completing an officer's course when the war broke out. Within two years he was made a colonel. In 1944, after successfully directing a twenty-seven-day tank battle in Poland, he was awarded the title Hero of the Soviet Union. In May 1945 he was given the title a second time for his heroism in Czechoslovakia and the storming of Berlin. In recent years Dragunsky has been active in the Soviet Anti-Zionist Committee.

RIGHT: Submariner Petr Krugliak. CREDIT: Vladimir Krugliak.

A photo made from a drawing, late nineteenth century. The older man, seated, is Hirsh Nissan Golomb, from Vilna. He published Hebrew primers and a Yiddish translation of one of Maimonides' works. His best-known work was *Kol khemdat Yisrael*, a biographical dictionary of famous Jews, which he is holding in this picture, and which he published with his son, Emanuel, who is standing. Golomb collected folk, Hassidic, and liturgical music, invented much of the musical terminology in Hebrew and Yiddish, and published several volumes on Jewish music. CREDIT: Benjamin Golomb.

Emanuel Golomb and his sons in "Maccabee" scout uniforms, Moscow, 1918. CREDIT: Benjamin Golomb.

Emanuel Golomb's sons during the war. On the left is Benjamin, a lieutenant in the engineering corps; Gershon, center, was a tank sergeant who took part in the battle of Kursk; Iosif was a naval photographer with the rank of senior lieutenant. CREDIT: Benjamin Golomb.

Two of the sons of this religious family, both standing at left, died at the front. The grandmother was a rabbi's daughter, married to a *shokhet*. She was shot by the Germans on May 29, 1942, in Yanushpol near Berdichev. Survivors reported that she shouted "Shma Yisrael" just before she was killed. CREDIT: Basheva Pevnaya.

nodar, saw the bodies of Jews exhumed from mass graves. On a stormy November night in 1943 his unit tried to make an amphibious landing under heavy fire on the Crimean peninsula. His landing craft destroyed, Felzenshtain swam ashore. He was seriously wounded on a special mission that he carried out alone. After two months in the hospital and a month's leave, he returned to his unit only to be wounded again in the battle of Sevastopol. In 1974, as a factory foreman in Kharkov, he became the first Hero of the Soviet Union to apply for emigration to Israel, to the great consternation of the authorities, but he succeeded in joining his family there.

RESISTANCE UNDER OCCUPATION

The civilians trapped in occupied territories had little chance to organize armed resistance because they were unprepared for the attack and because the mass killings began so quickly after it. More than half the ghettos and "concentration points" were destroyed by mass killings and deportations within nine or ten months. In Minsk a ghetto was established into which Jews from other towns and even other countries were herded.

Monument to 5,000 Jews killed near Minsk, March 2, 1942. CREDIT: Yad Vashem.

Jews with bundles awaiting deportation from the Kaunas ghetto. PHOTO: Zvi Kadushin.

Street scene in the Kaunas ghetto. Jews are wearing the yellow star. On October 28, 1941, 10,000 Jews were "selected" for deportation and were shot to death. PHOTO: Zvi Kadushin.

Corpses lying in the open, Kaunas. Of the 40,000 Jews in the ghetto, only 3,000 survived the war.

Genia Golovataia Peretiatko in Rostov after a battle. She was an eighteen-year-old cello student in the Odessa Workers' Conservatory when the war broke out. An expert markswoman, she volunteered for a sniper's battalion, was wounded, and returned to the front. By war's end she was credited with having shot 148 of the enemy. Her mother, two sisters, and all their children were killed in Domaniovka ghetto. CREDIT: Genia Peretiatko.

Peretiatko, center, in the Victory Day parade in Odessa, June 9, 1975. CREDIT: Genia Peretiatko.

About 100,000 Jews found themselves under a sadistic and depraved administration. An underground resistance developed, led mostly by Jewish Communists. In addition to sabotaging production for the German war effort, they managed to get about 10,000 people out of the ghetto and into the forests where they joined partisan groups and formed seven such groups of their own. There were also "family camps," consisting largely of women and children, who tried to hide in the forests. The Germans deployed about 8,000 troops to destroy the partisans in the area, and only about 5,000 of the escaped Jews survived the war. In July 1943 the Minsk ghetto was destroyed completely, and by the end of the war hardly a building was left intact in the capital of the Belorussian republic.

There were armed uprisings in several of the longer-lasting ghettos, most notably in Kaunas (Kovno) and Vilnius in

Lithuania, and in Bialystok, annexed to Belorussia. In Kaunas there were about 40,000 Jews in 1941, all but 16,000 killed by the fall. At least 600 active resisters concentrated on getting as many out to the forests as possible. In Bialystok the ghetto survived until August 1943. A resistance organization, led by the left-wing Zionist Mordechai Tenenbaum-Tamarof and the Communist Daniel Moszkowicz, included youth from several Zionist groups and the Bund. Before they could launch a planned uprising, the Germans entered the ghetto in order to destroy it. Nevertheless, 500 men and women fighters held out from August 16 to August 20, 1943, when all resistance was crushed and the surviving inhabitants were sent to death camps. Just before these events the resistance had posted a proclamation around the ghetto which read:

> We have nothing to lose. We are being driven to Treblinka. . . . Let us not behave like sheep going to the slaughter! Even if we are too weak to defend our lives, we are strong enough to defend our Jewish honor and human dignity, and thus to prove to the world that we are captive but not defeated. Do not go freely to your death! Make your enemy pay with blood for blood, with death for death![18]

A ruined Jewish cemetery in Minsk was the site where thousands were shot during the war.

Hirsh Smolar and Dora Halpern, former partisans, walking in the ruins of Minsk after the war. Smolar, was active in the Communist underground in Poland. He was one of the organizers of the resistance in the Minsk ghetto and published a book about it, in Yiddish and Russian, after the war. Following the war Smolar returned to Poland where he was editor of the Warsaw Yiddish newspaper *Folksshtimme* He left Poland after the 1968 anti-Semitic purges, now lives in Israel. CREDIT: David Cohen.

Jewish officers of Marshal Zhukov's staff. CREDIT: David Cohen.

Baruch Abramovich Tsirlin and his wife, Elena Isaakovna, in the 1970s. Both were partisans in the Minsk area, and he later served in the regular army. CREDIT: Baruch Tsirlin.

The ruins of central Minsk, 1944.

Fading Yiddish letters on factory wall in the Vilnius ghetto area. PHOTO: Grisha Talas.

In 1941 there were 57,000 Jews in Vilnius. Not until July 1942 did *Einsatzkommando* Number 9 arrive, but it killed 5,000 Jews in the first month, and 28,000 more by December. Until March 1943 there was a period of "stabilization," where mass murders were the exception and the Jews were deluded into believing that their labor was valuable to the Nazis and that as long as high levels of productivity were maintained they would remain alive. Of the 20,000 left in the ghetto, 14,000 were working. The second head of the *Judenrat*, the Jewish council appointed by the Nazis, was Jacob Gens. He was married to a Lithuanian and might have escaped the ghetto, but, according to his wife, chose to cast his lot with the Jews. He cooperated with the Nazis in two "small actions" in which the old and sick were deported, on the grounds that the Germans would have sent women and children away had he not sacrificed the others. At a ceremony awarding literary prizes—in the Vilnius ghetto Jews conducted an active cultural life—Gens began his speech with the following words:

Ruins of the Strashun Library, on the right, and of the "Shulhof," an area of synagogues and Houses of Study, Vilnius. CREDIT: Boris Feldblyum.

Ghetto street, Vilnius.
PHOTO: Jacob Roth.

Many of you consider me a traitor. . . . I, Gens, am leading you to your death; and I, Gens, wish to save Jews from death. I, Gens, order that hiding places be uncovered; and I, Gens, look for ways to make the ghetto useful, productive. *I make my calculations based on Jewish blood and not on Jewish honor.* If they demand a thousand Jews of me, I give them, because if we Jews don't give them ourselves, and the Germans have to come and take them by force, they will take not a thousand but thousands, and it will be open season on the entire ghetto. With hundreds I save thousands; with the thousand that I deliver, I save ten thousand. . . . that there be some remnant, I myself had to lead Jews to their death. And in order for some people to come out of this with a clean conscience I had to put my hands into filth, and trade without conscience.[19]

In January 1942 a United Partisan Organization (Fareinikte Partizaner Organizatsie) was formed in the ghetto by representatives of the Communist Party, several Zionist parties, and later on, the Bund. A second organization, "Yekhiel's Fighting Organization" (its leader was Yekhiel Sheinbaum), advocated flight to the forests rather than revolt, as planned by the UPO. In the spring of 1943 when the existence of the ghetto was clearly threatened, the two united.

Meanwhile the Gestapo had penetrated the local Communist underground outside the ghetto and learned that the leader of the UPO was Itzik Wittenberg, a Communist, and that he was hiding in the ghetto. They demanded his surrender. Jacob Gens, who was in constant contact with the UPO, whose activities he did not oppose as long as they did not threaten the ghetto, told the UPO that if Wittenberg did not surrender the entire ghetto would be liquidated. Learning of the Gestapo's demand, most Jews wanted Wittenberg to surrender. The UPO command had to choose between fighting a civil war against the rest of the ghetto with weapons they had intended to use against the Germans, or turning their leader in to a certain death. His comrades urged Wittenberg to turn himself in. He argued that since the Germans were going to liquidate the entire ghetto, starting with the leadership, it was time to begin the armed revolt. The others replied that this was not what the rest of the ghetto perceived. Wittenberg then proposed that he commit suicide and his body be handed over to the Germans. His comrades reminded him that the Gestapo demanded he be turned over alive. Abba Kovner, his successor, recalls:

Wittenberg asked each one of us: "What do you say?" Each one replied, "You have to decide." Then he asked Sonia [Madaisker] and Berl [Shershnevsky] [fellow Communists], "What should I do?" and they said, "You should go" [to the Gestapo]. Wittenberg asked them if this was the opinion of the comrades [Communists], and they said, "yes." His girlfriend broke down and accused the partisans of betraying him and sending him to his death. On July 16, 1943, in the evening, he turned himself in to the Judenrat who handed him over to the Gestapo.[20]

Ilya Ehrenburg meeting with Jewish partisans in liberated Vilnius, July 1944.

Three views of the Klooga death camp in Estonia soon after it was liberated by the Red Army. About 3,000 people, half of them Jews from Vilnius, were murdered here. Only 85 people survived. Of 84 children in the camp, 3 survived. The Red Army's advance was so unexpectedly rapid that the Germans did not have time to burn the corpses.

Ponary. At one of six mass graves, an inscription in Russian and Lithuanian says: "Here in 1941–1942 the fascists shot more than 15,000 Soviet citizens; in August 1944, 12,000 uncremated bodies were discovered here." No specific mention is made of Jews. PHOTO: Jacob Roth.

On the following day Itzik Wittenberg was found dead in his cell at Gestapo headquarters. He had committed suicide with cyanide given to him by Jacob Gens and another Judenrat official. He had not given the Gestapo any information.

In June, Heinrich Himmler, head of the German SS, had ordered that all ghettos in "Ostland" be liquidated, and in September the Germans surrounded the Vilnius ghetto, demanding the deportation of 5,000 Jews for labor in Estonia. At this point the UPO called for a mass uprising, believing that the liquidation of the ghetto was imminent. Clinging to desperate hopes that the deportations meant labor and not liquidation, the Jews of the Vilnius ghetto rejected the UPO's call. The UPO decided to leave the ghetto because of lack of popular support for its plans of revolt.

On September 14 Jacob Gens was shot by the Gestapo. Nine days later the ghetto was surrounded by German forces. Several thousand able-bodied men were sent to forced labor in Estonia, and 5,000 were sent directly to their deaths. About 600–700 partisans from Vilnius fought the Germans and many took part in the liberation of Vilnius in July 1944. In that same month most of the survivors in Estonian labor camps were killed. Of the 47,000 Vilnius Jews, only 2,000–3,000 lived to see the liberation.

In July 1944 a Polish woman brought a letter to Avraham Sutzkever, Yiddish poet and partisan of Vilnius, which she had found on Grodno Boulevard, the street that led to the Ponary death camp. It was addressed, "Deliver into Jewish hands":

Dear Brothers and Sisters,

We turn to you with a big request. First of all, please forgive us if we wronged you in any way. We don't know why our lives are being taken. That they are killing us is already nothing. [But] our children are being tortured in a most bestial way. They forced eight-year-old girls to have sexual relations, and the mothers were forced to stand by and make sure the children would not cry out. Later they made the mothers stand naked against a wall, hands up and tied, while they tore hair out of the bodies. They stabbed stretched-out tongues with needles. They cut off fingers and toes. It was forbidden to bind the wounds so that the blood poured out without a stop. We were tortured in this way for four days and then sent to Ponary. . . . I'm throwing this letter out on the road to Ponary so that good people will give it to the Jews. . . . If they would hang just one of them for us, 112 Jews, it would be a *mitzvah* for our people. With tears in our eyes, we beg, Revenge! Revenge!

Entrance to a ruined street in the Vilnius ghetto. The former Katsenellenbogen bookstore is on the left. CREDIT: Boris Feldblyum.

Inscription scrawled by an inmate on a prison wall in Hebrew/Yiddish, *nekomeh* (revenge).

I am writing in Polish, because if someone finds a Yiddish letter they would burn it. . . . We say good-bye to you, we say good-bye to the world, calling for revenge!

Gurvich and Ahs are writing.
June 26, 1944 [21]

JEWS IN THE PARTISAN MOVEMENT

The Soviet partisan movement included nearly 900,000 people according to Soviet historians, far fewer according to some Western historians. Whatever its number, the movement did not become very effective until 1943, by which time most of the Jews had been killed. Nevertheless it seems that thousands of Jews took part in it. Most Jews were unfamiliar with, and afraid of, life in the forest and they could not be sure of support by the local population. Close family ties made them reluctant to leave loved ones behind in the ghetto, and some were intimidated by the knowledge that the Germans would exact terrible reprisals for every partisan attack. Desperate escapees from the ghettos, escaped prisoners of war, and some people who had managed to hide out with peasants formed the nucleus of Jewish partisan detachments, many of which were ordered to merge with non-Jewish groups. Many of the Jewish partisans tried to conceal their nationality, since local inhabitants and even

Yaakov Chikvuashvili, a Georgian Jew, fought with the partisans in the Ukraine. This picture was taken in 1985. CREDIT: Gavriel Chikvuashvili.

Meeting of two partisan groups in the forest. From left to right: Khayim Shneider, Viktor Tsurkan, Yaakov Talis, Boris Saran, Naum Lodyzhensky, David Shor, Nikifor Druz. The latter is the only non-Jew in the group. CREDIT: Yaakov Talis.

Home and school for children of partisans, Gorky, 1942. The director of the school was Eva Isaakovna Schneider, center. Second from left in her row is Ida Solominska, a house mother. Solominska's father lived in the United States, but was drafted into the Russian Army on a visit to his parents in 1914 and was never able to return to the U.S. In 1941 he refused to evacuate because he remembered the Germans as "decent people" from World War I. He was killed in Kopyl, Belorussia. CREDIT: Ida Solominska.

Shalom (Shimon) Natanovich Zorin, partisan leader.

Yankl Moshkovich of Odessa, a furniture maker, was a partisan in the Vitebsk area when he was in his teens. He died in 1983. CREDIT: Grigory Moshkovich.

some of their comrades in arms were hostile to Jews. "Diadia Misha" (Uncle Misha) Gildenman, Shalom (or Shimon) Zorin, Tuvia Belsky and his two brothers, and Dr. Atlas are some of the better-known leaders of Jewish partisan units which operated mainly in the forests of Belorussia and Lithuania. Belsky's unit had 1,500 people in it, mostly noncombatant women and children. Only in Jewish units could noncombatants find a place, because the others saw them as a burden which they could not afford to carry. Gentile women and children generally had no reason to hide, but

Staff of the Vilnius orphanage, 1945. This was the only entirely Jewish orphanage after the war. CREDIT: Dora Ferdman Finefter.

the Jews had some chance of survival only if they hid in the forests. Of course, ruthless German pursuit, and at times the hostility of the local population, made life in the forest very precarious. A great many of the partisans and escaped families did not live to witness the defeat of Nazi Germany.

VICTORY AND UNCERTAINTY

On May 24, 1945, Joseph Stalin received the commanders of the Red Army in the Kremlin and toasted the victory over Nazi Germany and her allies. He praised the Soviet people, twenty million of whom had lost their lives in the struggle against the invaders. He singled out the Russian people, whom he called "the most outstanding nation among the peoples of the Soviet Union" and the "driving force" of the war. Proportionately, of course, the Jews had suffered more than any other Soviet nationality and their contribution to the war effort had been immense. About one and a half million Jews had been killed, not including those who had died in combat. Nothing could alleviate the tragedy, but Soviet Jews could be proud of the role played by their country in defeating Nazism. Many, particularly in the west-

Jews marching out of a synagogue in Rovno, Ukraine, carrying desecrated Torah scrolls to be buried, 1944. CREDIT: Robert and Martin Koby.

Burying the Torahs at the
cemetery. CREDIT: Robert and
Martin Koby.

ern territories, had reservations about the Soviet system
before the war. Some were opposed to it in principle, while
others were among its most enthusiastic admirers. Some had
suffered under the Soviet regime, but others had greatly
benefitted from it. At the end of the war, none could deny
that Soviet evacuation, and, ironically, Soviet deportation
and exile, had saved the lives of hundreds of thousands, and
the defeat of Germany had saved millions. In the struggle
against the enemy there could be no ambivalence. But already during the war Jews had felt the anti-Semitic expressions of part of the population. They were well aware of the
extent of collaboration with the Nazis, of hostility toward
Jews among some civilians and soldiers alike, and they came
increasingly to realize that the special tragedy of the Jewish
people was going largely unmentioned in the media, in literature, films, and the theater. They looked forward to
peacetime with a mixture of grief and relief, with hope, and
above all, uncertainty.

CHAPTER FIVE

THE BLACK YEARS AND THE GRAY, 1948-1967

V ictor Alter and Henryk Erlich, two leaders of the Jewish Labor Bund in Poland, were among the refugees from the German army who found themselves in Soviet-controlled territory in 1939. They were arrested and charged with cooperating with the "international bourgeoisie," Polish counter-intelligence services, and a Bundist underground in the USSR. Both were sentenced to death for their supposed anti-Soviet activities. However, they were released in September 1941 after pressure from the British and a thaw in relations between the Polish government-in-exile and the Soviet government. Erlich and Alter proposed to the Soviet government the formation of a Jewish Anti-Hitlerite Committee, including representatives from Nazi-occupied countries, the USSR, the United States, and Great Britain. The committee would wage anti-Nazi propaganda, care for Polish-Jewish refugees in the USSR, mobilize world Jewish support for the war effort, and form a Jewish Legion in the United States to fight within the Red Army, since the United States was not yet in the war.

Shortly after midnight on December 4, 1941, an NKVD (Soviet secret police) agent, Khazanovich, who happened to be a Jew, summoned Erlich and Alter to an urgent meeting. They never returned. Apparently the idea of an international Jewish organization and of a distinctly Jewish role in the war effort was unacceptable and considered dangerous by Stalin. Repeated inquiries by prominent figures in the international labor movement as to the fate of Erlich and Alter went unanswered until February 1943 when the Soviet government admitted that the two had been executed, ostensibly for appealing to Soviet troops to conclude peace with Germany.

Nevertheless the idea of a Jewish anti-Nazi committee proposed by Erlich and Alter found expression in a series of public meetings, involving leading Soviet Jewish personalities, which took place in 1941. Appeals were made to

Henryk Erlich (1882–1941), on the left, and Victor Alter (1890–1941) in a May Day parade in Warsaw, 1936. Erlich was a leader of the Bund, first in Russia, and after the revolution, in Poland. His wife, Sophia, was the daughter of the historian Simon Dubnow. Alter was active in the Bund in Russia and Poland and played a leading role in the Polish trade union movement. In 1921 he was arrested by the Bolsheviks but was released, and later became the Bund's representative to the Socialist International.

Poets and writers, members of the Jewish Anti-Fascist Committee, meet with Ben-Zion Goldberg, an American Yiddish journalist and son-in-law of Sholem Aleichem, 1946. Standing from left to right: Leib Kvitko and Dovid Bergelson. Seated, from left: Itsik Feffer, unidentified, Peretz Markish, Ben-Zion Goldberg, Shlomo Mikhoels, unidentified, Aron Kushnirov, Shmuel Halkin. CREDIT: L. Podriachik.

Anglo-American Jewry to support the USSR's fight against the scourge of world Jewry. In 1942 a "Jewish Antifascist Committee" was formed in the Soviet Union. Its primary purpose was to rally political and financial support for the Soviet war effort among Jewish communities in the West. The committee began publishing a Yiddish newspaper, *Eynikeit* (Unity), which appeared once every ten days, and later weekly and three times a week. The committee also supplied material and cultural support to Yiddish writers, including refugees from Poland, Romania, and the Baltic states. The JAC was the only official Jewish institution in the country. As such, it became the focus of many Jewish cultural and national aspirations. Some of its officials insisted that the committee restrict its activities to foreign propaganda, while others hoped to turn it into a domestically oriented institution which would be the "central address" of Soviet Jewry and organizer of its Yiddish cultural activities. Some members seem to have proposed that the Crimea, from which the Tatars had been exiled on grounds that they had collaborated with the Germans, be turned into a Jewish republic. This idea was opposed by the promoters of Birobidzhan, and more important, by Stalin himself. It was soon to cost its proponents dearly.

The JAC was quite successful in rallying foreign Jewish support. In 1943 the committee sent its chairman, Solomon (Shlomo) Mikhoels, renowned as the moving spirit of the Moscow Yiddish Theater and creator of the role of King Lear in Yiddish, to the United States, along with the Yiddish poet, Itsik Feffer, an ardent supporter of the Soviet system. During the course of several months they visited cities all over the country, with trips to Canada and Mexico as well. In general, they were enthusiastically received by largely

Mikhoels visits the grave of Sholem Aleichem, New York.

Itsik Feffer, left, and Shlomo Mikhoels meet with Albert Einstein in America, 1943. CREDIT: Aaron Kurtz.

Jewish audiences, though anti-Communist Jewish socialist circles refused to join in the general welcome. At a Polo Grounds (New York) meeting in July attended by nearly 50,000, the writer Sholem Asch praised the USSR for eliminating anti-Semitism, and Yiddish journalist Ben-Zion Goldberg, a son-in-law of Sholem Aleichem, spoke of the "the great leader Marshal Stalin." The rally was concluded by the actor Paul Robeson singing Yiddish and Russian songs. All told, several million dollars was raised for the Soviet armed forces.[1]

THE TIDE BEGINS TO TURN

Already in 1944 the Soviet press carried criticisms of excessive nationalism in the literature and press of several nationalities. In 1946 a campaign was launched against Ukrainian nationalism. In the same year, taking a cue from Andrei Zhdanov—at one time Stalin's heir apparent, head of the Leningrad party organization and ideological spokesman—*Eynikeit* began to criticize some Yiddish writers' preoccupation with Jewish history and Jewish themes. The writer Itsik Kipnis was criticized for his "*shtetl* attitudes" and for Jewish nationalism. In 1948 the critic Khayim Loitsker complained that "The works of the Soviet Yiddish writers abound with the word 'Jew' in its various forms," that too much use was made of biblical imagery and Hebraisms, and that there was "nationalist egocentrism" in several works. He concluded: "To outlive the remnants of narrow nationalism and nationalist egocentrism . . . to uproot all trace of bourgeois nationalism, to saturate the works with lofty Bolshevist ideology—that is the most urgent task of the ever developing and advancing Soviet Yiddish literature."[2] This rhetoric was typical of the *Zhdanovshchina*, the period of the late 1940s in which Stalin and Zhdanov led a militant campaign against all foreign ties and influences, and such vices as "bourgeois nationalism," "cosmopolitanism," and ideological laxity. At the same time, the special genius of the Russian people was emphasized. The West was degenerate and doomed to extinction, whereas the Russians, who according to the press of the time seemed to have invented everything worthwhile, were deserving of the highest praise.

On January 13, 1948, Solomon Mikhoels, who had been called to Minsk in connection with the award of some Stalin prizes, "died in tragic circumstances," in the words of the official announcement. People were led to believe that he had been run over by a truck or killed by thugs. Several months later, when other figures in the Yiddish theater were arrested and when state subsidies were withdrawn, it became obvious that he had been murdered by the authorities. The Soviet press admitted this only fifteen years later. Though a large public funeral was given Mikhoels, his death signalled the beginning of the massive repression of Yiddish culture and Jewish national expression. In retrospect, it became clear that Stalin had decided to liquidate the remnants of Soviet Yiddish culture. The logical place to begin was with the unofficial leader of Soviet Jewry, Mikhoels, who had brought fame and glory to the USSR for its Jewish culture.

Nina Sirotina, now living in the United States, was born in the Belorussian village of Podobrianka. In the 1930s she took up acting and auditioned before Mikhoels. He accepted her to GOSET, the State Yiddish Theater in Moscow. She ran home to tell her parents: "I shouted, standing at the door, 'I passed! I got through.' My father was sitting and pounding nails into the soles of shoes. . . . My father just looked up at me and I saw kind of . . . little stars lit up his eyes, but he immediately lowered his gaze, so that somehow I felt he was happy for me, that he approved. My mother asked 'What happened?' . . . 'Mama, I'm going to Moscow.' My mother was holding tongs in her hand and she came at me with the tongs and . . . said, 'I'll . . . break your legs, I'll break all your bones. What is this about Moscow? What is this about the theater? No, that's not going to be!' My father said to her, 'Sheine-Liebe . . . don't yell. Calmly, quietly we'll talk . . . then we'll talk to Nekhama as to how and what, because other times have come now, you can't keep all the children here or with you. . . .' "

From Moscow, on her stipend of 35 rubles a month, the aspiring actress sent food packages home: "Wheat, grain or some kind of dried fish because there they didn't have anything like that. . . . They were all barefoot, barely dressed. I sent little dresses for my younger sisters. The first time I sent a real pair of pants to my last [sic] brother . . . the first pants . . . he ever had."

During the war Sirotina was evacuated with GOSET, later returning to Moscow to resume her acting career, and working with Mikhoels all the time. She says of him: "He was not only an actor, he was also a director. He was incredible. He was a marvelous lawyer, he was a philosopher, he was an orator. He never had a paper and pencil . . . he had everything in his head, everything was fresh."

Important politicians and generals, Jews and others, came to GOSET's performances. Once, Lazar Moiseevich Kaganovich, the only Jew in the Politburo after 1930, came to see a play. Afterward he came to Mikhoels, "banged on the table and said, 'My people is not like this. Why are you showing me poor people, ragged people, people with *payes*

The gravestone of Mikhoels. It simply says "Solomon Mikhailovich Mikhoels," in Russian and Yiddish. PHOTO: Jacob Roth.

[earlocks], people like that?'" After that, says Sirotina, "we put on contemporary plays, partisans, heroes, how they work on the frontiers, and so on."

When Mikhoels was killed, all the actors understood that this was murder. There were lots of wounds on his neck, an arm was twisted out of joint, "his eyes were bulging . . . he was completely disfigured." A GOSET makeup artist and the son of the man who had embalmed Lenin worked on Mikhoels' corpse to make it presentable for viewing. "The hand, which had been wrenched out of joint, they also somehow put it so that he had his famous gesture with the index finger pointing. . . . He had extremely expressive hands, hands such as not a single actor in the world ever had. . . . There was a great deal he didn't have to say, his hands could say a great deal."

His body lay in state for three days and nights in order to accommodate the crowds who came to pay their respects. An old man stood on a nearby fence. He played the violin for a long time—selections from Mozart's Requiem, Kol Nidre, the Kaddish. "He was a virtuoso," and his playing forced the official orchestra to cease so that everyone could hear the old man.

After Mikhoels' death Jews stopped attending GOSET's performances because there was always a Black Maria parked near the theater. They bought tickets in order to support the theater whose subsidy had been withdrawn by the state, but they did not attend. All the actors feared arrest. One day, in 1949, a group of officials arrived, informed the actors that the theater was dissolved, arranged some severance pay for them, and suggested that they find other jobs. The State Yiddish Theater, the pride and showcase of Soviet Yiddish culture, ceased to exist.[3]

The Jewish Antifascist Committee continued to exist after the war, but at the end of 1948 it was dissolved and its leading functionaries were arrested. On November 17, 1948, the last Yiddish publishing house in the country

Peretz Markish (1895–1952) in 1943. The literary critic Sh. Niger wrote about Markish that he had introduced a "new theme and . . . new tone" to Yiddish verse—"the theme and tone of solemnity, fervor, and heroism."

was closed down. Esther Markish, wife of the Yiddish poet Peretz Markish, recalls: "The new linotype machines were humming away. The chief editor, Moisei Belenky, was in conference with Strongin, the director, when, without a word of warning . . . trucks filled with State Security agents pulled up in front of the house. Soldiers in civilian clothes burst into the printing plant and disconnected the machines. Everything came to a standstill; all was silence. 'Your publishing house is closed down!' one of the pogromists bellowed."[4]

"Markish lost all hope. He realized the end was near, that it was now only a question of time—days or, at best, months," his widow remembers. In late December, Itsik Feffer, Dovid Bergelson, and Leib Kvitko were arrested. During the next month Peretz Markish was followed by police agents who also stood guard at his apartment. On January 27, 1949, seven agents came for him a few minutes before midnight. To his agitated wife they said, "Our minister just wants to have a talk with your husband." He never returned.

Itsik Kipnis (1896–1974). A poet and children's writer, he was accused of being "apolitical and petit bourgeois." Kipnis was expelled from the writers' union for writing in 1947, "I wish that all the Jews now walking victoriously in Berlin should wear on their chests, along with their medals and orders, a small Jewish star. . . . I want everyone to see now that I am a Jew, and my Jewish and human dignity is no less than that of anyone else among freedom-loving citizens." Deported to labor camps in 1948, he was released after Stalin's death. CREDIT: Itsik Kipnis.

Borukh Veisman, a writer from Kiev, spent ten years in a labor camp, 1959. PHOTO: Yosef Schneider.

In the years 1948–1953 Yiddish culture was destroyed by the arrest of several hundred Jewish cultural figures—writers, actors, artists, sculptors, musicians, journalists, editors. Most were sentenced to ten years at hard labor on charges of "bourgeois nationalism," or slander of Soviet Union (for asserting that anti-Semitism existed there), or espionage on behalf of the West. The Jewish Section of the Soviet Writers Union was dissolved. Esther Markish recounts how, at a general meeting of the union's Moscow section, the writer Aron Kushnirov, a combat officer who had lost a son in the war, was called on to speak. He "knew only too well what

Dovid Bergelson (1884–1952), right, and Moshe Notovich (b. 1912). Bergelson, one of the most distinguished Soviet Yiddish prose writers, lived in Berlin from 1921 and traveled widely in Europe and America. In 1934 he went to Birobidzhan and remained in the Soviet Union, settling in Moscow. Arrested in 1948, he was shot in 1952. Notovich was associated with the Yiddish theater and the Antifascist Committee. CREDIT: Hirsh Osherovitch.

was expected of him, [and] was literally dragged onto the podium. Before he could utter a word, however, he burst into tears and was led away." Only his death soon after prevented his arrest; his wife was sent away to a camp.[5]

THE "ANTI-COSMOPOLITAN" CAMPAIGN

Just when Markish was arrested, a lead article in *Pravda* condemned "anti-patriotic" theater critics who represented a "rootless cosmopolitanism which is deeply repulsive and inimical to Soviet man."[6] The critics attacked were Jews, and it was hinted that they could have no proper understanding of Russian culture. "What kind of an idea can Gurvich have of the national character of Soviet Russian man?" Gurvich, a Jew, was accused of slandering "the national Soviet character." There was a general campaign against "cosmopolitanism" in the arts, literature, music, philosophy, and scholarship. Jews were singled out as "rootless" cosmopolitans, meaning that they were unpatriotic and had no attachment to the Soviet motherland. One scholar has calculated that 70 percent of the writers, artists, and scholars criticized in the press were Jews; among economists and athletes accused of cosmopolitanism the percentage was even higher—over 85.[7] Those accused were usually removed from their posts, expelled from professional organizations and from the Communist Party. In February 1949 the press began to reveal the original names of Jewish personalities who had adopted pen names. The original Jewish name was printed in parentheses following the name by which the person was known. Thus Melnikov (Melman), Burlachenko (Berdichevsky), and Yakovlev (Kholtsman) were "exposed." Even some Jews faithful to the party line whatever its direction, took part in the campaign. The philosopher Mark Mitin, the journalist David Zaslavsky (a former Bundist), and V. Lutsky, a scholar of the Middle East, published attacks on cosmopolitanism.

Ilya Ehrenburg later denied the rumors that he had testified against former JAC members and other Jewish cultural figures. Ehrenburg recalls that from February 1949 he was no longer allowed to publish anything. Only close friends called; many of them would hang up as soon as he answered, reassured that he had not been arrested. Ehrenburg, like many others, lived in constant expectation of arrest. "In March 1938 I used to listen anxiously to the lift . . . like many others I had kept a suitcase ready packed with two changes of underwear. In March 1949 I gave no thought to underwear and awaited the outcome almost with indifference. Perhaps it was because I was now fifty-eight and not forty-seven." Weary of rumors about his impending arrest, Ehrenburg dropped a note to Stalin asking to have his "position clarified." Georgii Malenkov, who was later to compete against Nikita Khrushchev for the post-Stalin leadership of the country, called Ehrenburg to dispel his fears. "Immediately the telephone came to life again: various editorial offices said there had been a 'misunderstanding,' that my articles would be published and would I write some more."[8]

The anticosmopolitan campaign extended far beyond the circles of the intelligentsia. The general public understood very well that an official campaign against the Jews had originated at the very top and that it was open season on the "rootless cosmopolitans." As Esther Markish recalls, "A prepogrom atmosphere reigned in Moscow. It was dangerous for Jews to venture out into the streets, and Jewish children were beaten in school."[9] Many lost their jobs or were refused admission to schools of higher education. Some frightened Jews burned their Jewish books, destroyed Jewish objects, and cut off all contact with relatives or friends abroad. One woman, a geology student at the time, recalls her professor's telling the class that he had received a meteorite fragment from a friend in Australia and he proposed to compare it with a fragment from Siberia. This was enough to have him arrested as a "cosmopolitan." A former conductor in the Bolshoi Theater was asked to make a speech at a general staff meeting in which he would deny that there was any anti-Semitism in the Soviet Union. He refused, was given a day to think about it, and when he refused again, he was dismissed on the grounds that since the Bolshoi was a "special organization," all its employees were to have political views beyond reproach.[10]

In July 1952, twenty-five prominent Jewish cultural figures were tried, and on August 12, about a score—including some of the best-known Yiddish writers—were executed. Among them were Markish, Bergelson, Kvitko, Shmuel Persov, Binyamin Zuskin, Mikhoels' close colleague and successor, and the literary critic Yitzhak Nusinov. Among the executed was also Itsik Feffer, the same poet who once wrote: "When I mention Stalin—I mean beauty, I mean eternal happiness, I mean nevermore . . . to know of pain." The victims were charged with trying to sever the Crimea from the USSR and establish a Zionist republic there "to serve as a base for American imperialism"; espionage for foreign states; "bourgeois nationalist activity and anti-Soviet propaganda"; and illegal activities. Their relatives, who did not know of their fate, were imprisoned and exiled.

At about the same time, as part of a drive against corruption, many Jews were being accused of theft of state property, embezzlement, currency speculation, economic sabotage, bribery, and other economic crimes. Their misdeeds were widely publicized in the press. The economy had not yet recovered from the immense hardships of the 1930s and the war, and charges against those working in the consumer industry—nearly all the publicized cases were of this nature—could not but arouse general public resentment against those who were depriving "honest Soviet citizens" of their fair share of the limited supplies. Stereotypes about the sharp business practices and fundamental dishonesty of Jews were reinforced. After a major economic trial involving Jews in Kiev in November 1952, three Jewish defendants were executed. A newspaper editorial commented that "all those khains and yaroshetskys, greensteins . . . perses . . . and kaplans, and polyakovs . . . arouse the profound loathing of the people."[11]

In the same month a sensational trial in Prague, Czechoslovakia, saw eleven prominent Communists tried as "apprentices of the Zionist movement," and as sympathizers of Trotsky and Yugoslav Marshal Tito (Stalin had broken with the latter in 1948). Eight were condemned to death and the others to life imprisonment. A few of the defendants were not Jewish, but among the prominent themes in the trial were the defendants' connections with Zionism and with American espionage; their worldwide Jewish connections; their economic crimes which lowered the general standard of living; and involvement in an attempt to murder by medical means a leading Czechoslovak politician. These same themes were to echo shortly thereafter in another sensational, and for Jews, most ominous, announcement made in Moscow on January 13, 1953.

On that day *Pravda* made known the arrest of a "group of saboteur-doctors." Nine doctors with obviously Jewish names were cited, six of them linked to the Joint Distribution Committee which was said to have been "established by American intelligence" for the purpose of espionage and terrorism in the USSR and other countries. Three other doctors "proved to be old agents of British intelligence." These "monsters in human form" were accused of having murdered medically two leading Soviet politicians, Andrei Zhdanov and Alexander Shcherbakov. They were also intending to murder several leading military figures. Further, it was charged that the JDC's orders had been transmitted via "the well known Jewish bourgeois nationalist, Mikhoels."[12] A *Pravda* editorial proclaimed that "The Soviet people wrathfully and indignantly condemn the criminal band of murderers and their foreign masters. They will crush like loathsome vermin the despised hirelings," but warned that "to end sabotage it is necessary to put an end to gullibility in our ranks,"[13] signaling a new campaign of "vigilance" and rooting out "enemies of the people." Such a campaign was a logical concomitant of the Cold War, then at its height. The Soviet people were told that the Western threat was extremely serious, and that the enemy had his agents and accomplices within the USSR itself. Jews, with their Western connections, were obvious candidates for the role of spies and collaborators with the Western imperialists.

All over the country people began to avoid Jewish doctors. The epithet "Poisoners!" was hurled at Jews riding the tramways and even sitting in the classroom. Stories "unmasking" corrupt and dangerous Jewish doctors began to appear in the provincial press. Rumors spread that the Jews were injecting poison into medicines, that they had infiltrated rest homes and vacation spots in order to carry out evil designs, and that there were "nests" of Zionist spies in governmental and academic positions. The most ominous rumor was that barracks were being constructed in Siberia on such a scale that it could only mean the deportation of the bulk of the Jewish population. This was expected by both Jews and non-Jews. Physicist Mark Azbel, then a university student, remembers that "The country was ready for murders, for pogroms. It was no secret. And shortly, word got around that an open letter by the most eminent Jewish writers and scientists was to appear in the papers, saying they understood the guilt of their people, that this guilt had to be somehow expiated. . . . They themselves would request, nay, urge the government to send the Jews to the far northeast of Siberia, where they might atone for their crimes . . . by their labor. Rumors arose that new labor camps were already in the making in Siberia. . . . It became harder to lead a normal life . . . to ignore the panic that filled the air."[14]

Raisa Palatnik, then in the ninth grade, recalls that she became acutely aware of her nationality at the time of the "Doctors' Plot." "It was scary to leave the classroom and go into the hallway because from all sides you heard, 'You Yids, you poisoned Gorky, you wanted to poison Stalin, you poisoned all our great leaders,' and the atmosphere was very tense. Even the teachers allowed themselves such remarks."[15] Jews who graduated from medical school were assigned to Kamchatka, the farthest possible point from the major European cities. Assignment to Yakutia in Siberia was considered a lucky break. "They decided to send all the Jews out of Russia proper." Also, "We had to take part in these political meetings at which the poisoner-physicians were damned and accused."[16] Professor Vovsi, a relative of Mikhoels (whose real name was Vovsi), was one of the accused doctors. "One day Professor Vovsi existed, the next day he ceased to exist. His name was taken off the lists in the library, his name disappeared, you weren't allowed to mention him . . . only when you accused him."[17]

Clearly, Jews as a group were now viewed as a potential fifth column. In line with this perception, the percentage of Jews in the party Central Committee was reduced from ten (1939) to two (1952). In the republics Jews disappeared from the upper echelons of the party. Their numbers in government posts, especially those dealing with foreign, security, and military affairs, declined drastically. Whereas in 1937 there were forty-seven Jews in the Supreme Soviet, the highest legislative organ, in 1946 there were only thirteen, and in 1950 only eight.[18]

THE USSR AND THE ESTABLISHMENT OF THE STATE OF ISRAEL

Paradoxically, at the very time that Soviet Jewry was being terrorized, the Soviet government was supporting the establishment of a Jewish state in Palestine. Apparently the Soviet position was influenced primarily by its desire to weaken British influence in the Middle East and its skepticism that the Arabs would be capable of doing so. The Soviets may have also calculated that a future socialist Jewish state would align itself with the USSR. On May 14, 1947, Deputy Foreign Minister Andrei Gromyko addressed a special session of the United Nations General Assembly. The representative of a government which was suppressing the story of Jewish martyrdom during the war spoke with pathos about the "exceptional sorrow and suffering" of the Jews which he characterized as "indescribable." Moreover, said Gromyko, this suffering did not end with the war. "Hundreds of thousands of Jews are wandering about in . . . Europe in search of means of existence and in search of shelter." Therefore the Jews aspire to establish their own state. "It would be unjustifiable to deny this right to the Jewish people, particularly in view of all it has undergone during the Second World War." In late 1947 the Soviet government advocated the partition of Palestine into Jewish and Arab states.[19]

The USSR went beyond political support for a Jewish state. It approved the sale of Czechoslovak arms to the Zionist forces and it did not interfere in the movement of Jewish survivors out of Eastern Europe toward Western Europe, and from there to Palestine (after May 1948, Israel) and North America. Yet a domestic campaign against Zionism was launched by the fall of 1948. In September 1948, less than half a year after the establishment of Israel, Ilya Ehrenburg published an article in *Pravda*—"at the editor's request," he says—in which he wrote that "The State of Israel is not headed by representatives of the working people." Moreover, in the USSR, "Jewish toilers, like all others, are strongly attached to the land where they were born and where they grew up." Citizens of socialist countries "can never envy" those who live under the "yoke of capitalist exploitation." Soviet Jews, who are "working to build up their socialist homeland . . . are not looking to the Near East."[20]

Ehrenburg's warnings came too late for young Soviet Jews who, thrilled by the establishment of the State of Israel and their country's support for it, had inquired of Soviet offices where they could volunteer to fight for Israel against her Arab attackers. Their names and addresses were carefully recorded, and sometime later they were arrested as Zionists.

Golda Meir, Israel's first ambassador to the USSR, surrounded by Moscow Jews outside the synagogue, Rosh Hashanah, 1948.

Even more cautious Jews could not suppress their joy at the establishment of a Jewish state. A former career army officer relates that "I personally welcomed it and any Jews I spoke with, officers or not, all welcomed it. We understood that . . . Jews could enter the international arena, that they would use their voice to defend Jewishness and Jewish rights, show Jewish culture, Jewish history and its worth, how we fought against the Germans." [21] Perhaps it was this very pride and hope that Israel's establishment aroused, even among highly acculturated and unquestionably loyal Soviet citizens, that made Stalin and his subordinates doubly alert to the dangers of "bourgeois nationalism" at home. If the calculus of Soviet foreign policy dictated support for Israel, stronger measures against Zionism would have to be taken at home.

RELIEF AND REHABILITATION, 1953–1964

On the evening of March 4, 1953, Mark Azbel had a bitter argument with his father and stomped out of their apartment in Kharkov. He dropped in at the central telegraph office, open twenty-four hours a day, seeking shelter from the cold. Very early in the morning there was a great commotion at the switchboard.

> The entire board was lit . . . the operators . . . in some kind of frenzy. Bells rang incessantly. Several of the operators began to scream; others hushed them saying: "Don't alarm everyone! Don't say anything! It couldn't be true!" . . . The screaming got louder; a few of the women burst into tears. . . . Everyone in the office surrounded the switchboard. "What's happened, girls?" "What's going on?" "Not—war?" "*Stalin is dead!*" one of the women managed to announce, between sobs. If a bomb had exploded in our midst, no one present could have been more astonished. . . . It had no more occurred to most of the population in all of Russia that he might die than it would occur to the devout that God might die. . . . Among the crowd were five or six Jews—they looked as bereaved and smitten as everyone else.[22]

Many people, including Jews, wept in both sorrow and fear, but not everyone reacted the same way. One emigré recalls that while she was crying, her husband went to the store, bought a bottle of champagne, and announced, "Now we shall live." The religious father of a Communist loyalist thanked

God that he had lived to see the death of "that thief, that murderer," and noted with satisfaction that "that Haman" had died right around the holiday of Purim (which celebrates the deliverance of the Jews in ancient Persia from mass annihilation at the hands of Haman).

Indeed, one month after Stalin's death, *Pravda* carried an announcement by the Ministry of Internal Affairs that those accused in the "Doctors' Plot" "were arrested by the former USSR Ministry of State Security incorrectly, without any lawful basis." The accused were exonerated and "The persons accused of incorrect conduct of the investigation have been arrested and brought to trial." One could almost hear the collective sigh of relief breathed by Jews all over the country.

The death of Stalin aroused hopes that the worst aspects of the system he had created would disappear with him. In the decade following his death there was a partial "return to Leninist norms," as Nikita Khrushchev liked to say, and Jews benefited from it to a limited extent. The threat to their physical survival was removed. The cultural leaders who had been murdered, imprisoned, or exiled were "rehabilitated." Those still alive were restored to their homes, given jobs or pensions, and had their records cleared. Those who had been killed at least had their honor restored, and their families were released from exile and imprisonment. But the cultural institutions of Soviet Jewry were never restored. Not a single Yiddish school was reopened—nor has one since. The theater was never fully restored, though amateur and semiprofessional troupes were permitted later on. Popular anti-Semitism was not condemned and, in contrast to the 1920s, no effort has been made to discuss it openly and try to overcome it.

Three years after Stalin's death Khrushchev found the courage and political opportunity to denounce Stalin. Symptomatic of the sensitivity of the issue was the fact that Khrushchev's revelations about Stalin's crimes were made to the highest party body, its Twentieth Congress, but only in secret session. His now-famous speech, smuggled out to the West, has never been published in the USSR, though its general contents became widely known there. In the speech, Stalin was criticized for deporting the Volga Germans and other nationalities, but no mention was made of his anti-Semitic policies. Khrushchev confirmed that the "Doctors' Plot" was an invention, initiated by a Dr. Lydia Timashuk who was much praised in the Soviet press and highly decorated. She supposedly wrote a letter to Stalin accusing the doctors. According to Khrushchev, Stalin then "personally

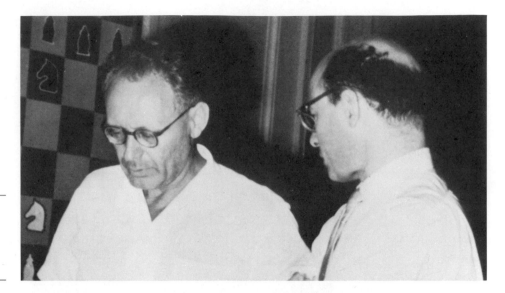

Mikhail Botvinnik, (left) and Mikhail Tal, both world chess champions. CREDIT: Rima Bendersky.

Pyotr Solomonovich Stoliarsky with his music students, Moscow, 1937. Seated, from left: Lisa Gilels, Stoliarsky, Mikhail Pikhtengoltz. Standing: David Oistrakh, (left) and Boris Goldshtain. CREDIT: Yaakov Soroker.

David Oistrakh, (left) and Arkady Raikin in Vilnius, 1967. Raikin is one of the most famous actors in the USSR. Oistrakh was one of the many world-famous Jewish violinists from Odessa. PHOTO: Yona Shishko.

issued advice on the conduct of investigation and the method of interrogation of the arrested." Stalin told Minister of State Security Ignatiev, "If you do not obtain confessions from the doctors we will shorten you by a head." Khrushchev, who had been the First Secretary of the Ukrainian Communist Party and a member of the Politburo in Stalin's day, said that Stalin personally called the investigating judge and told him which methods to use. "These methods were simple—beat, beat, and, once again, beat." In all the graphic description of the affair Khrushchev said not one word about the Jewish element in the case nor about its consequences for all Soviet Jews.[23]

Stalin's successors jockeyed for political position for four years. It was only in 1957 that Khrushchev succeeded in eliminating the "anti-party group," comprised of some of Stalin's closest associates, including Kaganovich, the last Jew to occupy a very high party post. Though often seen as an impetuous buffoon both inside and outside the Soviet Union, Khrushchev was a courageous politician who took enormous risks in order to eliminate the most irrational aspects of Stalinism, curb the secret police and the terror, revive Soviet cultural and artistic life which had fallen moribund under the weight of Stalinist orthodoxy and sycophancy, and make partial amends to many of those who had

LEFT: Maia Plisetskaia, prima ballerina of the Bolshoi Ballet, 1981. PHOTO: Yona Shishko.

RIGHT: Oistrakh conducting in Vilnius, 1970. PHOTO: Yona Shishko.

been victimized by the "cult of personality." Jews as individuals benefitted from these changes, though Jewish collective rights were only minimally restored. Whereas all Jews had been threatened by the hysteria of the late Stalinist period—and yet some still shed real tears at the "great helmsman's" death—in the late 1950s and 1960s Jews were more differentiated both in their treatment by the system and in their attitudes toward it. Many felt that justice was being done, and if not everything was set aright, it was sufficient to make life manageable. They felt that one ought be satisfied with that in view of all that had gone before. Others were highly ambivalent: true, things had gotten better, but there was no institutional or legal guarantee against a return to mass terror and rampant anti-Semitism. A third group, including many released prisoners, nationally conscious Jews, and young people, felt themselves aliens, not accepted by the population or by the elite, which only tolerated them. The inspiring visions of internationalism, "brotherhood of peoples," and social equality which had moved so many in the 1930s seemed hopelessly unrealistic three decades later. Some Jews accepted that as a fact of life and concentrated their energies on making the best life possible for themselves within the limitations of being a Jew in a society which no longer took "internationalism" seriously. Others found it difficult to make this compromise and began thinking about alternatives: reforming the system, abandoning their Jewishness, leaving the Soviet Union, struggling to restore Jewish culture, or "internal emigration"—that is, retreating into privatism and "dropping out" of the mainstream.

KHRUSHCHEV'S POLICIES AND SOVIET JEWS

In Stalin's last years many qualified Jews were demoted, fired, or refused employment or acceptance to higher educational institutions of their choice. One report has it that at the time of the "Doctors' Plot" 200 Jewish students were summarily expelled from the university in Odessa. With de-Stalinization, some people were restored to their old posts or given equivalent ones. Admission to higher education, though not based purely on merit and class background as it had been in the 1920s, was now easier for Jews. They found, however, that it was much easier to be accepted in scientific and technological fields than in the more ideologically sensitive ones, such as the humanities and social sciences generally, and fields related to security and foreign affairs in particular. Jews discovered that they were not welcome in the ministries of foreign affairs and foreign trade, in the military academies, the higher echelons of the party, and the secret police—all hierarchies in which they had been "overrepresented" up until the mid-1930s or later. Between 1952 and 1961 the number of Jews in the Supreme Soviet, a largely symbolic institution, also declined, and in the republic-level legislatures it fell considerably below what their proportion in the republic populations would have warranted. Jews were seriously underrepresented in the local soviets. In 1958–1961 there was not a single Jew among the many government ministers, the first time that had happened.

The restoration of Yiddish culture was slow, limited in scope, and of such modest dimensions that it had largely symbolic, not practical, value. In December 1955 Peretz Markish was "rehabilitated," followed in 1956 by other Yiddish literary and cultural figures. The first Yiddish book published since 1948 did not appear until 1959. For the rest of Khrushchev's reign, lasting until late 1964, only six other Yiddish books were published. In 1961 the first Yiddish journal since the "Black Years" was published. *Sovetish heymland* appeared initially as a bimonthly in an edition of 25,000

Curtain call, the cast of the Vilna Yiddish Drama Collective in *Hershele Ostropoler*, Vilnius, 1966. CREDIT: Khana Bederis.

copies. These gestures were made largely in response to inquiries about Yiddish culture posed to Soviet officials by foreigners, including Communists and socialists. When one compares the cultural situation of the Jews with that of other extraterritorial minorities—Germans, Poles, Hungarians, for example—it becomes clear that the Jews were being treated differently. In Kazakhstan in the 1960s, one-quarter of the German children were in German-language schools. Not a single Jewish school of any kind was ever reopened. In the decade following 1946, 2,417 books were published in Ger-

RIGHT: Yiddish and Russian actress Anna Guzik. PHOTO: Moisei Nappelbaum; CREDIT: Ilya Rudiak.

BELOW, LEFT: A Jewish amateur choir, Vilnius, 1968. CREDIT: Yona Shishko.

BELOW, RIGHT: Folk dance by an amateur troupe, Vilnius, 1968. PHOTO: Yona Shishko.

ABOVE: L. Podriachik giving Yiddish lessons at the Moscow theatrical studio, 1946. CREDIT: L. Podriachik.

BELOW: Yiddish writers drinking a toast in Moscow, 1965. From right to left: Hirsh Osherovitch, Esther and Moishe Teif, Polina and Yosef Rabin, Note Lurie. CREDIT: Hirsh Osherovitch.

Yiddish theater actresses Sidi Tal and Dina Roitkop, Riga, 1964. CREDIT: L. Podriachik.

man, 1,287 in Polish, and 719 in Hungarian.[24] The number of Yiddish publications was tiny, and, needless to say, Hebrew was still anathema. Moreover, Russian literature dealing with Jewish themes was very sparse.

Despite the lack of official sponsorship of Jewish culture, in the more relaxed atmosphere of the post-Stalinist era it was possible for Jews to initiate cultural activity on an amateur basis, though every such endeavor had to be cleared with the authorities. Amateur choirs and theatrical groups were founded in Latvia and Lithuania, where the Zapadniki were less assimilated and acculturated. About twenty theatrical and musical companies were established around the country. Binyamin Shvartser, a veteran of GOSET, set up a troupe in Moscow in 1962, and others were formed in Vilnius, Birobidzhan, and elsewhere. Though most of the groups seem to have been on a low artistic level, their performances were very important as statements that Jewish culture exists and as events around which Jews could meet and through which they could express their belonging to the Jewish people. This became especially important to younger people, who had no other tangible expression of their ethnic identity and few other links to the remnants of Jewish culture. Jews also took great pride in eminent Soviet artists of Jewish origin whose work was taken as evidence of the high cultural level of a people deprived of its original culture.

MILITANT ATHEISM AGAIN

Curiously, at a time when the anticosmopolitan campaign was in full swing and anti-Semitism was reaching into many aspects of Soviet life, the Jewish religion was treated with circumspection. During the war the government had adopted a more benign attitude toward Judaism, as it had toward other faiths, in order to rally both domestic and foreign support for the struggle against the invaders. Rabbi Shlifer of Moscow was even made a member of the Jewish Anti-fascist Committee. This official attitude and the renewal of Jewish consciousness spurred by Nazi persecutions returned many Jews, including youth and soldiers, to the synagogues, perhaps not so much because they had become believers but because they felt a need to express solidarity with their people and its fate. Though in the "Black Years" after the war Jews began to avoid the synagogue and visible expressions of religious observance, there was no official campaign against Judaism while the one against Jews was at its peak. Perhaps this was due to the authorities' reluctance to liquidate the sole surviving Jewish institution, the synagogue, because should public expression of religion be suppressed, it would only be driven underground, making it more difficult to monitor.[25]

The relatively benign posture toward Judaism continued after Stalin's death. Delegations of American rabbis began

At left is Rabbi Yehuda Leib Levin of Moscow, who succeeded Rabbi Shlomo Shlifer (center) as rabbi of the choral synagogue. At the right is Gedalia Pechersky, a lay leader of the Leningrad religious community. He lodged a complaint against illegal police operations in synagogues, and applied for permission to organize courses in Hebrew, Yiddish, and Jewish history. He was sentenced to twelve years in prison for spying for Israel and spreading anti-Soviet propaganda. Pechersky was permitted to emigrate to Israel in the early 1970s. CREDIT: Joint Distribution Committee.

Yaakov Lerner and Gilya Zaitsman, students in an underground Khabad (Lubavitcher) *yeshiva*, Samarkand, Uzbekistan, 1953. CREDIT: Vladimir Krugliak.

Rabbi Shlifer (center) with Georgian Rabbis Eliashvili (left) and Davarashvili, Kutaisi, Georgia, synagogue, 1950. CREDIT: Gershon Ben-Oren.

Yeshiva Kol Yaakov, Moscow, 1959, the students and faculty. Seated in the center (first row, third from right) is a rabbi from Tbilisi, Georgia. Next to him, right to left, are Rabbis Khayim Lubanov of Leningrad, Yehuda Leib Levin of Moscow, Khayim Katz, Shimon Trebnik, and Mordechai Khanzin. CREDIT: *The Day Morning Journal.*

to visit the Soviet Union where they met not only with fellow rabbis and co-religionists but even with Khrushchev. Rabbi Shlifer traveled to Paris, along with General Dragunsky, and spoke in Hebrew on the need for world peace. Most important, in January 1957 a theological seminary, the Yeshiva Kol Yaakov, was opened at the Choral Synagogue in Moscow, the first such institution established legally since the revolution. It began with ten students (the youngest of whom was twenty) and eight teachers, and was maintained exclusively with funds contributed by Soviet Jews. Since the generation of rabbis trained before the revolution was dying off, the *yeshiva* had the potential of assuring the survival of Jewish religious leadership. At about the same time the *yeshiva* was opened, a *siddur* (prayerbook) was published in an edition of 3,000 copies, and the Moscow religious community published a Jewish calendar. In mid-1957, however, there was a shift in policy, in line with a general antireligious campaign mounted by Khrushchev, and the "honeymoon" came to an end.

During 1957–1964 a multifaceted campaign against religion was carried out in most parts of the country. The campaign, which affected Judaism no less than other religions, included massive propaganda attacks, the closing of synagogues and expropriation of Jewish cemeteries, and harassment of religious observance. The propaganda campaign resurrected themes from the antireligious wars of the 1920s: Judaism was reactionary, diverting workers from their true interests; it was tightly linked to Zionism and "bourgeois nationalism"; it was unscientific and shot through with

В РОКИ ГІТЛЕРІВСЬКОЇ ОКУПАЦІЇ ВЕРХОВОДИ-СІО-НІСТИ ПРИСЛУЖУВАЛИ ФАШИСТАМ

The caption reads: "During the Hitlerite occupation the Zionist leaders served the fascists."

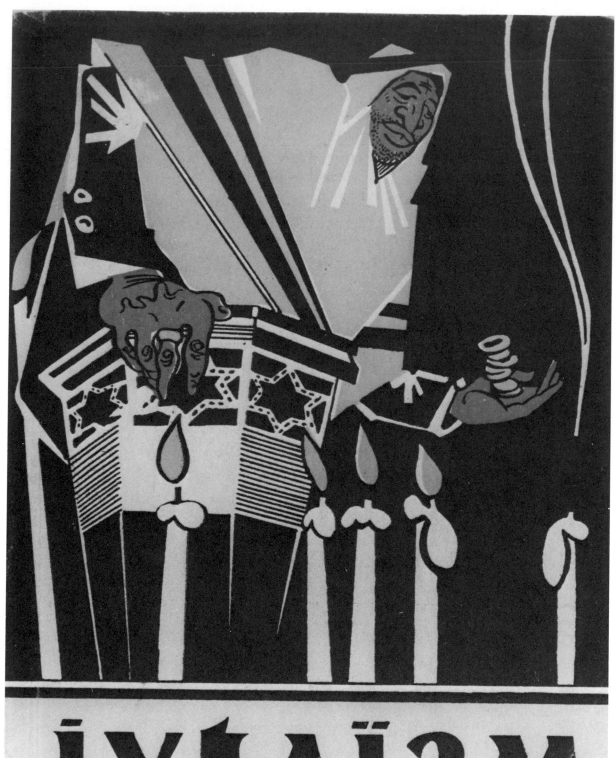

Cover of Kichko's *Iudaizm bez prikras* (Judaism Without Embellishment).

superstitions; it promoted hatred of non-Jews and the exploitation of Jews and Gentiles alike. Based on a wide-ranging search of the Soviet press of the period, Benjamin Pinkus, in *The Soviet Government and the Jews, 1948–1967*, concludes that there were over 300 articles attacking Judaism that appeared in 1960–1964.[26] Radio and television took up the same theme. There were fifty-four books published in Russian alone that attacked Judaism, and others were published in Moldavian, Ukrainian, and other languages. One of the crucial differences between this campaign and earlier ones was that attacks on Judaism were now published in languages that could be read by non-Jews, whereas previously most of the literature had been in Yiddish so that the "struggle against religion" had remained more of an intramural affair. In contrast to "universal" religions, such as Christianity and Islam, which are practiced by many peoples and nationalities, Judaism is associated with only one ethnic group, the Jews. Thus the attacks on Judaism that were being read by Russians, Ukrainians, Belorussians, and others could not but create negative images of Jews in general, whether or not they practiced their historic faith. Though much of the literature was written by people with obviously Jewish names—Belenky, Gulevich, Shakhnovich—non-Jewish "specialists" in Judaism used the genre as an officially sanctioned means of promoting outright anti-Semitism. The most notorious example is the book *Iudaizm bez prikras* (Judaism Without Embellishment), by Trofim Kichko, published in 1963 by the Ukrainian Academy of Sciences in 12,000 copies. The inside blurb, presumably written by the publishers, sets the tone when it states, "Judaism . . . incorporated and condensed all that is most reactionary and against humanity in the writings of present-day religions." Particularly galling were the many caricatures in the book which, while themselves reminiscent of Nazi anti-Semitic propaganda, explicitly linked Jews and Nazis as collaborators.

Kichko quoted from Karl Marx's essay "On the Jewish Question," usually a source of embarrassment to Marxists, in order to "prove" that "The entire Judaic religion is the translation of trade and commerce into the language of religion." Hypocrisy and bribery were said to be admissible in Judaism, as are "contempt and even hatred" for non-Jews. Foreign protest against the publication of such a diatribe brought mild criticism by the party Central Committee's Ideological Commission, which pointed to "erroneous statements" which "might offend the feelings of believers and might be interpreted in the spirit of anti-Semitism."

Wedding ceremony in Riga, 1965. CREDIT: Kalman Shaltuper.

The last synagogue in Lvov, Ukraine, turned into a club. PHOTO: Jacob Roth.

Odessa cemetery, 1956. This man recited prayers for the dead (*El moleh rakhamim*) for those who do not know the prayers themselves. PHOTO: Jacob Roth.

Sforim (religious books) in the synagogue in Kiev. CREDIT: Washington Committee for Soviet Jewry.

Entrance to a Jewish cemetery in Odessa.
PHOTO: Jacob Roth.

Minsk cemetery, with a traditional gravestone (Batia Ovseevich, daughter of a rabbi, died in 1917), next to a pile of gravel with a bulldozer in the background, apparently about to uproot the cemetery.
PHOTO: Jacob Roth.

Synagogue scene, Sukkoth, 1972, in Moscow.

Sign in the Minsk synagogue begging Jews to attend services in order to allow mourners to say Kaddish—if they do not come, the only synagogue in Belorussia will be closed. "Let us not allow that to happen." CREDIT: Washington Committee for Soviet Jewry.

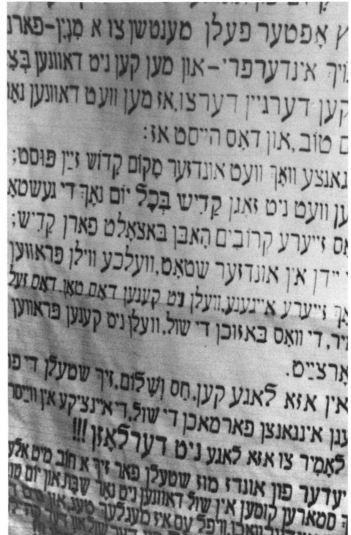

A small-town rabbi, Kiev region, 1969. PHOTO: Gennadi Smolyansky.

However, the commission hastened to say, the question of anti-Semitism "does not and cannot arise in our country." While Kichko was silenced for a while, he reappeared a few years later as an anti-Zionist and atheist propagandist.

More than fifty synagogues (and thousands of churches) were closed down in this period, mostly in the Slavic republics. The closures followed a consistent pattern, making it obvious that a campaign was being directed "from above." Exposés would appear in the local press "revealing" that the synagogue was a "nest of speculators," a place where Israeli diplomats "peddled their Zionist propaganda," where disgraceful fights broke out, and where "dirty dealings" played a much more important role than worship of the Lord. Then "indignant citizens" with obviously Jewish names—including "repentant" former worshipers—would write letters to the editor demanding that the synagogue be closed. Naturally, the authorities hastened to accede to the wishes of the "broad masses."

In the early 1960s the baking of *matza* for Passover was virtually banned all over the country, and other religious observances were hampered as well. Vigorous protest from abroad and the shipment of *matzot* from there, usually confiscated by the authorities, caused the regime to relent somewhat. By 1964 religious congregations in several major cities were permitted to resume the baking of *matzot*.

THE ECONOMIC TRIALS

In the early 1960s Khrushchev mounted a campaign against economic crimes, possibly out of a desire to reduce the flagrant cheating that had begun under Stalin as a matter of self-preservation—if you couldn't fulfill the plan, you had better fiddle with the figures—and had become at least partially routinized and institutionalized. "Anti-parasite" laws were passed and the death penalty was attached to conviction for certain crimes. Wide publicity was given to cases of economic crime, presumably for the didactic purpose of exposing the evils involved and deterring others from similar practices. Any Soviet reader would have been struck immediately by the extraordinary prominence of Jews in these cases. The Jewish character of their names was stressed— Ber Peisakhovich Frid, Leib-Khayim Yudovich Dynov, Abram Moiseevich Kantor, etc.—so there would be no mistaking their nationality. The stereotype of the Jewish speculator was not unknown to Soviet peoples, and the message was quite clear: Jews are heavily involved in speculation and are thereby making economic gains at the expense of others and the state. Over 400 trials for economic crimes which involved Jews prominently were reported in the press of several republics. Bribery, embezzlement, falsifying records, and foreign-currency speculation were the most frequent charges. The familiar themes of links to foreigners, Israeli diplomats, and the synagogue were often raised, further highlighting the distinctively Jewish character of these odious, anti-Soviet practices. Of the 117 people sentenced to death in the 512 trials analyzed in the Pinkus study, 91 (78 percent) were Jews. True, Jews were prominent in bookkeeping, retail trade, and the service sector—areas of the economy where hanky-panky was especially likely to occur—so that one might explain away the unusually high proportion of Jews arrested. But why was their proportion among those executed so much higher?

Evgeniia Evel'son, a defense attorney and highly placed teacher of law, analyzed 440 trials (1961–1967) in which 1,676 Jews were in the dock. Most of the cases involved embezzlement, bribery and currency speculation being the other two major categories. Of the Jewish defendants, 163 were shot, 801 got ten years' imprisonment, and 712 got ten to fifteen years. After examining hundreds of cases in detail—and she was professionally involved in several of them—Evel'son concludes dryly that "the principle of equality of all citizens before the law was violated. . . . The law punished Jews and non-Jews differently."[27]

ISRAEL AND ZIONISM

In 1955 Czechoslovakia signed an agreement with Egypt whereby this Soviet client state would provide substantial amounts of weapons to the major Arab country, led by Gamal Abdel Nasser. This was a turning point in Soviet policy toward the Middle East. It signified that the USSR was betting on a rising tide of Arab nationalism to sweep away British and American interests in the region. When Britain and France tried to halt Nasser's nationalization of the Suez Canal, and Israel joined in their attack because Egypt had closed off the canal to Israeli shipping and had permitted terrorists to cross from Egypt to Israel, the Soviet Union condemned all three countries and strongly supported the Egyptians. Soviet backing for the Arab cause grew as Khrushchev revised Stalin's "two camp" theory of international relations, which assumed that countries must be in either the socialist or capitalist camp, leaving no room for neutralism. Khrushchev now proposed that in the nuclear age, all-out war between the two camps would be catastrophic for all and that the former colonies emerging into independence, including Arab states, could not be forced to choose immediately between the two camps. They constituted a third camp for whose allegiance the socialist and capitalist worlds would compete politically, ideologically, and economically. The Arab nations of the Middle East were major prizes in the socialist-capitalist competition and the Soviet Union was going to try to win their allegiance.

One of the consequences of this commitment was a deterioration in Soviet-Israeli relations and an acceleration of anti-Israel and anti-Zionist messages in the media. Israel was accused of going over to the side of "imperialism," of seeking to acquire territory from her neighbors and expand her influence in Africa. Israel's socialist claims were ridiculed. She was depicted as a tool of "American imperialism" and "West German revanchism." Israeli diplomats accredited to the USSR, who tried to visit as many Jewish communities as they could, were accused of spreading Zionist propaganda and even recruiting Soviet Jews for purposes of espionage. Several diplomats were declared *persona non grata*. Soviet Jews who had contacts with them were often questioned and warned by the secret police, and a few were brought to trial on charges of having acted as Israeli agents. Indeed, Israeli diplomats and tourists did try to establish contacts with Soviet Jews, especially because they could sense a great deal of interest in Israel on the part of Jews of all ages. Concerts by visiting Israeli performers drew overflow audiences; visiting athletes were mobbed by people eager just to touch them or shout a hurried "Shalom" and melt back into the crowd; Israeli tourists were questioned

Unidentified Zionist political prisoners, 1963.

Elderly Jew and Soviet soldiers greeting Israelis at the 1957 international youth festival in Moscow.

Susanna Petchura, sentenced in 1952 to twenty-five years of forced labor for having been a member of an underground Zionist organization. The photograph was taken in 1955 at a camp in Mordovia where she was doing agricultural work.
CREDIT: Maia Ulanovskaia.

intensively about life in the Jewish state. Emotions that had to be suppressed during the "Black Years" came to the surface in the more relaxed atmosphere of the post-Stalin era. In 1957 an Israeli delegation participated in an international youth festival in Moscow. One participant described some of his encounters with a broad range of Moscow Jews: from people who could tell him the previous year's statistics from the Bank of Israel, to those who could not say a word in a Jewish language but wanted just to touch his hand; from a long letter written in elegant archaic Hebrew by a bearded old man who passed it to him, to a small scrap of paper thrust into his hand by a teenager, which read: "My name is . . . I want to learn Hebrew. Help me. Mama and I want to go to Israel. Good-bye, dear brothers. We are proud of you."[28]

In that same year, 1957, the gates of the USSR opened just slightly. As part of the political changes which brought Wladyslaw Gomulka to power in Poland, Soviet citizens who had been Polish citizens before 1939 were allowed to "repatriate" to Poland, something that had been permitted in 1945–1946 as well. It is estimated that as many as 30,000 Jews who were former Polish citizens, their spouses, and their immediate families took advantage of this to leave the USSR. Most used Poland as a revolving door, staying there only briefly and then continuing on to Israel, the United States, and other countries. This gave some hope to the minority of Soviet Jews who dreamed of emigrating to Israel. In the decade 1954–1964, only 1,452 Jews left the USSR directly for Israel. Several times Khrushchev, when pressed by foreign reporters and officials, denied that there were significant numbers of Jews who wished to go to Israel. "There are no files at our Ministry of the Interior with applications from persons of Jewish nationality or other nationalities who wish to emigrate to Israel. On the contrary, we have many letters from Jews in Israel, applying to us with the request to permit them to return from Israel to their homeland, the Soviet Union."[29]

The reality was that the national consciousness of part of Soviet Jewry had been aroused by limited exposure to Israelis and other foreign tourists, growing interest in Western Europe and North America in the condition of Soviet Jewry, and a greater sensitivity by Soviet leaders to world opinion. While some were contemplating what seemed to be the remote possibility of leaving for Israel, the majority were trying to establish themselves in the sectors still open to Jews. Though there was no public announcement, it was clear to all that certain hierarchies were no longer accepting Jews.

They could no longer think of making careers in the party, government, police, diplomatic, or military sectors. Their opportunities seemed to lie in science and technology, the retail and service sector, and to a more limited extent, in the professions.

The constriction of opportunity for Jews, a sharp reversal of the situation in the 1920s, probably resulted from a paradoxical combination of the remnants of the Stalinist mentality along with a profound change in the nature of the Soviet system and the outlook of its leaders. Stalin's suspicion of Jews as disloyal carried over beyond his death and was reinforced by the obvious interest in and sympathy for Israel displayed by large numbers of Jews. As Soviet and Israeli interests continued to diverge, their attachment to Israel became less tolerable. On the other hand, the new generation of leaders were not the Leninist internationalists who had dreamt of world revolution and the abolition of all states, but rather those who had been propelled into leadership positions as young men by the purge of their predecessors. They had come to political maturity under Stalin's regime of "socialism in one country." Their mentality was shaped by the xenophobia and chauvinism of the 1940s and 1950s, not the cosmopolitan atmosphere of the revolutionary period. Khrushchev, who had not traveled abroad until he rose to the top leadership, was a good representative of this generation, coming out of the peasantry and proletariat rather than the intelligentsia. Of course, Khrushchev's personal views of Jews must also be taken into account in analyzing the policies of the period. In an interview in 1958, he lamented the fact that the Jews had not settled Birobidzhan in large numbers, explaining it by the "historical conditions" that made Jews shun "mass professions" such as building or metallurgy. (He was apparently unaware that there was a disproportionately high number of Jewish workers and technicians precisely in these fields in the 1920s and 1930s.) "They do not like collective work, group discipline. . . . They are individualists. . . . Jews are essentially intellectuals. . . . As soon as they are in a position to, they want to go to university. . . . Their interests are too diverse. . . . The Jews are interested in everything, study everything deeply, discuss everything and finish by having profound cultural differences."[30]

In May 1956 Khrushchev granted an interview to a French socialist delegation. Questioned about the situation of the Jews, he revealed what was perhaps the underlying reason for their exclusion from sensitive posts: "At the beginning of the revolution we had many Jews in leading party and government organs. Jews were perhaps more educated, more revolutionary, than the average Russian. After that we formed new cadres. . . . [Pervukhin interjects] Our own intelligentsia. [Khrushchev]: If Jews were now to occupy the leading posts in our republics, this would of course arouse unhappiness among the indigenous population. . . . But we are not anti-Semites. . . . We fight against anti-Semitism."[31]

In his memoirs Khrushchev takes pains to describe his feelings of revulsion at pogroms he observed in his childhood and at blatantly anti-Semitic acts by his colleagues and subordinates in the Communist Party in the Ukraine. He describes instances of Stalin's anti-Semitism and admits that after his death "we arrested the spread [of anti-Semitism] a bit, but only arrested it. Unfortunately, the germs of anti-Semitism remained in our system, and apparently there still isn't the necessary discouragement of it and resistance to it."[32]

It may well be that Khrushchev sincerely thought of himself as free of anti-Semitism, but the phrase in his interview with the socialists, "we formed new cadres," reflects a sense of the Jews' being alien, not "our own intelligentsia," as his colleague Pervukhin put it. Anti-Semitism, especially in its physical and grossly manifest forms, was loathsome to him, but he still regarded the Jews as not "our own." They did tend to be individualists and intellectuals, not easily assimilated, often not "team players." Moreover, Khrushchev recognized that anti-Semitism was deeply ingrained in Soviet society and accepted it as a "fact of life"; he was unwilling to pay the political and social costs of combatting it and trying to uproot it. Given the realities of anti-Semitism and what he discerned as "Jewish characteristics," Khrushchev pursued policies that would not antagonize the population and would not allow the "Jewish traits" to disturb the system. On the other hand, where those traits could be useful— in science and technology, for example—some place could be found for Jews.

This ambivalence toward the Jews meant that while there were no violent national campaigns against them, neither could their presumed traits be ignored. They were no longer seen as equal members of society, but as a tolerated marginal group, excluded from much of the mainstream and best relegated to sectors where they could make some particular contribution and not harm the overall Soviet cause.

CHAPTER SIX

SOVIET JEWS, 1967–1987:
TO REFORM, CONFORM, OR LEAVE?

The removal of Khrushchev by his erstwhile political protégés and subordinates in October 1964 did not immediately affect Soviet Jewry. The new party leader, Leonid Brezhnev, had made no public statements about Soviet Jewry, and seemed content to maintain the status quo in policy. In a speech in Riga in 1965, Chairman of the Council of Ministers Alexei Kosygin did refer in passing to anti-Semitism, along with nationalism, racialism, and "great-power chauvinism," as "absolutely alien and contradictory to our world view." In an interview with a foreign correspondent a year later he denied the existence of anti-Semitism in the USSR, but said that "if some families wanted to meet or wanted to leave the Soviet Union, the road is open to them, and no problem exists here."[1] This remark caught the attention of some Soviet Jews, especially in Latvia and Lithuania, who had long thought about leaving for Israel. Indeed, while in the last year of Khrushchev's rule only 539 visas were issued for emigration to Israel, in 1965 there were 1,444, and in the following year, 1,892. As word spread about departures for Israel, more people began to consider it as a realistic possibility. At first it seems that they were mainly Zapadniki who had been involved with Zionist movements before the war and those who had close relatives in Israel. But there were larger trends developing which were to widen substantially the circles of those who would seriously consider leaving the USSR for Israel.

Khrushchev had allowed fresh breezes to invigorate the cultural atmosphere grown stale under the deadly conformity imposed by Stalin. Beginning with Ehrenburg's novel *The Thaw*, which gave its name to the immediate post-Stalinist period, some Soviet writers began to write more critically about their own society. Aleksandr Solzhenitsyn's *One Day in the Life of Ivan Denisovitch*, whose publication was permitted because it served Khrushchev's de-Stalinization campaign, gave a shocked Soviet public a glimpse of the world of the GULAG labor camp system. Even the taboo subject of anti-Semitism had been addressed by Yevtushenko's poem "Babi Yar." Soviet artists experimented in ways that sometimes aroused Khrushchev's ire, "daring" plays were mounted in several theaters, and Dmitri Shostakovitch, who had run afoul of Stalin's ideological vigilantes, was not only able to resume an active composing career, but incorporated Yevtushenko's "Babi Yar" in his thirteenth symphony. In 1966 the authorities caught up with two writers who had written pseudonymously and whose works had been published abroad, some of which were smuggled back into the country and others broadcast by foreign radio. Andrei Sinyavsky had written a trenchant critique of the official esthetic, "socialist realism," and satires on other aspects of Soviet life. Yuli Daniel had written in the same vein. Sinyavsky used the Jewish-sounding pseudonym "Abram Tertz" and Daniel was the son of the Soviet Yiddish writer Daniel Meerovich. Their arrest and trial in February 1966 marked out the limits of official tolerance of heterodox ideas in literature, and by implication, in other fields as well. Jews and others who had hoped that the trends begun under Khrushchev would continue and accelerate correctly interpreted the Sinyavsky-Daniel trial as a strong signal that the reins were being tightened and that there was no reason to expect a fundamental change in the cultural sphere.

Several types of dissident movements emerged parallel to and intertwined with the relaxation in culture. Some of the nationalities—Crimean Tatars, Germans, Ukrainians, Lithuanians, Jews, and even Russians—had begun to express their grievances. There were also groups which proposed political changes for the system as a whole, ranging from a return to a more "Leninist" socialism to the abolition of socialism altogether, and from the introduction of a full range of civil liberties to demands that Stalinist methods and principles be restored. The government was experimenting with economic reforms along the lines proposed by Prof. Evsei Lieberman. Jews were quite prominent among those who advocated democratization and liberal political reform. Such groups were composed largely of the urban intelligentsia, among whom the proportion of Jews was high. Moreover, as "marginals" in Soviet society, Jews were able to view the system from a perspective more removed and critical than that of others. Just like the Jewish revolutionaries half a century before, they were neither well established within a Jewish culture and community nor well integrated into the Russian society whose culture they had adopted. The illusions of full integration had been dispelled during the 1940s, reinforced by Khrushchev's view of Jews as not quite "ours."

Jews such as Alexander Ginzburg, Pavel Litvinov, Petr Yakir, and Mikhail Agursky sought once again to improve the society in which they lived so that it would conform to the old ideals and would provide a more secure home for themselves and all other nationalities. Arrests of dissidents and constant harassment by the KGB (secret police) persuaded some that their cause was probably hopeless and that the Soviet system was unlikely to change through initiatives from below. If that were true, a logical alternative was to give up on that system and try to leave it. Until the late 1960s the only way to do that would be "internal emigration," what Americans of the time would have called "dropping out" into private worlds—esoteric hobbies, religion, total involvement in non-ideological vocations and avocations. The modest emigration that had begun around 1965 offered Jews a possible new avenue of leaving the system, though it entailed abandoning one's birthplace, culture, social circles, and possibly family.

THE SIX-DAY WAR AND SOVIET JEWRY

The June 1967 war between Israel and several of her Arab neighbors was a catalyst that, for many, speeded up the growth of their Jewish national consciousness and, simultaneously, disillusionment with their position in Soviet society. The war spurred others to think for the first time of their Jewish identity and their status in the Soviet system. First came the shrill Arab propaganda before the war, echoed in the Soviet media, which painted the "Zionists" in the blackest terms and confidently predicted their crushing defeat. A second holocaust seemed to be within the realm of possibility, and not even the most assimilated Jew could remain indifferent to that. Then came the realization that their own government was unequivocally supporting those whose declared intention was to "throw the Jews into the sea." The Soviet government was supporting such rhetoric not merely with political backing but with the weapons that could accomplish this aim. "Until June 1967 Soviet Jews had illusions about co-existence with the regime, despite the fact that it wanted to destroy the Jews spiritually. But suddenly they realized that the Soviet government identifies itself with those who wish to destroy the Jewish state. . . . Russia spat on the Jewish people 'and then we knew that we would never be able to live under such a regime.'"[2]

Сионистский тенетник

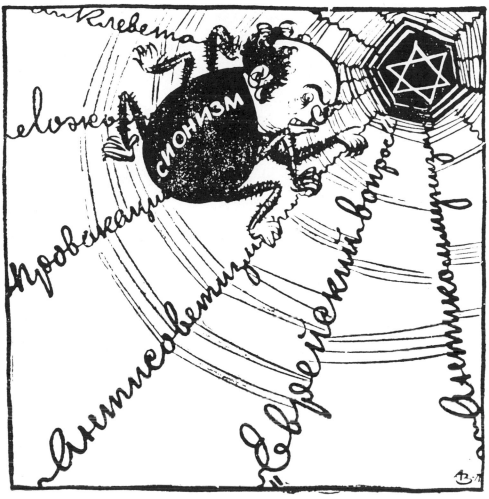

За любимой «работой».   Рис. А. Зенина.

The media attack on Zionism did not differentiate between the Zionists and Jews. Caricatures portrayed Zionists with the traditional figures of Jewish stereotypes. Thus even anti-Zionist Jews could not but feel uncomfortable during the constant bombardment in the press and on radio and television. The massive purges of Jews in Poland in 1968, and their subsequent exodus, showed where "anti-Zionist" campaigns could lead.

The stunning Israeli victory, accomplished within six days, came as a shock to those who had been following the Soviet media, although many Jews followed the events on foreign radio broadcasts, including Israeli ones. The impact of the Israeli victory was great throughout the world, nowhere more so than in the USSR, where the public was stunned by it. One emigré, calling it a "spiritual blast," commented that "The Soviet inheritors of Russia's . . . military glory had been preparing their Egyptian clients for an invasion of a remote, tiny patch of semi-desert, sparsely inhabited by freaks. . . . Nothing was believed to be funnier than a Jew

"The Zionist Spider," *Sovetskaia Moldavia*, August 27, 1971. The webs of the spider say "slander, lies, provocation, anti-Sovietism, Jewish question, anti-Communism."

Американский обозреватель Сайрус Сульцбергер писал в «Нью-Йорк таймс»: «Между Израилем и Южно-Африканской Республикой существует чрезвычайно тесное, хотя и малоизвестное, партнерство».

●

НА ДОЛЛАРОВОЙ ЦЕПОЧКЕ...

Рис. В. КОНСТАНТИНОВА.

"On the Dollar Chain," *Gudok*, August 4, 1973. The caption reads: "The American commentator Cyrus Sulzberger wrote in the *New York Times*: 'There is a very close, though little-known, partnership between Israel and South Africa.'" On the figure's chest are the words "international Zionism."

forced to fire a rifle."[3] If the Soviet media insisted on identifying Zionists and Israelis with all Jews, many Soviet Jews did the same—and with pride. One teenager now living in Israel, recalls:

> As kids . . . we used to shoot down birds. . . . That poor little dead bird we used to call *zhid* [kike]—yes even the Jewish boys did this. . . . We didn't stop to think that we ourselves were calling that miserable, helpless creature by the name we hated . . . that's how cowardly and helpless we had been. And all of a sudden when the Six Day War was over . . . we Jews realized that we didn't have to be like that . . . bird. We saw that there could be a different kind of Jew who was able to live like a human being.[4]

The Israeli victory affected all Jews, and in various parts of the country groups of Zionists began to gather. In the Baltic republics some of them had been Zionists before the Sovietization of their lands, or were the children of such people. In Moscow, Leningrad, Kiev, Odessa, Kharkov, Minsk, and other cities most of the Zionists were purely "Soviet products," younger people who had either come to Zionism from political and cultural dissidence or had become nationally conscious Jews because Soviet conditions had made them such.

Ever since the decline and later suppression of Yiddish culture—and perhaps since the suppression of traditional and Hebrew culture—the Soviet Jew had been placed in an intrinsically anomalous position. On the one hand, Jews are identified as a nationality group and registered as such on their internal passports. They are also regarded as a group apart by the rest of the population. On the other hand, they are progressively losing their distinct culture. Though they might retain particular styles of living, social and educational characteristics, and values, they are assimilating linguistically, and have no Jewish schools, significant newspapers, magazines, or other appurtenances associated with national cultures, even in the Soviet Union. Thus they are Russians (or Georgians, Ukrainians, etc.) culturally, but Jews legally and socially. Contrary to Lenin's expectations that Jews would melt rapidly into other nations, Soviet Jews today are acculturated but not assimilated, because while for the most part they have lost their Jewish culture, they have not lost their Jewish identity. Many Soviet Jews in the 1930s and 1940s had tried to reconcile the contradiction between Jewish identity and non-Jewish culture by relinquishing their identity. The "Black Years" taught them that this was not feasible. In the late 1960s and thereafter, many tried to recapture their culture rather than give up their identity. They began with efforts to revive Jewish culture within the USSR, but they quickly perceived the powerful limitations on such efforts. After 1967 they concluded that genuine Jewish culture and positive Jewish identity were possible in Israel, the Jewish state, and not in the place of their birth.

For some Jews, Jewish identity is a matter of indifference; for many others it is a source of shame and embarrassment, a mark of Cain carried for life. Two young Jews from Riga describe their experiences in the first grade. Yosef Mendelevitch, later imprisoned for trying to leave the country illegally, describes how he felt as the only Jew in a class of forty. He waited "like a hunted animal" as the teacher went around the room asking students their nationality. "'Jew,' I breathed with effort. The whole class burst into laughter. From that point I no longer grew up like an ordinary Soviet citizen and I did not like the Soviet Union."[5] Alla Rusinek, the daughter of Zionist leader Ezra Rusinek, one of Mendelevitch's mentors in Zionism, describes her dread each year when on the first day of school each child had to announce his or her name, nationality, and father's occupation. "She asks my nationality and then it begins. The whole class suddenly becomes very quiet. Some look at me steadily. Others avoid my eyes. I have to say this word . . . which sounds so unpleasant. Why? There is really nothing wrong with its sound, *Yev-rei-ka*. But I never heard the word except when people are cursing somebody. . . . Every time I try to overcome my feelings, but each year the word comes out in a whisper: *Yev-rei-ka.*"[6] Some children learned early on that they were quite different from all the rest, and that that difference was not in their favor. For others the awakening came later—when denied entrance to a university for which they qualified, or for a job for which they had all the credentials, or a promotion, or a trip abroad. Twenty years earlier they would have accepted their fate with resignation, but in the 1960s many were determined not to reconcile themselves to such treatment. During the campaign against "rootless cosmopolitans" the best people could do, even highly placed ones, was to make themselves as inconspicuous as possible. In a time when terror had receded, some reacted by taking the chance and asserting themselves rather than hiding. Parents of young militants sometimes looked with dismay at the younger "generation which knew not Joseph," but they also felt a twinge of admiration for their assertive children.

The Six-Day War did not by itself bring about the changes in Soviet Jewry. About a decade before, several of the leading Zionist activists in the Baltic had begun to create a new mood of national affirmation by forming amateur musical and dance groups. Jews of several generations began to sing in a choir or meet in small groups to learn Hebrew or discuss topics of Jewish interest. Their interest was piqued by visiting Israeli performers or by Soviet singers, such as Nekhama Lifshitsaite, who were allowed to include some Yiddish songs in their repertoires. In the 1960s Jews began to go out to the mass graves of those murdered by the Nazis in order to hold memorial meetings. At first attended by only a few dozen, from year to year the commemorations drew larger numbers. People of all ages thus remembered the fate

A memorial meeting in Rumbuli at Simon Dubnow's grave, December 1967. CREDIT: L. Podriachik.

Jews of all ages meeting at mass grave in Panevezys (Ponevezh), Lithuania, in the 1960s. PHOTO: Jacob Roth.

Young people clearing an area in Rumbuli in order to make a monument to Holocaust victims, 1969.

of their fellow Jews and could not help but ponder their own. A different kind of gathering also become popular at about the same time. In the major cities, where at best one synagogue remained open, young people began to congregate on the joyous holiday of Simkhat Torah. They turned it into a social and national occasion, where large numbers of Jews could meet and socialize, exchanging views, information, or simply telephone numbers. They did not come to pray, largely because they did not know how. They were coming together as a community of fate, not one of faith. From time to time some would venture into the synagogue itself, and they began to explore the religious origins of their Jewish peoplehood.

It was about 1968 that Jews in the Slavic republics became aware that some people had been allowed to leave for Israel, and they began to wonder if it would be possible to do the same. A former resident of Kiev describes a man who worked as a butcher by day and played the accordion at weddings and parties at night. He became almost a legend when it was discovered that he got permission to go to Israel.

> The artist-butcher . . . began to go to all the departments . . . and obtained quick permission to go to Israel. I do not know how to explain it. . . . In any case he got his visa and for several days all Jewish Kiev talked only about this. . . . The sensation that this artist made, no matter how you look at it, can only be compared with the sensation from the victory of Israel in the 1967 war. Our artist was only the stone that started the avalanche.[7]

If the Six-Day War supplied the "pull" of immigration to Israel for many, the Leningrad trial in December 1970 supplied the "push" for emigration from the Soviet Union. Eleven people, nine of them Jews, were tried for having planned to seize an aircraft and force it to fly them out of the country. They were arrested before they had made their attempt. Yet they were tried for treason rather than for attempting to cross the border illegally or for illegally seizing state property. Since they were convicted of treason, two of the defendants, Mark Dymshitz and Edward Kuznetsov, were sentenced to death. Yosef Mendelevitch was sentenced to twelve years of "strict regime." It was obvious that the Soviet authorities had chosen to make a test case of this incident, to use it in order to frighten off would-be applicants for emigration to Israel and roll back the rising tide of Jewish national assertion. However, since a trial of nationalist Basques was going on in Spain at the same time and the issue of oppressed national minorities was brought to public attention, the Leningrad trial succeeded only in placing the issue of Soviet Jewry on the international agenda. A transcript of the trial was circulated in *samizdat* and abroad, highlighting the issues involved and drawing the attention and sympathy of many toward the young Jews. Subsequent trials in Leningrad, Riga, and Kishinev served only to dramatize the extent of Soviet Jewry's discontent. Rather than suppressing the Jewish national movement, the trials strengthened it. As one woman explained, "When the first Leningrad trial began . . . we read every word . . . and were ashamed. . . . Here are Jews that don't simply talk about Israel . . . but they *do* something, and are not afraid of the danger and punishment."[8] The thin trickle of applications to go to Israel began to swell into a flood.

The trials had mobilized public opinion in the West, which in turn prompted political leaders there to make representations to their Soviet counterparts. The pressures from Soviet Jews combined with external pressure became effective because Leonid Brezhnev and his colleagues had embarked on a policy of détente. This policy was aimed at gaining Western credits, accelerating trade with the West, and reaching arms control and other kinds of agreements. The Soviet leadership realized that these could be achieved only if American and West European public opinion were not militantly hostile to the USSR. In order to create a propitious climate for the pursuit of its goals, the Soviet leadership decided in early 1971 to allow a limited number of Soviet Jews to leave for Israel. Perhaps they calculated that there were only a few thousand "troublemakers" who could be gotten rid of by emigration. That done, pressure would ease and the nascent movement would die a natural death.

Like the Leningrad trial, this, too, proved to be a miscalculation. "Old Guard" or "classical" Zionists, as they were sometimes called, were joined by younger ones who had been molded by their experiences in the USSR. Former political dissidents also found their way to the movement for emigration, and the dissident movement to some extent served as a model for the Zionists. Yuli Telesin, son of two Yiddish writers prominent in *Sovetish heymland*, noted that "from such as Bukovsky, Litvinov, Grigorenko, Amalrik . . . [dissidents] who had nothing in common with Zionism, I learned how to struggle for my legal right to live in my historic homeland."[9] To be sure, there were differences among the members of what had become a national movement. Some urged cooperation with the democratic dissidents, while others argued that reform of the system was hopeless. Besides, Zionists were to be concerned only with going to Israel. Tactically, they said, cooperation within the dissidents would only make it easier for authorities to portray the *aliyah* (immigration to Israel) movement as anti-Soviet. Other tactical disputes were whether to act strictly within the letter of the law or to engage in activities outside it; whether to confront the authorities head-on or to avoid confrontation as much as possible; whether to renounce Soviet citizenship and declare themselves Israelis or to declare that they had nothing at all against the Soviet system and simply wished to go to their ancestral homeland.

Aliyah activists in Riga, Vilnius, Kiev, Moscow, and Leningrad had been in touch with each other since the late 1960s. Applications for immigration to Israel began coming from all parts of the country. Petitions and manifestoes on the subjects of Jewish cultural rights and the right to emigrate were appearing in Georgia, where entire extended families

Jews departing for Israel from the Riga rail station, spring 1967. CREDIT: Yosef Schneider.

Exit visa of a man who left the USSR in November 1971. CREDIT: National Conference on Soviet Jewry.

The Liubelchik family leaves Riga for Israel, April 1967. CREDIT: Yosef Schneider.

were signing them, as well as in Moldavia, Kazakhstan, Uzbekistan, and Kirghizia. The signatories ranged from unskilled laborers to members of the Academy of Sciences. To the authorities' surprise, the number of emigrés was increasing geometrically. Not having permitted emigration for so long, the Soviets did not realize that, once started, emigration would not wane but grow. Chains of migrants, linked by family and friendship ties, became ever more extended. As the movement out of the country encompassed tens of thousands, it was no longer fed only by ideologically committed Zionists. Emigration became a social pattern, a fashion. As a woman from Kiev put it simply, "everyone was going, so I went too. I was afraid of being alone, without Jews. All the Jews are going, so should I stay behind?"[10]

Of course, far from "everyone" was going. The Soviet government did its best to dampen people's ardor for emigration. Between 1970 and 1974, 134 books sharply critical of Israel and Zionism were published. From 1967 to 1980 at least 2,262 articles on Zionism, Israel, and the situation of Soviet Jews appeared in the Soviet press.[11] These publications condemned Israel and Zionism in the sharpest terms, painting grim pictures of economic hardships, constant war-

Col. and Mrs. Efim Davidovich of Minsk. Davidovich was a decorated war hero whose repeated applications to emigrate to Israel were denied. He died in the Soviet Union. CREDIT: National Conference on Soviet Jewry.

fare, terror, and discrimination against Soviet immigrants. Already in the late 1950s several pamphlets and articles had appeared, written by disappointed Soviet immigrants who had returned to warn their fellow Jews not to go to the "promised land," which was in reality a "Zionist hell." In the 1970s and 1980s the number of such publications rose steeply and they were supplemented by radio broadcasts and television shows. One cannot know how many would-be emigrés were dissuaded by propaganda, how many by fear of punishment for applying or simply reluctance to leave the familiar for the unknown, and how many by objective circumstances, such as age, infirmity, dependence, or family ties. But the number of applicants for *vyzovy*, an invitation from relatives abroad, was far greater than expected by either Soviet authorities or foreigners. Many had assumed that Soviet Jews were so highly acculturated, perhaps even assimilated, that only small numbers, marginal types, would ever think of leaving. Yet by the mid-1970s emigration had become a mass phenomenon, and was paralleled by similar developments among Armenians and Soviet Germans. From the 14,310 Jews who left in 1971, the first year of substantial emigration, the numbers climbed to over 30,000 each in 1972 and 1973, fell in the middle of the decade, but climbed again in 1978 and peaked at over 51,000 in 1979.

At the same time, the number of those refused permission to leave was also growing. If persuasion could not stem the tide, other measures would be devised. The very process of applying to leave is sufficiently complicated and fraught with uncertainty as to present a barrier in itself. Applications to OVIR, the office of visas and registration, must be accompanied by a *vyzov* from a relative abroad; a declaration of intent to leave; an autobiography; character attestation from one's place of employment; permission from one's parents, regardless of the age of the applicant; permission from a former spouse in cases of divorce; a certificate from the house committee in one's residence; copies of all important documents (birth certificates, educational degrees, death certificates of relatives, etc.), and photographs.

But the applicants kept coming. By the mid-1970s emigration of Soviet Jews became a well-publicized item on the agenda of international human rights. The Helsinki agreements in 1975 and the human rights policy of the Carter administration in the United States had raised the salience of the issues and gave legal, moral, and political support to those Soviet Jews who wished to emigrate. The Helsinki accords and at least two other international agreements signed by the USSR provided for free emigration. Soviet authorities were therefore compelled to find indirect ways of restricting emigration. The authorities declared in 1972 that anyone who had received any form of higher education would have to pay back the costs of his or her education, in addition to the passport fee of 300–400 rubles and the 500-ruble fee for the privilege of renouncing Soviet citizenship, which is obligatory for all emigrants. (The average monthly wage in the 1970s was about 150 rubles.) This "diploma tax" was vigorously protested in the USSR and beyond, since it would have effectively barred the emigration of at least one-third of the Jews. The Soviets stopped collecting it, although it remained the law. In 1980 a further provision was implemented restricting the *vyzov* to first-degree relatives (parents, spouse, child). Though this was not formally codified and announced until 1987, it was strictly enforced for seven years before, serving as an effective device for reducing emigration substantially. Many legitimate *vyzovy* never reach their addresses. Even those who have all the necessary documents can be denied permission to leave on the grounds that they possess "state secrets," to which they had access in their work or military service — even if that work or service were performed so long ago as to make their knowledge obsolete. Some are given no reason at all for their refusal and others are simply not answered. By the mid-1980s the number of "refuseniks," those who had been denied permission to leave more than once, was estimated at over 10,000. Another 400,000 or so were said by Israeli authorities to have requested *vyzovy* but had not yet gone through the entire process of application.

In the period 1968–1987, nearly 270,000 Jews, or 12.5 percent of those enumerated in the 1970 census, left the USSR as emigrants. At first nearly all of them immigrated to Israel, but following 1973 a rising proportion chose to immigrate to other countries, primarily to the United States, where about 90,000 have resettled. Israeli authorities and officials of the Jewish Agency, responsible for arranging the transportation of immigrants to Israel, were deeply disturbed by the fact that, beginning in 1977, more than half the emigrants chose not to go to Israel. In the 1980s more than two-thirds "dropped out" at the Vienna transit point and immigrated to North America, Australia, and Western Europe. Israeli and Agency spokesmen tried to blame the "drop-out" trend on the "seductions" offered by American Jewish organizations, especially HIAS, the major agency responsible for Jewish immigrants to the United States. More likely the change in direction by those leaving the USSR was due to the depletion of the reservoir of ideologically committed Zionists by the mid-1970s, as they were the first to leave and were the ones most "pulled" to Israel. Second, over 80 percent of the immigrants to the United States came from the Russian and Ukrainian republics, areas which had been under Soviet rule for five decades or more and where acculturation was far more extensive than in the Baltic or in Georgia and Central Asia. By contrast, more than one-third of those who went to Israel came from the the non-Ashkenazic communities of Georgia, the north Caucasus, and Central Asia, where Jewish traditions are more widely observed, and another third were Zapadniki, also less acculturated than those from the Slavic republics. These groups were more "pulled" to a Jewish state, whereas the third- and fourth-generation Jews from Russia and the Ukraine, who constituted only about a third of the Israeli immigrants, were more "pushed" from the Soviet Union. They chose to go to countries of greater size and more complex economies, where they felt their educational and economic opportunities, and those of their children, would be greater.

The mass emigration reinforced Soviet suspicions that the Jews are fundamentally ambivalent, or decidedly negative, about the Soviet Union. They were confirmed in their belief that Jews ought to be removed to the margins of society because they simply could not be trusted to be loyal citizens. Parallel with the emigration came a sharp reduction, on the order of 40 percent, of the number of Jews admitted to

Alexander Volpe's in-laws in the Soviet Union listening to a cassette tape message from their daughter and family, now living in Chicago. CREDIT: Alexander Volpe.

Alexander Volpe, his wife Julia, and their five-year-old son leaving from Sheremetyevo airport, Moscow, for the United States, 1981. The family is originally from Siaulai (Shavel), Lithuania. They were exiled by the Soviets, and Alexander's father was imprisoned from 1941 to 1955. After his release, the family lived in Siberia. Also in the photograph are relatives of Julia who came to see the Volpes off. CREDIT: Alexander Volpe.

institutions of higher education. After all, why should Soviet institutions train professionals for Israel or the United States? This reduction had a boomerang effect, because many Jews who had no previous intention of leaving concluded that they or their children had no long-term prospects in a system which closed up the only channels of social mobility that remained open in the 1960s. Once again the system alienated its own products.

Some of those refused permission to leave did their best to reintegrate into society. Their efforts were eased somewhat by an apparent moderation of discrimination against Jews seeking higher education in the 1980s. Others began to create a kind of Jewish counterculture, either by choice or because they were deliberately left in a limbo, without employment in their professions. People began to study Hebrew informally but intensively, at first in preparation for *aliyah*, but also as an end in itself. Hebrew had been suppressed during the *Kulturkampf* mounted by the *Evsektsii* in the 1920s, though it was never made "illegal" and is taught in universities in Moscow, Leningrad, and Tbilisi (but only to small numbers of carefully selected students). Hebrew teachers and their students were harassed by the KGB on the grounds that they were engaged in "anti-Soviet activity" (the link between Hebrew and Zionism was appreciated by

Yosef Radomyslsky, Vladimir Kaberman, and Sasha Rozman around a sign announcing Hebrew classes, with the phone numbers of the teachers.
CREDIT: National Conference on Soviet Jewry.

the police as well as by the others). Powerful motivation, determination, talent, and courage enabled the Hebraists, probably several thousand around the country in the 1970s and 1980s, to overcome the lack of textbooks and other materials. The result was that not a few immigrants arrived in Israel with an impressive command of Hebrew. The classes also served to bring Jews together and to give them the tools to delve into classical sources, as well as to communicate more easily with Israelis and other non-Soviet Jews.

Study circles expanded their scope from the Hebrew language to Jewish history and culture. Soviet sources were combed for the few scraps of information they would yield on Jewish history. One Western analysis of history texts used in Soviet elementary and high schools found that hardly any mention was made of Jews in connection with the ancient Near East, medieval and modern European history, or even the history of Russia, Eastern Europe, and World War II. The *Great Soviet Encyclopedia* devoted 117 pages to Jewish history and culture in its first (1932) edition, but only two pages in the 1952 edition.[12] Nevertheless, those with access to better Soviet libraries could sometimes find pre-revolutionary materials, such as the *Evreiskaia Entsiklopediia* published just before World War I, which yielded nuggets of information to be shared with others. One way of doing that was to emulate the dissident movements and produce *samizdat* ("self-published") literature. The *Iton* (Hebrew: newspaper), disseminated in the Baltic, was followed by publications such as *Jews in the USSR*, *Tarbut* (culture), and others. Other publications included over 2,000 petitions and manifestoes regarding Jewish culture and the right to emigrate. These were signed and disseminated in the USSR and the West.

The Soviet Zionists and Jewish activists engaged in political activities as well. In the absence of approved means of making their views and desires known, they courageously organized demonstrations demanding emigration. They even dared to mount a sit-in protest in the Kremlin in February 1971, followed by another one in March involving 156 Jews from eight cities. Militantly confronting successive waves of ever-higher Soviet officials, the demonstrators were finally addressed by Minister of the Interior and member of the party Central Committee Colonel-General Shchelokov. He promised to reexamine their applications for emigration. By June almost all the participants had arrived in Israel. The Soviet minister of the interior had conceded to the Soviet Zionists.[13]

Scientists who were refused emigration permits were usually fired and forced to take menial jobs. This was devastating, not only economically but also professionally and psycho-

A scientific seminar organized by refuseniks. In the audience are, from left, Ilya (Eliahu) Essas and Andrei Sakharov. At the extreme right is Benjamin Fein. Essas and Fein are now in Israel. CREDIT: National Conference on Soviet Jewry.

logically. As the refusenik physicist Alexander Voronel pointed out, referring to the Jews, "Having exchanged their traditions for this one value—education—when they are deprived of it, they are deprived of everything. When intellectuals who have built their lives on professional achievement perceive barriers to their advancement, they find themselves in a crisis that is tantamount to loss of the meaning of life."[14] In order to stay alive professionally they organized scientific seminars among themselves, invited foreign scientists to speak to them, and tried to boost each other's morale and knowledge. Important personalities from other nonconforming movements, such as Andrei Sakharov, also attended such meetings, demonstrating solidarity with colleagues. The atmosphere in these circles was a heady mixture of pride in their self-assertion, belief in the justice of their cause, and determination to see it triumph. This buoyant climate was tempered by uncertainty about their future and painful awareness that arrest, imprisonment, hard labor, and exile were just as likely outcomes of their struggle as emigration.

THE END OF THE ERA OF EMIGRATION

At the end of December 1979 a "limited contingent of Soviet forces" invaded Afghanistan in order to halt political developments there seen as harmful to Soviet interests. Soon there were more than 100,000 Soviet troops engaged in a cruel war with Afghan resisters. The United States reacted by placing an embargo on the shipment of grain to the USSR and cutting back sharply on cultural and trade agreements. The era of détente had ended, and with it, apparently, the era of mass emigration. In 1980 Jewish emigration was cut back by 60 percent, and in the following year again by more than half. From 1983 through 1986 the average annual number of emigrants was just above 1,000, whereas in the 1970s it had been over 25,000. Apparently once Soviet-American relations turned sour, Soviet leaders no longer saw any point in playing up to American opinion by permitting emigration. In the last years of Brezhnev's rule there was a general conservatism and stagnation in politics, culture, and the economy. Brezhnev had stood for "stability of cadres," meaning that officeholders could remain in their positions indefinitely. He himself had lost the vigor of his earlier years, and the country as a whole sank back into conservatism, comfortable for longtime officials and for a leadership increasingly aged and infirm. Disturbances to the system were most unwelcome. When groups were formed in Moscow, the Baltic, the Ukraine, Georgia, and elsewhere in order to check on Soviet compliance with the Helsinki agreements, they were broken up by the authorities. One member of the Moscow group, Anatoly Shcharansky, was particularly obnoxious to them because he was also a Jewish emigration activist and an articulate and popular spokesman for both causes to Western press representatives in the Soviet capital. A fellow Jewish "activist," who was actually cooperating with the KGB, reported that Shcharansky was working for American intelligence. Shcharansky was arrested in 1977 and tried for treason. Despite a public statement by Amer-

Alexei Magarik and Aryeh Volvovsky entertaining, Sukkoth, 1978. CREDIT: National Conference of Soviet Jewry.

ican President Jimmy Carter that Shcharansky was not an American spy, he was held in solitary confinement for sixteen months and then sentenced to thirteen years' imprisonment. His wife, Avital, who was allowed to leave the USSR the day after their marriage, began a tireless international campaign to free her husband.

In 1980 Yosef Mendelevitch, last of the nine Jewish defendants in the Leningrad hijacking trial, was released and arrived in Israel. At same time, however, new Zionist activists were being arrested on charges such as "slandering the Soviet Union," "hooliganism," possession of drugs, forgery, and draft evasion. Ida Nudel, known for caring for these "prisoners of Zion" and their families, displayed a sign asking to be allowed to join her sister in Israel. For that she was sentenced to four years of exile in a remote area in extremely primitive conditions. When she was released she was forced to live in the small Moldavian city of Bendery

LEFT: Ida Nudel, who helped many refuseniks before her own exile. Upon release, she was forced to live in the provincial Moldavian city of Bendery, until allowed to emigrate in 1987. CREDIT: National Conference on Soviet Jewry.

RIGHT: Yosef Begun in exile. CREDIT: National Conference on Soviet Jewry.

and was still denied permission to emigrate. Yosef Begun, who taught Hebrew to many who themselves became Hebrew teachers, was sentenced three times, the last time in 1983 for "anti-Soviet agitation and propaganda." He was given seven years in a labor camp and five years of exile following that.

Such actions and the severe curtailment of emigration visas discouraged new applicants for emigration, but committed activists, bolstered by visits from foreign tourists and radio broadcasts that told of efforts being made on their behalf, did not give up the fight. In 1984, 200 Jews in eleven cities participated in a hunger strike to protest arrests of Hebrew teachers and other activists, among them Yuli Edel-

Departure of a refusenik from the airport in Moscow. Among those gathered are Anatoly Shcharansky (front row, second from left), now in Israel, and Vladimir Slepak (second row, fifth from left), who was allowed to emigrate in late 1987. CREDIT: National Conference on Soviet Jewry.

shtein and Alexander Kholmiansky, on fabricated charges such as trafficking in drugs and possession of weapons.

In the 1970s the prominent solution to the dilemmas of Jewish identity and culture was emigration. In the 1980s, when this option was practically closed, new directions in Jewish identity and culture were sought. As a prominent Soviet ethnographer has noted, "The 'grounds' for national identification change, but people continue nevertheless to identify themselves with some national group, and as their general competence and knowledge grows, they do so even more freely. . . . Thus, the objective base of national self-awareness does not disappear, it simply changes. Indeed, the foundations for its continued growth expand."[15] In fact, many nationally conscious Jews came to the conclusion that all of Jewish culture was ultimately rooted in religion. To understand Jewish culture and history, one had to go back to the sources and confront religion.

A second source of the religious impulse was the closing down of emigration. Energies that were earlier devoted to demonstrations, sit-ins, petitions, and jumping through the bureaucratic hoops of the emigration process were directed toward study and the exchange of ideas and knowledge. It is as if Jews who could not emigrate abroad were once again moving toward "internal emigration." If one's Jewish life could not be lived in Israel, at least for the moment it could be put together in an alternative community within the USSR. Great ingenuity and devotion were required to set up study circles, provide kosher meat, and arrange for prayer and the fulfillment of other *mitzvot* (religious commandments). The newly religious, mostly young, number perhaps only in the

Ilya (Eliahu) Essas, now in Israel, teaching two young men in Moscow. CREDIT: Washington Committee for Soviet Jewry.

Lighting Sabbath candles in the home of Yuri Shpeizman, Leningrad, 1980. Shpeizman was finally allowed to emigrate in 1987, but died on his way to Israel. CREDIT: Rita Levin.

Hanukkah play at the home of Yitzhak Kogan, a leader of the religious refusenik community in Leningrad. The picture was taken in 1985, a year before Kogan and his family arrived in Israel. CREDIT: Rita Levin.

A Passover seder in the Moscow synagogue, 1976. CREDIT: Zeev Vagner.

A family seder in Moscow, 1974, led by ninety-three-year-old Khayim Shneider. Shneider was in the Red Army when the Germans invaded his home in Uman, Ukraine. He later found out that his wife and eight children—another one was in the Soviet paratroops—were hiding at home when the Germans ordered all Jews to assemble. They were betrayed by a neighbor. The soldiers made them dig their graves in their own backyard. The children were severely beaten in sight of their mother, who lost her mind from grief when ordered to bury them alive. The neighbor helped finish off the wounded children. The mother was shot and left sprawled over the mound. Shneider never returned to Uman and settled in Kharkov. In 1974 he suddenly appeared in Moscow and asked his relatives to gather for a seder "because you people have never seen a proper seder, so before I die I want to show you how to conduct one." At the extreme right is Gary Berkovich, an architect. This was his first seder. He now lives in Chicago. CREDIT: Gary Berkovich.

Purim celebrations in Moscow. CREDIT: Evgenyii and Roza Finkelberg.

At the end of morning services in Kishinev. PHOTO: Brian Blue.

A woman has come to the Odessa synagogue to ask the *shammes* if he will say the Kaddish in memory of her deceased husband and turn on the *yortseit* light. PHOTO: Brian Blue.

Two men pass each other, one leaving the early *minyan* and the other arriving for the later one, Kishinev. PHOTO: Brian Blue.

hundreds, but their visible Jewishness and alternative way of life no doubt have an impact on many others in an officially atheistic society. Even those who are not religious continue to make Simkhat Torah a Jewish national holiday. Purim is an occasion for social gatherings and merry-making, and the old tradition of humorous plays, *Purimshpiln*, has been revived by people whose grandparents and great-grandparents had already abandoned it. Passover *sedarim* are celebrated with gusto, the participants well aware that the themes of exodus, liberation, and entry into the Land of Israel are as relevant to them as they were to their remote ancestors. In Moscow and Leningrad such activities have not been disrupted often, but in other places even such essentially private and nonpolitical ceremonies have been repressed. For example, on March 21, 1986, eight houses in Odessa were raided and the Purim parties being held there were broken up. The same happened in Kishinev. Any activity not organized "from above" makes the Soviet police mind uneasy; and all the more so anything that can be connected with "Zionism."

NEW LEADERS, NEW HOPES

The Brezhnev era ended politically not with his death in 1982, but with the rise of Mikhail Gorbachev to the leadership of the party in March 1985. Gorbachev, the youngest

Soviet leader since Stalin and the youngest member of the Politburo, conducted a peaceful purge of the state and party hierarchies, retiring almost half the government ministers within two years of his attaining office and replacing at least half the provincial party secretaries and many other high party functionaries. But they were replaced by people with very similar backgrounds and training, only younger. Significantly, of more than fifty new ministers appointed, only one was a non-Slav (Foreign Minister Shevardnadze) and not a single Central Asian was given a major post in the central government or party. Over 1,200 officials in Uzbekistan were removed for corruption, and the press portrayed all the Central Asian republics as shot through with corruption. Riots broke out in Kazakhstan when Dinumukhamed Kunaev, an ethnic Kazakh, was replaced as party first secretary of the republic by a Russian. Thus, despite all the talk about *"glasnost"* (openness), "reconstruction," and "democratization," at least in the area of the nationalities Gorbachev was not introducing any liberalizing reforms.

Over the previous twenty years policy toward the Jews had come to be more a function of foreign policy than of nationalities policy, so that Gorbachev's nationalities policy might affect them less than his relationship with the United States and Israel. Tentative probes were extended in the direction of each. Several brief meetings were held by Soviet diplomas with Israeli counterparts; Poland and Hungary opened interest sections in Israel, after having had no diplomatic relations with her since 1967; anti-Zionist propaganda was somewhat toned down; in 1987 almost all Zionist prisoners were released and there was some increase in emigration. Summit meetings with President Ronald Reagan at Geneva and Rejkyavik produced few concrete results, though around those meetings some prominent refuseniks were released, drawing the desired media attention in the West. Anatoly Shcharansky was suddenly released and received a tumultuous hero's welcome in Israel in early 1986. In February 1987, Yosef Begun was released in an amnesty to dissidents, and was finally allowed to emigrate to Israel, as was Ida Nudel. The return of Andrei Sakharov to Moscow from exile in Gorky was perhaps the centerpiece of Gorbachev's attempt to rally the intelligentsia to his side in the battle against the very bureaucracy from which he had come, but which now seemed to be the major impediment to any reforms he would try to implement. All this had no immediate impact on Jewish emigration. Even while internationally known refuseniks were being released, the total number of Jewish emigrants in 1986 was the second lowest in twenty years. On the other hand, there was a significant increase in emigration in the early part of 1987. Also, the replacement of some elderly Jewish cultural figures—curators, librarians, artists—by younger people, usually their students, signalled the intention to maintain the vestiges of an officially approved culture, some of which indirectly aids the Jewish counterculture. For example, books on Israel, though they have a negative slant, do provide some factual information; the synagogues, though closely watched and staffed by a few younger clergymen trained at the Budapest Jewish Theological Seminary (the only such institution in the socialist countries) who cooperate fully with the authorities, still serve as the "Jewish address" for many. The twenty-fifth anniversary issue of *Sovetish heymland* (1986) presented 31 Jewish writers and artists born after 1945. Directors of Yiddish theatrical ensembles in Moscow, Vilnius, Kaunas, and Birobidzhan debated whether or not to introduce Russian dialogue and commentary, thus hinting at the possibility of Jewish culture in the Russian language. So far, then, Gorbachev, aside from a few spectacular, and welcome, gestures, seems to be maintaining the status quo. This leaves the would-be emigrants in limbo. The "silent majority" of Soviet Jews, those who are simply trying to get along as best they can and see their future in the USSR, remain in a continuing state of marginality and uncertainty. Most Soviet Jews are not "refuseniks," though thousands would emigrate if given the chance to apply without repercussions. They would do so not necessarily because they are Zionists or even committed to a distinctly Jewish way of life, but because they seek to join family members or to find economic opportunities. Some seek to escape anti-Semitism or leave a political system they do not support. Others see themselves as well integrated into the Soviet system and have no desire to leave it. Their careers, their friends, and their cultural life are in the USSR, and they are comfortable with them. But even among these types there are those who understand that, however they may think of themselves, much of Soviet society regards them as outsiders.

Years ago the widow of the recently deceased political prisoner Anatoly Marchenko expressed their position most poignantly:

> Who am I? . . . Unfortunately, I do not feel like a Jew. I understand that I have an unquestionable genetic tie with Jewry. . . . A more profound, or more general common bond is lacking . . . community of language, culture, history, tradition. . . . By all these . . . I am Russian. . . . and nevertheless, no, I am not Russian. *I am a stranger today in this land.*[16]

CHAPTER SEVEN

THE "OTHER" JEWS OF THE USSR:
GEORGIAN, CENTRAL ASIAN, AND MOUNTAIN JEWS

The non-European Jews of the Soviet Union constitute less than 10 percent of the total Jewish population. Their history has been different from that of their European co-religionists, as their territories came under Russian rule only in modern times, and even in the Soviet period they have maintained differences in family structure, religious tradition, language, culture, and social structure. While each of the major non-Ashkenazic (non-European) communities—Georgian, Central Asian ("Bukharan"), and Mountain Jews—has a distinct culture and history, they have some common features which set them off from the Ashkenazim. To this day they maintain patriarchal families, especially in rural areas and smaller towns. The head of the family, usually an older man, makes many decisions for all the rest, or at least is consulted about them. The families are both larger and more extended than European ones. Cousins several times removed will know each other, and in Central Asia they are likely to live near each other, even within the same group of connected houses surrounding a courtyard. These patterns and many others are shared with the non-Jewish populations among whom these communities have lived for centuries. Tradition and custom are highly respected, as they are in the Georgian Christian and Central Asian Muslim communities. The kind of collective revolts against tradition represented by the Haskalah, the socialist movements, and the enthusiasm for building Communism that have been observed among the European Jews never appeared in the non-Ashkenazic communities. The one modern movement that did enjoy great popularity was Zionism, especially among the Georgian and Mountain Jews. This exception is explained by the fact that it fit into the religious tradition of praying for a return to Zion, which was always taken seriously by these communities. In the nineteenth century, both independently of the modern Zionist movement and as part of it, Jews from these areas immigrated to the Holy Land, usually settling in Jerusalem, but in some cases founding new agricultural settlements such as Beer Yaakov, established by Mountain Jews.

Before the revolution Jews in all three communities were concentrated in commerce, the artisan trades, and agriculture. They suffered from some of the same economic limitations imposed on European Jews and thus were concentrated in some of the same kinds of professions and vocations. To this day they appear to be well represented in the service and retail sectors in Georgia and Central Asia. Over the years a professional intelligentsia emerged, trained in the institutions of higher education established by the Soviets, although among the Mountain Jews this did not occur to the same extent. Despite their entry into the professions and their climb up the social and political ladders, the non-Ashkenazic Jews have not intermarried with non-Jews to any significant extent. Their attachment to religion and tradition, and the strong sense of ethnicity in the Caucasus and Central Asia generally, held them back from marrying out of the faith. Because only the Mountain Jews suffered very much at the hands of the Nazis, the population of these communities has not declined as rapidly as that of the European communities. Their intermarriage rates are much lower and their fertility rates higher than among the Ashkenazim, though since the 1970s substantial numbers have immigrated to Israel, counterbalancing natural growth.

THE GEORGIAN JEWS

Some hold that Jews first arrived in Georgia, located in the Caucasus Mountains between the Black and Caspian Seas, at the time of the Assyrian conquest of Israel in 722 B.C.E. Others believe that they did not make their appearance until the fourth or fifth century of the Common Era (Jewish tombstones from that period have been found in Georgia). In any case, there has been a Jewish presence there for many centuries. Though they never abandoned Hebrew as the language of prayer and study, Georgian Jews seem to have adopted the Georgian language for everyday affairs long ago, though there are distinctly Jewish traces in their speech and they preserve some archaic Georgian forms. Unlike Mountain and European Jews, Georgian Jews did not experience violent anti-Semitism, except in isolated cases. Georgian Jews maintained unquestioning allegiance to their faith and Jewish peoplehood and simultaneously developed a strong sense of Georgian patriotism. Some Georgian immigrants in Israel maintain an active interest in the welfare and culture of the Georgian republic, and there are active cultural ties between the republic and the community in Israel.

In the 1920s the Georgian Jewish community was greatly impoverished by the radical transformation of the economic system which affected most severely those occupations that were characteristic of Georgian Jews. Most remained petty traders and artisans, though they moved into various sorts of cooperatives. Attempts were made to establish collective farms for Georgian Jews, and by 1936 there were nineteen such *kolkhozy*, but with only 1,376 inhabitants. Zionist activity continued longer among the Georgian Jews than among Europeans, but in the late 1930s some of the most prominent Zionists were arrested and tried for their political activity. Among them was Rabbi David Baazov, whose son, Herzl, was a famous writer. Nor did Georgian Jews escape anti-religious measures, though they managed to hold onto their synagogues and religious schools longer than Ashkenazic Jews. The synagogue is even more central to religious life in Georgia than it is in Europe. For example, circumcision ceremonies, usually conducted at home among Ashkenazim, are held in synagogues among the Georgians. The synagogue has long been a social center as well as a place of religious instruction. The *khacham* (literally, a wise man) has a wider range of functions than the Ashkenazic rabbi, serving also

A wedding in Kutaisi, 1952.
CREDIT: Tsiyon Matsumashvili.

Georgian Jewish women in front of the synagogue in Batumi, 1956. PHOTO: Jacob Roth.

Typical Georgian Jewish couple, Kutaisi, 1920s. CREDIT: Gershon Ben-Oren.

A meeting of Georgian Jewish cooperatives (artels), Borisoglebsk, 1939. CREDIT: Gershon Ben-Oren.

Khacham (Rabbi) Khayim (left) with Rabbi Shlifer, Kutaisi, 1954. CREDIT: Mikhael Mirilashvili.

A Jewish home in Oni. CREDIT: Khayim Khaichiashvili.

Passover seder, Kutaisi, 1956. CREDIT: Tsiyon Matsumashvili.

as a teacher and cantor. When about forty synagogues in Georgia were closed in the 1950s and 1960s, this was a severe blow to the communities. Georgian Jews recall with justifiable pride the incident in Kutaisi in 1952 when the authorities tried to expropriate a synagogue. The community, some 20,000 strong, organized a mass sit-in, placing their bodies in the way of the trucks that had come to take the synagogue's furnishings. Although this was just before the "Doctors' Plot" was "uncovered," and all citizens, let alone

Women's party for a bride, Oni, 1952. Credit: Rivka Shimshiashvili.

The synagogue in Kutaisi, 1949. Credit: Mikhael Mirilashvili.

First group of people from Oni to depart for Israel. CREDIT: Rivka Shimshiashvili.

Jews, would be taking their lives into their hands by such actions, the authorities retreated and the Jews of Kutaisi retained their synagogue and their honor. Until the 1940s Sabbath observance was universal in the Georgian communities, and though in the last forty years this has eroded, Georgian Jews adhere to religious practices more than any other Jewish group in the USSR. In 1960 when many Jews in other parts of the country found it difficult to obtain *matzot*, the synagogue in Tbilisi, the Georgian capital, baked ninety-three tons.[1]

Until 1937 officially Jewish schools existed in Georgia, and until the 1970s one school in Tbilisi carried a Jewish name. Even after Jewish schools formally ceased to exist, the fact that many Georgian Jews concentrated in certain neighborhoods created *de facto* Jewish schools. One young girl, now in Israel, described School Number 67 in Tbilisi:

> This is our school, because only we, students at this school, could eat *matza* and *kharoset* [on Passover] during the ten-minute break, with pride and without hesitation. . . . The non-Jewish students in our school were not afraid to eat *matza* because they could be sure there was no blood of a kidnapped child in it. . . . Only in our school could we discuss Rosh Hashanah and Sukkot without hesitation. . . . Only in our school was it possible to dare tell a teacher, "Teacher, today is Yom Kippur and I will not do any written work." In no other school would they dare. . . .[2]

Of course, anti-religious agitation and propaganda were carried out among Georgian Jews as well. A Jewish historical-ethnographic museum was established by the government in Tbilisi in 1933. Its expeditions gathered about 16,000 Jewish artifacts and 4,000 books from around Georgia with the aim of promoting atheism through lectures and exhibitions that would demonstrate the "reactionary" character of Judaism. The museum's three permanent exhibitions were history, ethnography, and "socialist construction." The director of the Museum, Aharon Kricheli, was a party member, energetic and talented. Nevertheless he was arrested as a nationalist in 1949 and the museum was closed to the public, never to be reopened.[3]

By the 1960s Jews were well established in Georgia. Their economic situation was improved considerably, and they were part of the fabled "second economy" of Georgia which seemed to flout the socialist strictures against private enterprise. Several Jews were highly placed in the republic's state and party apparatuses. Anti-Semitism was not nearly the problem it was elsewhere in the country. Yet Georgian Jews felt the pull of Israel, as they had for centuries. In August 1969 eighteen Georgian families sent a letter to the Human Rights Committee of the United Nations. In simple language

Three men of Batumi who received their visas for Israel, 1973. CREDIT: Rivka Shimshiashvili.

it asked assistance for "eighteen religious Jewish families from Georgia who ask you to help us emigrate and go to Israel, as it is written, 'If I forget thee Jerusalem, let my right hand fail.'" They outlined the history of the Jews and their contributions to world civilization, and stressed that Israel was the culmination of the hopes, not only of the twelve million Jews of the world, but of "those who are no longer here. . . . They are marching together, undefeated and eternal, for they have given us the tradition of struggle and faith. That is why we wish to leave for Israel. . . . We believe our prayers will reach God; we believe our cries will reach people. We are not asking much—only to be allowed to leave for the land of our forefathers."[4]

This was the first collective public declaration in the struggle for emigration. It had a major effect in Israel, where it prompted Prime Minister Golda Meir, a former ambassador to the Soviet Union, to give the first official public Israeli endorsement to the open struggle for *aliyah*.

The Georgian fight for *aliyah* was remarkably successful. Over 30,000 Georgian Jews of a total of 55,000 counted in the 1970 census had reached Israel by 1980. Some see this as a "messianic" immigration, moved by purely religious motivations. More likely, while it draws on age-old yearnings for Zion, for many it is a way of preserving their religious and ethnic identity and solidarity, both of which were beginning to erode under the pressure of secularization and the transformation of the social structure. Georgian Jews fought a successful battle to avoid assimilation, and when they reached Israel they continued to insist on maintaining their distinctive culture and community, adding to the rich mosaic of the Jewish state.

THE JEWS OF CENTRAL ASIA

Jews appeared in Central Asia in ancient times, but the present population, often referred to as "Bukharan Jews" (at one time the center of the Jewish population was in the city of Bukhara in Uzbekistan) began arriving from Parsi-speaking lands in the fourteenth century. Their language is a dialect of Tajik, part of the Iranian language group, and they are concentrated mainly in the republics of Tajikstan and Uzbekistan, both overwhelmingly Muslim. "Judaeo-Persian" (sometimes called Farsi and "Bukharan") was originally written in Hebrew letters, but when the Soviets transferred the Central Asian languages to Latin and then to Cyrillic letters, the Jewish dialect was transferred to

Traditional types of "Bukharan" Jews.

Traditional types of "Bukharan" Jews.

The Bachaev family in Mari,
Turkmenia, 1911. CREDIT:
Mordechai Bachaev.

Simkha and Miriam Pinkhasov,
Samarkand, Uzbekistan, 1930s.
CREDIT: Moshe Pinkhasov.

Miriam Pinkhasov and her
children, 1928. CREDIT: Moshe
Pinkhasov.

The Pinkhasov family, Samarkand, 1931.
CREDIT: Moshe Pinkhasov.

An old woman in traditional dress, Tashkent,
Uzbekistan, 1955. CREDIT: Aaron and Frida
Moshiakhov.

Mordechai Bachaev, member of the editorial
board of *Rushnoi*, the newspaper in Judaeo-
Persian which he is holding, Samarkand, 1928.
CREDIT: Khayim Khaichiashvili.

Funeral in Samarkand, 1978. The men are wearing photographs of the deceased pinned to their chests. CREDIT: Spanel Yitzhakbaiev.

A "letter" written in Judaeo-Persian on a sheet sent by Sarah Yitzhakbaieva to her husband, Michael, imprisoned in 1938. He was serving a term of twenty-five years in prison because he had received a letter from an uncle in Tel Aviv. CREDIT: Spanel Yitzhakbaiev.

Wedding in Dushanbe, Tajikstan, 1980. CREDIT: Spanel Yitzhakbaiev.

Wedding in Dushanbe, Tajikstan, 1980. CREDIT: Spanel Yitzhakbaiev.

Latin but never to Cyrillic, so that the last publication in Judaeo-Persian appeared in the 1940s.

There was a short-lived Jewish theater, cultural clubs, and a historical-ethnographic museum in Samarkand, but the purges of the 1930s repressed Central Asian Jewish culture even before Yiddish culture was stifled in the European USSR. Nevertheless, a strong sense of identity and solidarity remained. Jews tended to live in ethnically homogeneous neighborhoods. The ethnic boundaries between them and the Muslims were quite sharply drawn, so that intermarriage was rare. Though not as devout as the Georgian Jews, Bukharan Jews maintained a strong attachment to religious customs, transmitted down through the generations. The removal of Ashkenazic refugees, including Polish and Lithuanian Jews, to Central Asia during the war brought Bukharan Jewry in contact with knowledgeable Jewish people. In both Georgia and Central Asia the Lubavitcher Hassidic movement tried to provide Jewish education and spiritual sustenance, though most of this had to be done in a clandestine way.

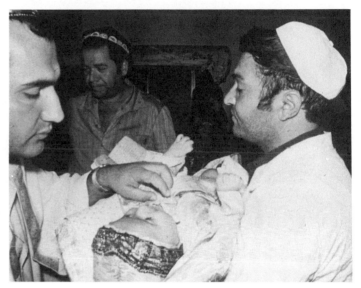

Circumcision ceremony in Samarkand. CREDIT: National Conference on Soviet Jewry.

Bechor and Roza Khanimov, Dushanbe, 1973. CREDIT: Mordechai Bachaev.

A funeral in Central Asia. Men and women sit on different sides of the room, a coffin, with pictures of the deceased, between them. CREDIT: Spanel Yitzhakbaiev.

A Bar Mitzvah in Samarkand, 1979.
CREDIT: Tamara Failaeva.

Dvora Abramovna, Samarkand, 1955.
CREDIT: Moshe Pinkhasov.

Wedding of Yura and Tamara Bachaev,
Dushanbe, 1953. CREDIT: Mordechai Bachaev.

Funeral of Simkha Pinkhasov, Samarkand, 1977. CREDIT: Moshe Pinkhasov.

Jewish cemetery, Samarkand, 1960. CREDIT: Moshe Pinkhasov.

Simkha Pinkhasov's grave. CREDIT: Moshe Pinkhasov.

ABOVE, LEFT: Women with a bride, Tashkent, 1973. CREDIT: Aaron and Frida Moshiakhov.

ABOVE, RIGHT: Tsvia Aminov in national costume, Samarkand, 1969. CREDIT: Tamara Failaeva.

LEFT: Mourners at a funeral, Samarkand, 1974. CREDIT: Frida Aminova.

BELOW: Farewell dinner for Azair Khaimov, departing for Israel, Tashkent, 1971. CREDIT: Aaron and Frida Moshiakhov.

Jews from Central Asia had established a community in Jerusalem in the nineteenth century. To this day one of the neighborhoods of the Israeli capital is known as the "Bukharan quarter." In the early 1970s a significant *aliyah* began to come from Central Asia. By the 1980s over 15,000 immigrants had arrived, a substantial proportion of the estimated 60,000 Central Asian Jews. Like the Georgians, most Bukharan Jews who left went to Israel, though one-third of those leaving Tashkent, the capital of Uzbekistan, did not continue to Israel and immigrated to the United States and, to a lesser extent, Western Europe. In the patriarchal family structure the decision of the head of the family to emigrate often was sufficient to bring along several others, even beyond the immediate family. The post-1967 atmosphere in the Muslim republics was less comfortable for Jews, since many Muslims associated them with Israel, portrayed in the media as an enemy not only of Arab states but also of Islam. There were cases of blood libel accusations, as there had been in isolated instances in Georgia, adding to the tension between Muslims and Jews.

THE MOUNTAIN JEWS

Sometimes called "Caucasus Jews," or "Tats," after the language they speak, these Jews are spread over the north Caucasus in the Daghestani Autonomous Socialist Republic, in the Azerbaijani Republic, and in the Kabardino-Balkar and Chechen-Ingush autonomous republics. They seem to

Writers Itsik Feffer, Avrom Veviorka, Peretz Hirshbein, and his wife, Esther Shumiatcher, visiting Mountain Jews in the Crimea. CREDIT: Joseph Rosen.

A domestic scene in Dzhankoi, Crimea, 1929.

A family in Agricultural Colony No. 36, Crimea. The mother is only fourteen years old. CREDIT: Joseph Rosen.

A Mountain Jew.

Sowing grain in the Smidovich *kolkhoz*, early 1930s. CREDIT: Joseph Rosen.

Capt. Shatiel Semenovich Abramov, Hero of the Soviet Union. Born in Derbent, Daghestan ASSR in 1918, he was drafted into the army in 1941, served on various fronts, and was wounded six times. When his battalion commander was killed in the battle for a fortress in Poznan (Poland), Abramov took command. He scaled the wall and led the way to the conquest of the fortress, for which he received the highest military award. After the war he received a doctorate in geology and mineralogy and worked in the oil industry.

An ensemble of Mountain Jews, 1967. CREDIT: National Conference on Soviet Jewry.

have arrived in the area in the fifth century. Their language, Tat, is an Iranian one. Over the centuries many of these Jews were converted to Islam and some to Christianity. In the Soviet period "Tat" came to mean a nationality, not just a language, and today most of those identified as Tats by nationality are not Jews. Badly treated by Muslims in the nineteenth century, the Mountain Jews evolved a warrior tradition. They sided with the Russian conquerors of the Caucasus, deepening the enmity of their Muslim oppressors. Relations with Muslims were further exacerbated by Mountain Jews' support for the Red Army. One Soviet source asserts that 70 percent of the Red Guard in Daghestan were Jews. In 1926 and 1929 there were serious blood libels against the Mountain Jews. In World War II they were heavily engaged in fighting the Muslim collaborators of the Nazi invaders, and distinguished themselves in the ranks of the partisans and Red Army. The Red Army soldier who planted the Soviet flag on the Reichstag in 1945 was a Mountain Jew.

Mountain Jews have been carpenters, locksmiths, artisans, and peasants. There are few professionals among them, and they are perhaps the least educated and poorest segment of Soviet Jewry. Zionist traditions are strong among them. They were represented at early Zionist congresses, and contributed watchmen to the early Jewish settlements in Palestine. They celebrated the founding of the State of Israel with great enthusiasm and public displays, which cost them dearly; some were taken by the police for interrogation, and imprisoned for having engaged in "anti-Soviet propaganda." In the 1970s over 10,000 Mountain Jews, representing probably one-quarter of the community, immigrated to Israel.

CHAPTER EIGHT

A CENTURY
OF AMBIVALENCE

The last hundred years have been a period of great ambivalence and profound contradictions for the Jews of Russia and the Soviet Union. They have reached heights in Soviet society which could not be imagined before 1917, and they have plunged into even more unimaginable depths as victims of the Holocaust and of Stalin's terror. They have been in the eye of some of the stormiest economic, political, and cultural transformations in history, and they have both reaped benefits and suffered losses from them. Liberated from their state-imposed disabilities by the revolutions of 1917, many Jews became among the most ardent enthusiasts and builders of Soviet socialism, only to find themselves among the most prominent victims of Stalinism. Little wonder that the Jewish minority has brought forth some of the most passionate defenders of the Soviet system as well as some of its most trenchant critics. On whatever side of the barricades Jews stood, they did so with passion and commitment, dedicating themselves unreservedly to the pursuit of their different, and often contradictory, utopias.

Some Jews and Russians saw, and continue to see, the future of Russian Jews in the land of their birth, accepted by the larger society and making important contributions to it. Over the past century many Jews gave all of their energies, and in many cases their lives, to strengthening and improving the country. They were pioneering entrepreneurs before the revolution, building railroads, developing the sugar and textile industries, arranging for foreign loans and trade, linking urban industries with a largely rural population. After the revolution, when their talents and energies could find freer expression, they contributed as planners, workers, administrators, technicians, and managers of Soviet industry. When given the chance, Jews contributed their creative talents to art (Levitan, Chagall, Lissitsky, Antokolsky), literature (Babel, Ilf and Petrov, Mandelshtam, Pasternak), music (Oistrakh, Gilels, Kogan, Kremer), dance (Plisetskaia), the theater (Mikhoels), science and technology (Landau, Gelfand, Gurvich, Luria), and many academic areas. Jewish creative talents had once been channeled almost exclusively into Jewish culture. The flowering of religious culture and of Yiddish and Hebrew literature, as well as of political and social thought, was the result. Perhaps because Jews were confined within their own communities, an intensive Jewish life evolved, suffused with traditional customs, rituals, and values. When cracks developed in the walls holding the Jews back, some eagerly sought to escape into the world beyond, often to be peremptorily rejected, while others preferred to remain within the Jewish environment. Time and again the assimilationists have been rebuffed. Following the pogroms of a century ago, Lev Levanda, who might have been speaking for future generations as well, expressed the pain of Jews who sought to be Russians. "Our best people," he wrote, "have done everything in their power to advance a *merging* in which they saw the most reliable cure for our ills and for the sake of which they were ready even to give up our traditions and social peculiarities. . . . But what can one do if those with whom one so wants to merge shun the merger. . . . with crowbars and clubs in their hands?" Even the Zionists, he claimed, dreamed of an independent Jewish state only because they were driven to despair in the "kingdom of darkness." If conditions were different, Zionists would "join the chorus" and sing "I am a Russian and love my land."[1] A Russian writer marveled at the affection Jews displayed for Russia. "Wherefore should they love Russia, who is so harsh and inhospitable toward them? Strange as it may sound, there are children who love their cruel stepmothers. . . . The Jews love the same Russia that is so cruel to them."[2]

But far from all Jews could ignore the treatment they received. No political system in Russia has been able to change for very long the popular perception of Jews as aliens. Some Jews struggled mightily to change that view, whether by changing themselves or by changing Russia, whereas others accepted this as an immutable fact of life and either tried to get along as best they could or left the country in search of a place where they could feel at home. This century has been framed by the quest for acceptance and by the strategies devised to attain it. But so far, even when Jews have been granted full citizenship and equality under the law, they have not been treated as equals of the national groups who dominate the state. The origins of hostility toward the Jews lay in Christianity, but it was compounded by economic competition and cultural differences. Russian and East European societies have not traditionally been enthusiastic about heterogeneity and cultural pluralism. Many of the peoples in the Russian Empire and its successor states had long-standing disputes over religion, territory, economics, and culture. Mutual suspicion has been the norm. Few of the ideologies that have competed for the peoples' allegiances in the last century have advocated the toleration of diversity in thinking or behavior. The mere fact that Jews differed in religion, speech, social values, even food and dress, was sufficient to make them targets of a hostility born of fear and incomprehension. When they have been welcomed, they have eagerly seized the extended hand and repaid the welcome manyfold. Whether they will be shunned or welcomed in the future remains an open question.

PEERING INTO THE FUTURE

The future of Soviet Jewry will be decided both by official policy and by internal developments within the Jewish population. At present the prospects for change in the Soviet Union are better than they have been in decades, but there is powerful opposition to Gorbachev's proposed reforms, and their fate is highly uncertain. Even if they were to be implemented it is not clear what the consequences would be for Soviet Jews. The extension of *glasnost* could conceivably open up a realistic, frank discussion of the Jewish situation, leading to its amelioration. Thus far, however, *glasnost* has resulted only in the public expression of some Russian nationalist sentiments which, some Soviet commentators have pointed out, are tinged with anti-Semitism. Criticizing the Russian group calling itself "Memory," a Soviet writer observed that their "kind of patriotism turns into nationalism in the twinkling of an eye. Touch the lighted match of anti-Semitism to it, and you will see 'Memory.'"[3] If freedom of expression is truly broadened, once again the voices of anti-Semitism and philo-Semitism will contend for the allegiance of the Soviet peoples.

Perestroika, or reconstruction, is the second pillar of Gorbachev's program. This will be a more difficult goal to achieve than *glasnost*. One structural reform that would signal an important change in policy toward Jews would be the restoration of Jewish schools, institutions not seen anywhere in the country for nearly half a century. This would require no great change in ideology and could be presented as a "return to Leninist norms." No doubt, much of the Jewish population would today prefer to organize their own Jewish educational institutions and would find little attractive in the

Sovietized, de-Judaized Yiddish schools such as existed in their grandparents' time. But whatever gesture the Soviet government might make in this direction would have at least symbolic value and could touch off meaningful changes in Jewish culture, perhaps broadening its conception to allow cultural activity in Russian, Yiddish, or even Hebrew.

One element of *perestroika* being discussed now is to de-emphasize ethnic criteria for admission to higher education, employment, and promotion. The central government and party have been highly critical of the practice, apparently especially prevalent in Central Asia, of reserving places and granting promotions largely on the basis of ethnicity rather than merit. Since Jews are nowhere in their own republic and are everywhere a small minority, the use of ethnic criteria generally works to their disadvantage. Should such criteria be de-emphasized and merit considerations become more important, perhaps more channels will be open to Jews, as they were in the 1920s. However, it may well be that Jewish emigration has permanently limited their chances for mobility, on the grounds that their loyalty is suspect, and that they will remain barred from many "sensitive" areas and impeded from rising above specified levels in others. They are likely to remain a marginal element, regarded by the state as alien and forced to regard themselves the same way.

Whatever their political fortunes, it is quite clear that the Jews will decline in number. Between 1959 and 1979 the number of Jews declined by nearly half a million, with emigration accounting for less than half of the decline. The Jewish population is shrinking, not only as a result of emigration, but also because of a very low birth rate, high mortality rates, an increasingly aged population, and intermarriage. Already in 1959 the average Jewish family in the Soviet Union consisted of only 3.1 persons—that is, one child per family was the norm, not enough to replace population.[4] One demographer has estimated that in the Russian and Ukrainian republics, which contain three-quarters of the Jewish population, the median age of the Jews is around fifty.[5] Moreover, several Soviet studies have shown that when Jews marry non-Jews—and perhaps a quarter to a third of Jews marrying do "marry out"—the children of such marriages overwhelmingly choose a non-Jewish nationality when they get their own internal passports. Finally, as is usually the case, younger people are overrepresented among the emigrants. In 1980, for example, the median age of Jews leaving the USSR was 35.7. This means that Jewish fertility will decline even further, as people in their childbearing years have left the country in greater proportions than other age groups. Thus the Soviet Jewish population is very likely to shrink rapidly in the coming years.

It would be wrong to conclude on the basis of the demographic outlook and the policy prospects that Soviet Jewry is likely to disappear in the near future. One of the ironies of the Soviet Jewish situation is that Jewish identity is probably stronger in the USSR that in most Western democracies, thanks largely to Soviet policy. The Soviet practice of officially identifying each citizen by nationality has maintained Jewish identity and reinforced it, often against the wishes of those who carry it. Jews identified as such on their internal passports are reminded of who they are on the many occasions that they have to produce those documents. In the eyes of society as well they are considered Jews. Many Soviet Jews do not actively identify as such: they do not practice their religion, speak a Jewish language, attend Jewish cultural events, educate their children in Jewish culture, wear distinctively Jewish clothes, or eat Jewish foods. But they have a passive identification conferred by the state and reinforced by anti-Semitism. As a Soviet scholar notes, "The distinctive feature of the sociopolitical situation in which a national community finds itself determines how clearly people perceive their national identity."[6] The Jews have a very distinct "sociopolitical situation" which defines their belonging to a group just as sharply as a common language or territory would.

The last twenty years have shown that passive identity can be turned into active identity. Large numbers of Jews have tried to infuse content and meaning into the identity imposed upon them by state and society. They have filled that identity with Jewish culture, religion, and activity. For a time the most dramatic expression of active Jewish identity took the form of emigration, and it may well do so in the future. But just as predictions of irreversible Jewish assimilation in the USSR have proved wrong, so would it be foolhardy to predict the fate of Jewish identity and culture in that country.

Still, one is struck by how much continuity in the midst of cataclysmic change there has been for Russian and Soviet Jewry in the last century. Just before the revolutions of 1917 some distinguished Russian writers lamented Russia's treatment of the Jews and warned that Russia's own future depended on how she would treat them, among others. Leonid Andreyev lamented the fact that Russia "has been too long playing a miserable part on Europe's stage and in its own conscience." He suggested that the way Russia had treated the Jews was the way Europe was treating Russia, and only better treatment of the Jews could bring Russia respectability. His words have an eerie relevance today. "We are still barbarians, the Poles still mistrust us, we are a dark terror for Europe, a baffling menace to her civilization, we long for purity and reason. . . . The Jews' tragic love for Russia finds a counterpart in our love for Europe. . . . Are we not . . . the Jews of Europe, and is not our frontier—the same 'Pale of Settlement'—something in the nature of a Russian Ghetto? . . . Here is the punishment by means of which impartial life takes revenge on the Russians for the Jews' sufferings. . . . We must all understand that the end of Jewish sufferings is the beginning of our self-respect, without which *Russia cannot exist.*"[7] A prominent economist asserted that "The Jewish question is a Russian question. Full rights for the Jews. . . . are an indispensable condition for our peaceful cultural development."[8] Despite the assertions of Soviet spokesmen, many people inside the Soviet Union and beyond it believe that both the Jewish question and the Russian one await their full resolution. With remarkable prescience, the writer Fyodor Sologub noted, "Our country is feared for its military might and loved for the fine qualities of its people, but it will be respected only when it becomes a land of free men."[9]

And the Jews? How do they see the future? Perhaps the final word belongs to that quintessential Russian Jew, Sholem Aleichem's simple dairyman, Tevye. In 1916 Sholem Aleichem ended his cycle of Tevye stories with the following observation, still a fitting commentary on the Russian Jew's fate and future.

> *Ashrekho Yisroel*—I am lucky I was born a Jew, and so I know the taste of exile and of shlepping around the world, and of *vayisu vayakhnu*—"and they went forth and they encamped." Wherever we spend the day, we don't spend the night. Since they taught me that lesson in *lekh-lecho*—"go forth"—I've just kept going and I haven't found the place about which I could say, "Here, Tevye, you can settle down." Tevye asks no questions. When they tell him to go, he goes. You see, Mr. Sholem Aleichem, today we meet right here, on the train. Tomorrow it might take us to Yehupetz. A year from now it might throw us off to Odessa, to Warsaw, or even to America. Unless the Lord above would look around and say: "You know what, *kinderlekh*? I'll just bring down the messiah to you." I wish He would do that, if only out of spite, that old Lord of the Universe! Meanwhile, be well, have a good trip, and give my regards to our Jews, and tell them over there they shouldn't worry: our old God is still alive.[10]

NOTES

[*Author's Note:* Unless otherwise indicated below, quotations in the text in English that have been taken from foreign-language sources are my translations.]

INTRODUCTION

1. John Doyle Klier, *Russia Gathers Her Jews* (Dekalb, Ill.: Northern Illinois University Press, 1986), p. xviii.

1. CREATIVITY VERSUS REPRESSION: THE JEWS IN RUSSIA, 1881–1917

1. Michael Stanislawski, *Tsar Nicholas I and the Jews* (Philadelphia: Jewish Publication Society, 1983), p. 10.

2. Alexander Herzen, *My Past and Thoughts*, quoted in Stanislawski, *Tsar Nicholas I and the Jews*, p. 27.

3. Quoted in Stanislawski, *Tsar Nicholas I and the Jews*, p. 103.

4. Lev Mandelshtam, "Avtobiografiya," *Perezhitoe*, vol. 1 (1908), quoted in Lucy Dawidowicz, *The Golden Tradition* (New York: Schocken Books, 1984), pp. 157–58.

5. Pauline Wengeroff, *Memoiren einer Grossmutter* [Memoirs of a Grandmother] (Berlin, 1908–1910), quoted in Dawidowicz, *The Golden Tradition*, pp. 163–64.

6. Quoted in Dawidowicz, *The Golden Tradition*, p. 428.

7. Quoted in Dawidowicz, *The Golden Tradition*, pp. 443, 446.

8. Quoted in Dawidowicz, *The Golden Tradition*, p. 167.

9. Louis Greenberg, *The Jews in Russia* (Two Volumes in One) (New York: Schocken Books, 1976), 2:46.

10. Quoted in Dawidowicz, *The Golden Tradition*, p. 168.

11. Quoted in Dawidowicz, *The Golden Tradition*, p. 428.

12. Quoted in Dawidowicz, *The Golden Tradition*, p. 434.

13. Quoted in Avrahm Yarmolinsky, *Road to Revolution* (New York: Macmillan, 1959), p. 250.

14. Quoted in Greenberg, *The Jews in Russia*, 1:148.

15. Quoted in Yarmolinsky, *Road to Revolution*, pp. 307–309.

16. Quoted in Yarmolinsky, *Road to Revolution*, p. 310.

17. T. M. Kopelzon, "Evreiskoe rabochee dvizhenie kontsa 80-kh i nachala 90–kh godov" [The Jewish labor movement in the late 1880s and early 1890s], quoted in Henry J. Tobias, "The Bund and Lenin Until 1903," *The Russian Review* 29, no. 4 (October 1961): 344–45.

18. Quoted in Zvi Gitelman, *Jewish Nationality and Soviet Politics* (Princeton, N.J.: Princeton University Press, 1972), p. 30.

19. Quoted in Dawidowicz, *The Golden Tradition*, pp. 128–29.

20. Quoted in Salo Baron, *The Russian Jew Under Tsars and Soviets* (New York: Schocken Books, 1978), p. 71.

21. Henrik Sliozberg, *Dela minuvshikh dnei* [A Record of Days Gone By] (Paris, 1933), quoted in Dawidowicz, *The Golden Tradition*, p. 473.

22. Simon Dubnow, *History of the Jews in Russia and Poland* (Philadelphia: Jewish Publication Society, 1920), pp.128–29.

23. Quoted in Alexander Tager, *The Decay of Czarism* (Philadelphia: The Jewish Publication Society, 1935), p. 216.

24. Sholem Aleichem, "Bandits," in *The Best of Sholem Aleichem*, edited by Irving Howe and Ruth R. Wisse (Washington, D.C.: New Republic Books, 1979), pp. 216–17.

25. Zalman Yefroikin, ed., *Fun Peretzes oytser* [From Peretz's Treasure] (New York: Workmen's Circle, 1952), pp. 248–50.

26. Quoted in Dawidowicz, *The Golden Tradition*, pp. 205–6.

27. Mendele Mokher Sforim, *Mayn lebn* [My Life] (Warsaw, 1926), quoted in Dawidowicz, *The Golden Tradition*, pp. 279–80.

28. Irving Howe and Eliezer Greenberg, eds., *A Treasury of Yiddish Stories* (New York: Schocken Books, 1973), p. 53.

29. Michael Florinsky, *Russia: A History and an Interpretation* (New York: Macmillan, 1961), 2:1223.

30. Quoted in Baron, *The Russian Jew*, p. 105.

31. *Novy Voskhod*, July 10, 24, 1914, quoted in Greenberg, *The Jews in Russia*, 2:94–95.

32. Adapted from Baron, *The Russian Jew*, p. 197.

2. Revolution and the Ambiguities of Liberation

1. "Ben Khayim," "Di role fun di idishe arbeiter in der rusisher revolutsie" [The role of the Jewish workers in the Russian Revolution], *Funken*, 1, no. 8 (March 25, 1920).

2. L. Shapiro, *Bakalakhat haRusit* [In the Russian Cauldron] (Jerusalem: Lustigman, 1952), pp. 44–45.

3. Anonymous report, Joseph Rosen Archive, YIVO Archives.

4. B. Friedland, "Partai politik und folks-interesn," [Party politics and the interests of the people], *Di varheit*, May 1, 1918.

5. Y. Blumshtain, in *Kavkazer vokhenblat*, April 14, 1919.

6. Quoted in John Shelton Curtiss, *The Russian Church and the Soviet State* (Boston: Little, Brown, 1953), p. 69.

7. Shapiro, *Bakalakhat haRusit*, p. 62.

8. Ibid., p. 160.

9. *Der emes*, February 2, 1922.

10. W. R. Grove to Col. W. N. Haskell, May 1, 1922, Rosen Archives, Box 70, "Agro 18," YIVO Archives.

11. "Der krizis in Bund" [The crisis in the Bund], *Folkstseitung*, February 19, 1919.

12. *Folkstseitung*, February 15, 1919.

13. "Tsu unzer diskusie" [For our discussion], *Der veker*, February 18, 1921.

14. "Birger krig oif der idisher gass" [Civil war on the Jewish street], *Kommunistishe fon*, July 8, 1919.

15. Aleksandr I. Solzhenitsyn, *The Gulag Archipelago, Three* (New York: Harper and Row, 1978), p. 345.

16. Rabbi Jacob Mazeh, *Zikhronot* (Tel Aviv: Jalkut, 1936), 4:13.

17. Y. Opatoshu, "Drei Hebrayer" [Three Hebraists], *Zamlbikher*, no. 8 (1952).

18. Letter to Daniel Charney, 1925, YIVO Archives.

19. A. Zeldov-Nemanskii, *Di religie iz a privat zakh* [Religion Is a Private Matter] (n.p., 1917), p. 13.

20. Moishe Litvakov, "Habokhur hazetser" [The printer's devil], *Der emes*, October 2, 1921.

21. Letter of May 9, 1922, Levitas Archive, II-1, YIVO Archives.

22. Itsik Feffer, "So What If I've Been Circumsized," in *A Treasury of Yiddish Poetry*, edited by Irving Howe and Eliezer Greenberg (New York: Schocken Books, 1973).

23. "Di anti-religieze kampanie" [The anti-religious campaign], *Der emes*, October 18, 1922.

24. Quoted in Yakov Lestschinsky, *Dos sovetishe idntum* [Soviet Jewry] (New York: Yidisher Kemfer, 1941), p. 313.

25. Quoted in Boris Bogen, *Born a Jew* (New York: Macmillan, 1930), p. 329.

26. Itsik Feffer, "I've Never Been Lost," in *A Treasury of Yiddish Poetry*, edited by Irving Howe and Eliezer Greenberg (New York: Schocken Books, 1973).

27. Belorussian Academy of Sciences, *Di shtetlekh fun V.S.S.R. in rekonstruktivn period* [The *Shtetlekh* of the Belorussian Soviet Socialist Republic in the Period of Reconstruction] (Minsk, 1932), pp. 42–43.

28. Ibid., p. 37.

29. Ibid., p. 39.

3. Reaching for Utopia: Building Socialism and a New Jewish Culture

1. *Der emes*, September 12, 1918.

2. Y. Dardak, "Undzere dergraykhungen far 15 yor oktiabr afn gebit fun folk-bildung" [Our achievements in education in the fifteen years since the October Revolution], *Tsum XV yortog fun der oktiabr-revolutsie—sotsial ekonomisher zamlbukh* (Minsk, 1932), p. 173.

3. Y. Reznik, ed., *Programen fun der einheitlikher arbet shul* [Programs of the Uniform Labor School] (Moscow, 1928), pp. 41, 64, 86.

4. M. Kiper, "Oyfgabn in der kultur oyfkler arbet" [Tasks in cultural enlightenment work], *Shtern*, June 28, 1927.

5. Harold R. Weinstein, "Language and Education in the Soviet Ukraine," *The Slavonic Yearbook*, vol. XX of *The Slavonic and East European Review* 20 (1941): 138.

6. *Oktiabr*, January 28, 1928.

7. *Der veker*, February 16, 1923.

8. *Der emes*, April 6, 1924.

9. Quoted in *Alfarbandishe baratung fun di Idishe sektsies fun der Al.K.P.(b)* [All-Union Conference of the Jewish Sections of the All-Union Communist Party] (Moscow: Shul un bukh, 1927), p. 127*ff*.

10. Quoted in *Ershter alfarbandisher tsuzamenfor fun "GEZERD": Stenografisher barikht* [First All-Union Congress of GEZERD, Stenographic Report] (Moscow: GEZERD, 1927), p. 41.

11. Semën Sumny, "Tsvishn a natsminderisher natsmerheit" [Among a national minority which is in the majority], *Shtern*, May 26, 1927.

12. Quoted in *Alfarbandishe baratung . . .* , p. 129.

13. A. Gilman, *Vos darf visn an ibervanderer vegn der yidisher avtonomer gegnt* [What a Settler Should Know About the Jewish Autonomous Provinces] (Moscow: Der emes, 1939), pp. 44–45.

14. *Revoliutsiia i natsional'nosti*, November 1936, pp. 146*ff*.

15. Av. Epstein, quoted in Yaakov Lvavi, *HaHityashvut HaYehudit beBirobijan* [Jewish Settlement in Birobidzhan] (Jerusalem: Historical Society of Israel, 1965), p. 127.

16. *Der emes*, January 26, 1930.

17. *Di Yidishe bafelkerung in Ukraine* [The Jewish Population in the

Ukraine] (Kharkov: Melukhe Farlag, 1934), p. 34.

18. Personal interview, Chicago, 1981.

19. I. I. Veitsblit, *Di dinamik fun der Yidisher bafelkerung in Ukraine far di yorn 1897–1926* [The Dynamics of the Jewish Population in the Ukraine for the Years 1897–1926] (Kharkov: Literatur un kunst, 1930), p. 50.

20. Yankl Kantor, quoted in Solomon Schwarz, *The Jews in the Soviet Union* (Syracuse: Syracuse University Press, 1951), p. 139.

4. The Holocaust

1. Z. Segalowicz, *Gebrente trit* [Burned-Out Footsteps] (Buenos Aires, 1947), p. 96.

2. Quoted in Alexander Dallin, *German Rule in Soviet Russia, 1941–1945* (2nd ed.; London: Macmillan, 1981), p. 9.

3. Quoted in Matthew Cooper, *The Phantom War* (London: Macdonald and James, 1979), pp. 171, 173.

4. Raul Hilberg, *The Destruction of the European Jews* (Chicago, Quadrangle, 1961), p. 189.

5. *The Black Book* (New York: Duell, Sloan and Pearce, 1946), p. 354.

6. Ibid., pp. 354–55.

7. Ilya Ehrenburg and Vasily Grossman, *The Black Book* (New York: Holocaust Library, 1980), p. 191.

8. Ibid., p. 193.

9. Hilberg, *The Destruction of the European Jews*, p. 203.

10. Dallin, *German Rule in Soviet Russia*, p. 121 n.3.

11. Ibid., p. 598.

12. Based on the testimony of one emigré; see Bohdan Krawchenko, "Soviet Ukraine Under Nazi Occupation, 1941–44," in *Ukraine During World War II*, edited by Yury Boshyk (Edmonton: University of Alberta Press, 1986). Krawchenko argues that the number of Ukrainians fighting with the Germans has been exaggerated because the Allies "described all of the Wehrmacht's eastern units (Osttruppen), whatever their national origin, as 'Ukrainian'" (ibid., p. 25).

13. Taras Hunczak, "Ukrainian-Jewish Relations During the Soviet and Nazi Occupations," in *Ukraine During World War II*, edited by Yury Boshyk (Edmonton: University of Alberta Press, 1986), p. 42.

14. In a footnote Hunczak admits: "In fairness to the reports read by this author at Yad Vashem, it should be noted that they tell mainly the story of Ukrainian persecutors of Jews. The reports about righteous Ukrainians are almost an exception to the rule. That, of course, does not mean that all the reports are true. . . . On the whole, the depositions or reports of the survivors are tainted with anti-Ukrainian bias" (ibid., p. 44 n.50).

15. Dallin, *German Rule in Soviet Russia*, p. 215.

16. Dovid Bergelson, *Yidn un di foterland milkhome* [Jews and the Fatherland War] (Moscow: Ogiz, 1941), p. 23.

17. According to *Pravda*, May 6, 1965, 107 Jews got the award; according to the Soviet historian Yankl Kantor, 121 did ("Yidn oyf dem grestn un vikhtikstn front" [Jews on the largest and most important front], *Folksshtimme* [Warsaw], April 18, 1963, quoted in Reuben Ainsztein, "Soviet Jewry in the Second World War," in *The Jews in Soviet Russia Since 1917*, edited by Lionel Kochan [London: Oxford University Press, 1970], pp. 174–75. Gershon Shapiro enumerated 138 Jewish winners during the war, and 10 others who received it before or after 1941–1945. Shapiro's book tells the story, from official

Soviet sources, of every winner; see his *Evrei—geroii Sovetskogo Soiuza* [Jews—Heroes of the Soviet Union] (Tel Aviv, 1982).

18. Quoted in Yuri Suhl, *They Fought Back* (New York: Schocken Books, 1967), p. 143.

19. Quoted in Mark Dworzecki, *Yerushalayim d'Lite in kamf un umkum* [The Jerusalem of Lithuania in Battle and Death] (Paris, 1948), p. 308.

20. Quoted in Yitzhak Arad, *Vilna haYehudit bemaavak uvekhilayon* [Jewish Vilna in Struggle and Annihilation] (Tel Aviv: Sifriat Poalim, 1976), p. 314.

21. Quoted in A. Sutzkever, *Vilner getto* [The Vilna Ghetto] (Paris, 1946), p. 227.

5. THE BLACK YEARS AND THE GRAY, 1948–1967

1. Shimon Redlich, *Propaganda and Nationalism in Wartime Russia* (Boulder, Colo.: East European Quarterly, 1982), p. 119.

2. Loitsker's article is translated in Benjamin Pinkus, *The Soviet Government and the Jews* (New York: Cambridge University Press, 1984), pp. 165–72.

3. Nina Sirotina, oral history, William Wiener Oral History Library, American Jewish Committee, New York.

4. Esther Markish, *The Long Return* (New York: Ballantine, 1974), p. 149.

5. Ibid., pp. 165–66.

6. Quoted in Pinkus, *The Soviet Government and the Jews*, pp. 183–84.

7. Ibid., p. 159.

8. Ilya Ehrenburg, *Post-War Years: 1945–54* (Cleveland: World, 1967), pp. 132–33.

9. Markish, *The Long Return*, p. 173.

10. Boris Halip, oral history, William Wiener Oral History Library, American Jewish Committee, New York.

11. Quoted in Yehoshua Gilboa, *The Black Years of Soviet Jewry* (Boston: Little, Brown, 1971), p. 291. All names were spelled with lowercase letters, implying types, not individuals.

12. The *Pravda* article is translated in Pinkus, *The Soviet Government and the Jews*, pp. 219–20.

13. Quoted in Gilboa, *The Black Years of Soviet Jewry*, p. 296.

14. Mark Ya. Azbel, *Refusenik* (New York: Paragon House, 1987), p. 98. Whether or not the letter actually existed is not clear.

15. Irina Kirk, *Profiles in Russian Resistance* (New York: Quadrangle, 1975), p. 166.

16. Vladimir Golyakhovsky, oral history, Wiener Oral History Library, American Jewish Committee, New York, p. 13.

17. Ibid., p. 12.

18. Binyamin Pinkus, *Yehudai Russiya uBrit Hamoetzot* [The Jews of Russia and the Soviet Union] (Beer Sheva: Ben Gurion University, 1986), p. 316.

19. Quoted in Yaacov Ro'i, *From Encroachment to Involvement* (New York: John Wiley, 1974), pp. 38–39.

20. Quoted in Pinkus, *The Soviet Government and the Jews*, pp. 41–42.

21. Leonid Shekhtman, oral history, Wiener Oral History Library, American Jewish Committee, New York, p. 46.

22. Azbel, *Refusenik*, pp. 99–100.

23. Khrushchev's speech is translated in Russian Institute, *The Anti-*

Stalin Campaign and International Communism (New York: Columbia University Press, 1956), pp. 1–90.

24. Pinkus, *Yehudai Russiya uBrit Hamoetzot*, pp. 416, 420.

25. Pinkus, *The Soviet Government and the Jews*, pp. 310–11.

26. Ibid., p. 314.

27. Evgeniia Evel'son, *Sudebnye protsessy po ekonomicheskim delam v SSSR* [Economic Crimes Trials in the USSR] (London: Overseas Publications Interchange, 1986), pp. 336–37.

28. Natan Shakham, *Pgishot beMoskva* [Meetings in Moscow] (Merkhavia: Sifriyat Poalim, 1957), p. 12.

29. *Pravda*, July 9, 1960, quoted in Pinkus, *The Soviet Government and the Jews*, p. 71.

30. Interview with Serge Groussard, *Le Figaro*, April 9, 1958, quoted in Pinkus, *The Soviet Government and the Jews*, pp. 62–63.

31. *Réalités*, May 1957, p. 104, quoted in S. Schwarz, *Evrei v Sovetskom Soiuze* [Jews in the Soviet Union] (New York: American Jewish Committee, 1966), p. 261.

32. Nikita S. Khrushchev, *Khrushchev Remembers* (Boston: Little, Brown, 1970), p. 269.

6. Soviet Jews, 1967–1987: To Reform, Conform, or Leave?

1. *Pravda*, December 5, 1966, translated in Benjamin Pinkus, *The Soviet Government and the Jews* (New York: Cambridge University Press, 1984), p. 78.

2. David Giladi, summarizing statements made by Soviet immigrants to Israel at the Twenty-Eighth World Zionist Congress, *Haaretz*, January 25, 1972.

3. Lev Navrozov, "Getting Out of Russia," *Commentary* 54, no. 4 (October 1972): 50.

4. Quoted in Chasya Pincus, "Family and School: Some Preliminary Observations on Adolescent Russian Immigrants in Israel," *Jewish Social Studies* 34, no. 3 (July 1972): 256.

5. Yosef Mendelevitch, *Mivtza Khatunah* [Operation Wedding] (Jerusalem: Keter, 1985), p. 14.

6. Alla Rusinek, *Like a Song, Like a Dream* (New York: Charles Scribner's Sons, 1973), p. 20.

7. Izrail Kleiner, "Anekdotichna tragediia" [An anecdotal tragedy], *Suchastnist'* 78 (July–August 1973): 225.

8. Sonia Lerner-Levin, interviewed by Dov Goldstein, *Maariv*, March 18, 1977. Ms. Lerner-Levin is the daughter of Prof. Alexander Lerner, an eminent scientist, who since 1971 has been denied permission to emigrate from the USSR.

9. Quoted in Peter Reddaway, ed., *Uncensored Russia* (New York: American Heritage Press, 1972), p. 511.

10. Personal interview, Israel, 1975.

11. Binyamin Pinkus, *Yehudai Russiya uBrit Hamoetzot* [The Jews of Russia and the Soviet Union] (Beer Sheva: Ben Gurion University, 1986), pp. 398–99.

12. William Korey, *The Soviet Cage* (New York: Viking, 1973), pp. 85–89.

13. Ibid., pp. 181–82.

14. *Evrei v SSSR*, vol. 1 (October, 1972). This *samizdat* essay is translated as "The Social Preconditions of the National Awakening of the Jews in the USSR" in *I Am a Jew* (New York: Academic Committee on Soviet Jewry, 1973), p. 29.

15. L. M. Drobizheva, "Natsional'noe samosoznanie: baza formi- rovanie i sotsial'no-kulturnye stimuly razvitiia" [National self-con- sciousness: The basis for its formation and the social-cultural stimuli of its development], *Sovetskaia etnografiia* no. 5 (1985), translated in *Soviet Law and Government*, Summer 1986, p. 55.

16. Larissa Bogoraz, "Do I Feel I Belong to the Jewish People?" in *I Am a Jew* (New York: Academic Committee on Soviet Jewry, 1973), pp. 63–64 (emphasis added).

7. The "Other" Jews of the USSR: Georgian, Central Asian, and Mountain Jews

1. Mordechai Neishtat, *Yehuday Gruziya* [The Jews of Georgia] (Tel Aviv: Am Oved, 1970), p. 85.

2. Quoted in Gershon Ben-Oren, "Bet hasefer haYehudi be- Gruziya haSovietit" [The Jewish school in Soviet Georgia], *Peamim* no. 9 (1981), p. 42.

3. See Gershon Ben-Oren, "Hamuzeon hahistori-etnografi li Ye- huday Gruziya" [The Historical-Ethnographic Museum of the Geor- gian Jews], *Peamim* no. 15 (1983).

4. Quoted in Neishtat, *Yehuday Gruziya*, pp. 120–24.

8. A Century of Ambivalence

1. Quoted in Jonathan Frankel, *Prophecy and Politics* (Cambridge: Cambridge University Press, 1981), p. 87.

2. Fyodor Sologub, "The Fatherland for All," in *The Shield*, edited by Maxim Gorky, Leonid Andreyev, and Fyodor Sologub (New York: Alfred A. Knopf, 1917), pp. 148–49.

3. Ye. Lesoto, "In a Frenzy of Forgetfulness," *Komsomolskaia pravda*, May 22, 1987, translated in *Current Digest of the Soviet Press* 39, no. 21 (June 24, 1987): 1.

4. On Jewish population trends, see Zvi Gitelman, "Correlates, Causes and Consequences of Jewish Fertility in the USSR," in *Modern Jewish Fertility*, edited by Paul Ritterband (Leiden: E. J. Brill, 1981); and Mordechai Altshuler, *The Jews in the Soviet Union Since World War Two* (Westport, Conn.: Greenwood Press, 1987).

5. See Joel Florsheim, "Mifkad haukhlusin kemakor lemispar haYehudim biVrit haMoetsot" (Censuses as a source for the number of Jews in the Soviet Union], *Yahadut zmaneinu*, vol. 1 (1984).

6. L. M. Drobizheva, "Natsional'noe samosoznanie: baza formi- rovanie i sotsial'no-kulturnye stimuly razvitiia" [National self-con- sciousness: The basis for its formation and the social-cultural stimuli of its development], *Sovetskaia etnografiia* no. 5 (1985), translated in *Soviet Law and Government*, Summer 1986, p. 55.

7. Leonid Andreyev, "The First Step," in *The Shield*, edited by Maxim Gorky, Leonid Andreyev, and Fyodor Sologub (New York: Alfred A. Knopf, 1917), pp. 32, 34.

8. M. Bernatzky, "The Jews and Russian Economic Life," in *The Shield*, edited by Maxim Gorky, Leonid Andreyev, and Fyodor Sologub (New York: Alfred A. Knopf, 1917), pp. 90–91.

9. Sologub, "The Fatherland for All," p. 151.

10. Sholem Aleichem, "Vekhalaklakos," in *Ale verk fun Sholem Al- eichem* [The Complete Works of Sholem Aleichem] (2 vols.; New York: Sholem Aleichem Folksfond Oisgabe, 1925), 2:229–30.

INDEX OF NAMES

INDEX OF PLACES

Page numbers in *italics* refer to illustrations or captions.